Profits

Patricia Franklin grew up in San Diego, California, the youngest of a combined family of fourteen children. She came to the UK on a postgraduate scholarship to the London School of Economics. Her journalism has appeared in the *Sunday Times*, *Sunday Correspondent*, *Business*, *The Economist*, *Newsweek* and *Los Angeles Times*. She has worked as a programme and series consultant with the BBC and Trans World International and is managing director of Intrepid Productions Limited, an independent video/film production company. She lives with her husband in Richmond, Surrey.

PROFITS OF DECEIT

Dispatches from the Front Lines of Fraud

PATRICIA FRANKLIN

Mandarin

A Mandarin Paperback
PROFITS OF DECEIT

First published in Great Britain 1990
by William Heinemann Ltd
This edition published 1991
by Mandarin Paperbacks
Michelin House, 81 Fulham Road, London SW3 6RB

Mandarin is an imprint of the Octopus Publishing Group,
a division of Reed International Books Limited

Copyright © Patricia Franklin 1990

A CIP catalogue record for this title
is available from the British Library
ISBN 0 7493 0993 8

Printed and bound in Great Britain
by Cox & Wyman Ltd, Reading, Berks.

To my mother and father
and all those who loved them

Contents

Acknowledgements

The author wishes to thank:

The Motion Picture Association of America (Australia, Hollywood)

Commercial Trademark Services (Hong Kong, Taipei, Thailand, Singapore) Ltd

Carratu International (London)

The Securities and Exchange Commission

The Commonwealth Secretariat Crime Unit

The International Stock Exchange

The Commercial Crime Bureau of the Royal Hong Kong Police Force

The Independent Commission Against Corruption

The Hong Kong Banking Commission

The Research Laboratory for Archaeology and the History of Art at Oxford

The Los Angeles County Musuem of Art

John Maxfield/Boardscan

The National Centre for Computer Crime Data

The Southern California Fraud Task Force

US Postal Inspection Service

Orange County District Attorney's Office

City of Newport Beach, California Police Department

MCA/Universal Studios Pictures Ltd

New York Police Department

New York District Attorney's Office

Securities and Fraud Unit, New York US Attorney's Office

Hong Kong Customs and Excise Department

Attorney General's Chambers, Hong Kong

Arthur Andersen & Co.
Arthur Young
Ernst & Whinney

The professionals who contributed to this book. Thank you for your time and instruction; for the adventures, vicarious and otherwise.

Bill Hamilton, who got the ball rolling.

Dan Franklin, whose confidence lead to a commission.

Stephen Fay, whose encouragement allowed me the freedom to write the book.

Tom Weldon, whose editorial instincts kept me on track.

Helen Fraser, whose assuredness provided calm.

Kathleen Horton, Margaret Wiedower, Rita Gourlay and the many transcribers who patiently typed their way through assorted accents and reams of paper.

Barry Barnett, who met me three weeks before my journey and became my husband by the final draft. Your patience, love and support have been my lifeline.

The baggage handlers.

Introduction

Fraud pervades every corner of commercial life from the passage of super tankers bearing false bills of lading to forged art; from fake Rolexes to the illicit computer transactions of multinational banks.

The scale of commercial deception is huge. Counterfeiting alone counts for 9 per cent of world trade – roughly $80 billion. The International Maritime Bureau estimates fraud on the high seas totals $3 billion each year. Some experts double that figure. Museums and galleries house an embarrassment of forgeries for an unwitting public. The racket in fake Dalis alone is said to exceed $400 million.

More than half the banks and financial institutions in the City of London have been subject to commercial deception. In 1988 City of London police investigated cases of proven and attempted fraud totalling £477 million. It's a crime that presently costs UK companies £5 billion a year. Almost half the incidences of fraud discovered during 1989 were committed by managers. People in positions of power are perhaps more prone to fraud investigation than other crime as the investigations into Guinness, Barlow Clowes and Blue Arrow attest. In the European Community, an embezzler's paradise, an average £6 billion disappears annually.

Fraud is an invisible crime, touching our lives in unseen ways: from counterfeit heart pumps and space rocket parts to the exploits of a 6-year-old who after watching his father operate an automatic till, banked $1 million into his dad's account by inserting the tin foil wrap from a bar of chocolate. Fraud is rarely boring.

Using its worldwide information network, the financial and economic division of Interpol has classified thirty different types of commercial deception. When I first covered the topic, I looked at fraud through the eyes of five London-based investigators covering different beats. But fraud is an international problem and if one is serious about documenting any aspect of it, a global itinerary becomes inevitable.

What struck me from the outset of my research was the diversity of roles played by the detectives. No one had really focused on the investigators before, only the passing frauds. In the jetsam of the daily press, what makes headlines today is forgotten by tomorrow. I could not justify writing a book on forgettable cases. They needed to be remarkable in some unifying way. My objective was to let the investigators tell the story, making them the focal point, the common thread throughout the book.

Ninety hours of transcribed interviews and 25,000 miles later, what you are holding in your hands is the fruit of my adventures on the front lines of fraud. My guides were an extraordinary group of people culled from over a hundred law enforcement personnel, government investigators, police and private detectives. Regarded by their peers as the best in their fields, this book is about them and the crimes they solve. Their professionalism was more than admirable. At times, my life depended on it.

Like many a fraud investigation, this book has taken longer than expected to complete. Initially my plan was to spend six months on the road, another six writing. Hong Kong, my first destination, absorbed two and a half months' work. There, I went under cover and observed raids. Hong Kong provided more than an opportunity to learn about product-counterfeiting cases. When I wasn't gathering evidence under an assumed identity, a task force walked me through one of the biggest fraud cases of all time.

Whether it's an indication of the lax regulatory procedures in Hong Kong's financial markets that fostered cases of serious fraud, or simply good timing, I had plenty to write about in the colony. Bangkok was tranquil by comparison. By the time I made it to Taipei, I went undercover on my own.

These acts were not character-building quests. Fraud, I've found, is a highly personalised criminal act. Getting to the root of it is hearing the ruse first hand. As I made my way through South-East Asia, Australia, America and Europe, I targeted the cases I was chiefly interested in and met the appropriate investigators along the way.

Having over-packed in the first place, my wardrobe was gradually replaced with documents and cassettes. The volume of research grew and much of it was highly confidential. Because the raw data was irreplaceable, it was important that it was at hand during travel. The night I left Kuala Lumpur for Sydney, I crossed the tarmac to board the plane. Seeing my bloated luggage, the airline rep said it was too heavy to take on board. As the roar of the plane engines increased, I told him why it had to be allowed as carry-on baggage. He shook his head. The big valise, containing half the research for the book, remained on the concrete between us.

Two airport workers grabbed the movable steps to the plane. Everyone had boarded already. It was time to go. The propellers kicked in, whining louder. The gusts of air felt like a dry typhoon. I was in a cold sweat. He grabbed the bag, slipped a checked luggage tab around it and dragged it to the handlers. As I entered the plane, the stairs were wheeled away. I ordered a drink and prayed it would not get lost. Without realising it, I had accumulated 150 lbs of research and I was only half-way through the trip. At airports I put them on scales with care, weighing in like some boxer before a fight.

The only contests I had travelling alone were with flying cockroaches and the occasional bat. Gaining access to some subjects presented major dilemmas. It wasn't so much red tape

3

as crammed schedules and suspicion. I was attempting to make people who make a living getting others to talk, to reveal things they had never told anyone else. Achieving that took more than providing referrals, declaring credentials, stating my business. It took trust and that took time.

The results of those candid interviews is buttressed by a variety of different sources, mostly documentary. This is not a collection of war stories told by has-been heroes waxing lyrical over hard-won cases. More than anything, I've tried to make this as genuine a portrayal of fraud investigations as possible. There is no infusion of adventure, danger or excitement on these pages that does not genuinely exist in the lives of the portrayed subjects. As they would probably appreciate, truth is stranger than fraud or fiction.

What's the password?

'They want to put me out of business. I could be murdered by hackers in the next couple of months. They know I know their identities. I have 7,000 of them logged on my computer. They laugh at the FBI, the Secret Service, but they don't laugh at me. I was one of them.

'They live in a world in which they are gods. I force them to recognise themselves for what they are. I'm the one who rips off their masks.'

JOHN MAXFIELD, computer security consultant
and former FBI informant

Burnt-out buildings rub shoulders with banks that have gone bust on Detroit's north side. Here, on forgotten avenues dotted with abandoned cars, sheets of plywood board up businesses that have packed up and left, in search of customers that have gone before them. Two motorcycle gangs, the Scorpions and the Forbidden Wheels, provide deafening tributes to horsepower for members of the nearby First Psychic Church of Brightmoor. Even the quiet of tree-lined streets is punctuated by fire bombs and gunshots. Vacant flats have been converted to crack houses, drug dens for the severely addicted. In the local high school, as a means of reducing violence by confiscating weapons, students pass through metal detectors before entering the classroom.

Amidst this study in urban decay, John Maxfield operates out of an old distribution warehouse sandwiched between the faded storefronts of two beauty parlours. The harsh odours of permanents and hair colourants mix with the hot fat smells of a fried-chicken outlet located at the mouth of the alley that Maxfield drives down each day. Arriving at the guarded entrance of his headquarters, Maxfield parks his dented white Dodge van and dials a secret code on a telephone by a jailhouse door. He pushes two buttons in sequence and the barred door releases. With another formula of codes, Maxfield opens a thick, battleship-grey door made of steel. As it closes, it automatically locks behind him. In the dim light, shadows of machinery emerge in an ante-room the size of a small factory, leading to his office. Some of the hobbies Maxfield stores here have collected dust for decades. Over a thousand pieces of wood are assembled in a six-foot-long model of a street car that shares a table with dog-eared blueprints. An old-fashioned telephone booth from the 1940s, fully operational, is nestled in a corner. A machinist's lathe occupies another. Thick snakes of bright telephone wire coil round milk crates, filled with electronic switches, resting on a cold, concrete floor.

Maxfield's office illustrates his early life's passion for telephones, computers and *Star Trek*. His desk resembles the bridge of the Starship Enterprise. A bank of six monitors, green, black and white, and amber-screened, form an L-shaped console. There is a field of buttons, switches and blinking lights surrounding telephones, intercoms, disc drives and recording equipment. A Tokyo subway map lies next to a button warning, 'My Laser is Set on Stun'. Resting above the console a model of the USS Enterprise scans the surroundings. A voice communication cabinet bears the sticker, 'Star Fleet Computer Division'. Nearby, an entire telephone exchange, suitable for a small town, hums and clicks. Maxfield built it when he was 18, from salvaged equipment that included parts from a Japanese PABX switchboard from Vlasic Foods Inc., a company famed for pickles.

Across the hall, a huge storage room is filled with computer and telephone equipment Maxfield has purchased from businesses upgrading their technology or going into liquidation. Nearby is a collection of hacksaws, chisels and sledgehammers used to prise open the old computers. Maxfield, apart from living out the fantasy of a frustrated PC user, hacks away at them to retrieve valuable circuitry containing fragments of gold. When he has extracted enough, he takes the circuit board and chips to a smelter in Chicago.

Ribbons of connector cables drape over diodes, chips and wiring crammed on to steel shelves that take up an entire wall of Maxfield's storage room. A thick coat of dust shrouds a teletype machine from the 1930s. A collection of old black telephones stand silently to attention by a model train from the Mohawk Valley Electric Railway. Amidst all the machinery, dust and salvage, there is a sentimental reminder of what John Maxfield was up to when he was a kid. Alongside a crate filled with old headsets, sits the computer he built in 1953 out of an old pin-ball machine. He was 12 at the time.

A small room adjacent to Maxfield's console houses the heart of his operations. A bank of high-powered computers, $5^{1/2}$ feet tall and 4 feet wide, gently whir. For his own personal computer, Maxfield uses what amounts to an aging mainframe. A Hewlett Packard 2000 Access System flexes its strength with 99 megabytes, a 64K memory and, unlike an ordinary microprocessor's 8 megahertz, Maxfield's HP sports 27.5. Three disc drives, the size of small refrigerators, spin at 3,600 r.p.m. Maxfield keeps a humidifier next to the high-speed printer that is capable of printing 450 lines per minute. The steam keeps churning print-outs from jamming. Maxfield uses the energy of his computers to warm his office in winter. Apart from their central-heating value, the machines are worth about $300,000.

The only bugs in Maxfield's system appear to be the rubber centipede and cockroach he has glued to a printer. On another, a bright-orange furry doll of Garfield, the cartoon cat, poses with nonchalance while Captain Kirk, three gold stripes on the cuff of his mustard uniform, stares out from a poster. A life-size cardboard cut-out of Mr Spock lends a logical feel to the place. The word THINK looms out above the twenty-one switches on the HP 2000. Next to a disc drive a bumper sticker implores 'Beam Me Up Scotty – There's No Intelligent Life Here.'

When he was tested for intelligence, Maxfield discovered he had an IQ of 179. Whether by choice or consequence, Maxfield has always been somewhat of a loner. In high school, while everyone else was learning the Twist, he was building a telephone exchange. That sense of isolation still exists in Maxfield's work. In a building without windows, Maxfield gets input from the outside world through a panel of blinking lights attached to a photocell and an anometer on the roof. Red indicates the weather outside his office is cold; yellow, stormy; green, warm; blue, fair.

On a 'green' morning in May, Maxfield wears his only uniform: a white short-sleeved shirt, two pens and black spectacle pouch in the pocket, a black leather belt, dark-blue trousers, black socks, and black leather utility shoes. Maxfield's black hair shines with grease and he wears black horn-rimmed spectacles. His mouth is framed by a thick moustache and goatee. The man rarely leaves his office and it shows: his skin has the pallor of a submariner. 'I'm your basic nerd,' he explains. 'I was always the runty one the kids picked on.'

The only child of two librarians, Maxfield grew up in Ann Arbor, Michigan. Each day after school, he used to visit the telephone exchange with the same devotion other kids had for baseball practice. When he was 9, Maxfield invented a crude switchboard. Three years later he built his first computer. It was when Maxfield's attention turned to telephones that he installed his own telephone exchange. One day he dialled up all of the circuits from Ann Arbor to Chelsea, Michigan, in tandem until all of the phone lines of the two towns were fully engaged. It took Maxfield, then 15, all of ten minutes.

Soon afterwards, he began teaching his high-school class-mates electronics. One day, Maxfield spotted an intriguing advertisement in the *Saturday Evening Post*. It amounted to a public-service announcement placed by the telephone company. It proclaimed that operators could finally establish long-distance connections without having continuously to relay calls from one operator to the next. 'When they printed the ad,' recalls Maxfield, 'they also printed the musical notes represent-ing the tones of the numbers.'

Using what was available to him, Maxfield held the mouthpiece of his telephone against the sounding board of his parents' piano and played the corresponding notes. 'I was able to connect my call, free of charge. You didn't need anything electronic.' Maxfield escaped being billed for his call because, 'They made the mistake of publishing, for all the world to see, exactly how the long-distance system worked,' he says. 'The engineer that designed the system warned them that, if people started using home-made tone generators, they could start making free calls.'

In 1961, using pieces from scrap bins and pointers from a Bell System technical journal, Maxfield invented one of the first 'blue boxes', a sort of push-button keypad connected to amplified tone-generating circuitry. With it he was able to make illegal, long-distance calls. For Maxfield, it amounted to a portable piano.

He became what's known in the trade as a 'phone phreak'. 'Phreak' was coined in the early 1970s as the title given to someone who is able to make free but illegal long-distance telephone calls. Maxfield says his brief phreaking career came to an abrupt end when a man from Michigan Bell's special audit department stopped by his house for 'a chat about the facts of life and the phone company'.

Curious company executives who had never seen anything like Maxfield's invention decided to make a deal with him. They would not press charges as long as Maxfield co-operated. 'They

9

gave me three conditions. One: Don't do it again. Two: Tell us how you did it. Three: Don't tell anyone else.'

Besides inventing a blue box, Maxfield simultaneously created the first black box that permitted a user to receive incoming calls free of charge to the dialer. Because the caller could not be disconnected until the receiver of the call hung up, the black box proved very useful as a trap-and-trace device for police dealing with bomb threats. In 1964, at the age of 23, Maxfield received a patent for his black box.

He applied his knowledge of electronics to a career that would keep him in constant contact with the machines he had mastered. He began installing his own telephone systems and servicing facsimile and teletype machines. Maxfield travelled a daily 200-mile circuit around Detroit, mending and maintaining machines that sent information and images from satellites to television screens, from offices to overseas branches. During the day he carried a tool box, and at night he played with his computer.

In 1976, Maxfield joined a new club for computer enthusiasts. Instead of meeting in a coffee shop, the club met electronically, accessing time on a local school-district's computer, provided for their use, after hours. The club created one of the first electronic bulletin boards systems (BBS). A BBS is much like the notice board found at a local shop – a place where messages are displayed. Maxfield was elected treasurer of the club and supervised the bulletin board and the system's software, most of which was written by him and his friends.

As the years went by, more bulletin boards were set up by computer users. All that was required to operate a BBS was a computer, some software and a modem (a device enabling computers to receive and transmit information via telephone lines). Some of the bulletin boards were exclusive, requiring users to enter secret passwords before gaining access. Sometimes prospective members of a BBS had to pay an entrance fee in the form of a software package. In turn, the new member might receive five software packages from existing members. Almost without exception, all of the proprietary software exchanged was illegally copied, or pirated. Soon bulletin boards became the central source of software piracy in America.

Feeling the pinch of lost sales, software publishing companies sought legal remedies to the pirate problem. Because the stolen software was being transmitted through telephone lines (via a modem, connected to a computer), the crimes being committed were copyright infringement and computer fraud, then known technically as wire fraud. At the time, these cases were handled by the Federal Bureau of Investigation (FBI). In years to come, computer fraud and abuse would fall under the jurisdiction of the Secret Service following the passage of the US Computer Crime Bill in 1984.

In August of 1982, the FBI began making enquiries at computer stores in the Detroit area. One day an agent approached the president of Maxfield's computer club, explaining that he was chasing down leads in a software piracy case. The president of the club told Maxfield about the visit. 'They are looking in the wrong place,' said Maxfield.

'At that time,' he says, 'we were getting advertisements for pirated software on our BBS, but it was of no interest because we wrote our own.'

His curiosity piqued by the agent's visit, Maxfield called up local bulletin boards and ran print-outs of their messages. Users boasted about computer systems they had gained access to and Maxfield documented some illegal software swaps.

On an early September morning, he loaded up his van with tools and drove to the Ann Arbor weather bureau. Finished with his monthly equipment check, Maxfield wandered down the hall and entered the regional office of the FBI. He introduced himself to the agent who had approached the president of the computer club and said, 'I've got information on the pirates you're looking for.' Maxfield pulled out the sheaf of computer print-outs detailing illegal software transactions.

The man wanted to know how Maxfield had obtained such incriminating evidence. Maxfield explained that by hooking up his computer to a modem and using some software, he was able to dial up local bulletin boards and retrieve information for the price of a telephone call. 'Wait a minute. Stop right there,' said the agent. 'What's a modem?'

Maxfield suddenly looked around the room and noticed there was not a single computer in the office. 'How do you keep track of criminals without computers?' he asked. The agent pointed to a card file. Maxfield started from scratch, explaining what he knew about bulletin boards, modems and software piracy.

'At least half of all computer bulletin boards exist solely for the purpose of piracy. There are hundreds of software pirates operating on the boards, each one trying to out-do the other and be first with the latest version. Do you know what the street life of an average video game is?' he asked the agent. 'Well, it's negative two weeks. The pirates have it two weeks before it hits the stores because they get it right from the wholesalers or from the publishing house directly.

'I've seen stuff that wasn't even finished product, just partially completed games, that the pirates had three months before the stores had it. The bottom line is that many of the computer criminals start out as software pirates. The hacker underground is their introduction to the world of crime.' Maxfield didn't know if the agent understood a thing he had said. The man just nodded, expressionless.

Two weeks later, a young man who looked like a university student knocked on Maxfield's door. He was an FBI agent from the Detroit office, in charge of the software piracy case. Maxfield explained how the bulletin boards were used by pirates to trade illegal software and showed him the BBS print-outs. 'Going back to my experience as a phone phreak, in the 1950s and 1960s, I knew what could happen,' recalls Maxfield. 'You could invade military and private data bases.'

Maxfield began at the beginning, telling the FBI agent about

Cap'n Crunch, a phone phreak named after the breakfast cereal that contained the prize of a little whistle. The whistle identically mimicked the radio frequency tone used to tap into telephone lines. Cap'n Crunch used whistles illegally to wiretap and wound up serving jail time as a result. Then there was the Roscoe gang in Los Angeles, the first reported group of computer hackers to hit the scene. 'I was shocked the FBI didn't know anything about computers and their potential for crime,' recalls Maxfield.

It was a detailed meeting with Maxfield decoding computer jargon to an agent trying to refrain from legalese. Maxfield had access to this foreign world of computer hackers, and he wanted to help. After all, he was already providing evidence. The agent made a proposition that would change Maxfield's life: 'Could you be an informant for us?' Maxfield agreed, on condition that he would not be billed for his long-distance calls to the bulletin boards.

After the agent had gone, Maxfield remembered the promise he had made to the telephone company when they took his blue box away. He had kept the three conditions for over twenty years; now he was being given permission to break them. 'The FBI gave me an excuse to recreate what I had as a boy,' he says. 'I was given a licence to phreak and hack. To do what I always wanted to do but was afraid to. Suddenly I was able to return to 1961 and pick up where I left off.' Maxwell adds, 'I was an amateur. I had no legal or law enforcement background. In the beginning, it was the blind leading the blind.'

Within a matter of weeks, Maxfield was introduced to a vast society of hackers, each of whom had a different mission, achievable with the help of computer technology. Some were harmless thrill seekers who broke into complicated systems for the sake of penetrating a new sphere of technology. Others cared not so much about the artistry of cracking codes as creating chaos once on the inside. The ramifications were serious enough to draw the attention of federal agents. Their fear was that the power of computer technology had fallen into dangerous hands.

Maxfield began to see the evidence of criminal and malicious hacking: espionage, extortion, theft and credit-card fraud. He began to monitor the hackers and recorded their recipes for explosives and poisons. 'Logic bombs', 'viruses', 'worms' and 'trojan horses' were the heavy artillery of the computer anarchists under his surveillance. The hackers, with names like Brain Tumour, Dr Death and Axe Murderer, had crossed the divide of fun and games and had entered what Maxfield termed 'the dark side of the force'. For the next eighteen months, Maxfield would enter their world and, ultimately, fight for his own survival.

In the early days of computers, a hacker was a pioneer – someone intimately involved with the internal makings of a computer; someone who attempted, like the captain of the Starship Enterprise, to 'boldly go where no man had gone before'. The term 'hacker' was originally used to describe Massachusetts Institute of Technology (MIT) students in the 1960s who became obsessed with the computer. Their aim was to make the computer a beneficial tool for society. Later, 'hacker' applied to a computer user whose path of discovery involved trespassing on unguarded systems. In the traditional sense of the word, Maxfield is a hacker, whereas the new breed of hackers he was about to chase were guided, in his opinion, by two fundamental principles: that knowledge is power, and that there should be unrestricted access to computers, particularly those with sensitive data bases.

The sense of harmless exploration and invention embodied by early hackers gradually devolved into exploitation of data communication facilities by the new generation of whiz-kids who cared little about how a computer actually worked. The electronic machine was no longer a 'learning tool'. It had become a vehicle for criminal activity.

The criminals were not easy to catch. Their computers gave

them the chance to commit a kind of ephemeral larceny: silent, undetected, rarely punished. It was a safe form of robbery and extortion with no trace of fingerprints and, without ever encountering the victim, no guilt. 'Hacking is a completely impersonal, dehumanised crime,' says Maxfield. 'None of them would dream of taking a knife or a gun and mugging someone on the street. The hacker doesn't know his victim and the victim never knows the hacker. There is never any physical risk involved. They are introverted thrill seekers.' It's mob psychology but with an electronic twist.

Maxfield began to notice a form of electronic schizophrenia on bulletin boards. 'Face to face, the hacker is perfectly nice, well mannered, well behaved and polite. Someone who has never been in trouble, someone who is introverted. But when they get behind the keyboard, they unleash their imaginations and hidden personalities and they turn into Genghis Khan or Adolf Hitler. A 12-year-old I knew called himself Napoleon Bonaparte.'

On a BBS he noticed a certain equalisation taking place. 'There are no class distinctions,' says Maxfield. 'A hacker becomes just a voice on the phone or just a message on a bulletin board. It's like the Walter Mitty syndrome carried to the ultimate extreme. With a computer, hackers can carry out their wildest fantasies. And there is no one supervising them. It's the alternative to a street gang. The hacker is a street-corner hood, except today the meeting place is a bulletin board.'

Operating with an electronic anonymity, hackers key into boards named 'Sanctuary', 'Futureworld', 'Darkside', 'Death Trap' or 'Speed Demon Elite'. A BBS is an equaliser, upon which the physical appearance of the hacker is never called into play. Instead, what counts is the level of daring he performs in 'cracking' into sensitive computer systems. His hacking skills are displayed when he posts on the BBS the secret passwords to the restricted data base he has broken into.

The British science-fiction writer Arthur C. Clarke expressed that high technology is indistinguishable from magic. Maxfield believes hackers understand the power of magic. 'They live in a fantasy world where a computer password is the equivalent of a magical incantation, like an old-fashioned wizard might use,' says Maxfield.

Passwords allowed computer users to go certainly where no teenager had gone before. Demographic studies conducted on known hackers reveal that they are for the most part teenage boys, although 10-year-olds, college professors and a few girls have also become hacker gang members. An FBI agent described them as 'bright, affluent and bored'. Being a hacker became the perfect remedy for adolescent ennui. What could be more exciting than marauding sophisticated computer systems with an alias such as the Stainless Steel Rat, King Blotto, Satan's Stronghold or Black Knight – especially when your voice has not yet broken?

Maxfield's initial brief was to identify hackers who traded illegally copied software. He would gain access to a bulletin board and methodically write down their details on recipe cards. 'Then I called a BBS in New York City, where the real hackers hung out,' says Maxfield. He was in for a surprise. 'I have a friend who is installing a new computer at the Pentagon,' read one. 'He's giving us the password next week.'

'This was thirty days after I started working for the FBI,' recalls Maxfield. 'So, suddenly, we went from little kids passing around illicit software to someone who was now threatening our defence policy. We were playing hardball. That's when I decided it had to be more than a part-time activity. I felt a sense of obligation. What really concerned me was this lack of understanding of what a computer could do,' says Maxfield.

'When you're talking about a true hacker, you are talking about an explorer. The problem is that in the course of your explorations you find out not only how things work but how things are flawed. You think about how to exploit the flaw, to make things work to your benefit and, at that point, you've crossed into that grey area. If you continue further you're into the criminal area. You're into what I call the "Dark Side of the Force". The dividing line is not very clear,' says Maxfield, 'but I've always known where the line was. I always knew when I crossed the line and I think the hackers know, but they don't care. If something happens, if they think someone is on their trail, all they have to do is hang up the phone, disconnect the line and they're gone. In a sense, they are untraceable. They are invulnerable to any detection. I was the only person who volunteered to help. I became the Lone Ranger out there.' Following the Pentagon disclosure, Maxfield knew he could no longer remain on the sidelines. 'I've got to join this underground,' he told himself. The question was, how?

While gathering intelligence, Maxfield discovered a bulletin board featuring a section for the exchange of stolen long-distance dialling codes and information on hacking. He made friends with the BBS operator to find out what was going on. After several telephone conversations and bulletin-board messages, the BBS operator said, 'Look, you know much more about hacking and phreaking than I do. Why don't you run the hacking and phreaking section of the bulletin board?'

Maxfield accepted and soon the FBI gained an insider's look into the computer underground. 'We were running it as a sting,' says Maxfield, 'unknown even to the bulletin-board operator himself.' He developed a handle and called himself Cable Pair, the first phone phreak, and then devised an enticing gimmick for his prey. He set up a 'training school' for hackers on the newly created 'sting board'.

'I was going to teach them the basics of how the telephone system operated. I wasn't going to teach them anything that wasn't already in a technical manual. But I had to make it sound like they were going to learn something really super nasty. I had never had any training as an actor, never had any thoughts of doing anything like that and, suddenly, I was involved in acting, role playing. I did what I thought I should do and it worked.' Within seventy-two hours, Cable Pair received calls from the Glitch, the Sprinter and the Wizard, and two dozen more hackers from around the US.

'The objective was to penetrate through the alias to the real person and in order to do that all I needed was their home phone number,' says Maxfield. 'For instance, if the Mad Hacker was posting Sprint (an American-based long-distance telephone company) codes, we had all we needed to find out his real identity. We would make friends with him somehow through introductory messages. He would log on the bulletin board a day or so later and read my message that I had sent privately to him and he would call my phone number, using one of the stolen Sprint codes. We had a back trace if we needed, but, more importantly, I would be talking to him one-on-one over the phone, on a little more personal basis.'

During the telephone conversation Maxfield could find out what the Mad Hacker was doing, how he was doing it, what kind of equipment he had, what sort of computer, what other bulletin boards he was calling. Maxfield would say, 'Hey, I gotta go, it's dinner-time. Can I call you back later? What's your number?' And the Mad Hacker would unwittingly become an entry in Maxfield's FBI file.

Beginning in September 1982, Maxfield gathered evidence from hackers eager to learn about phreaking. Hackers soon discovered that 'BBSing', while fun and absorbing, can be terribly expensive, carrying the equivalent costs of marathon long-distance calls. One hacker spent sixteen hours a day on the telephone lines, accessing BBSs all over the world. Using stolen long-distance codes he ran up a bill of $400,000 before being caught. The simple solution for hackers was to learn how to make free telephone calls. Maxfield's 'training school' drew eager hackers ready to learn the fine art of blue boxing and phreaking. While he spun together vague abstracts on telecommunications, Maxfield gleaned valuable tricks of the hacker trade.

Maxfield monitored numerous boards, each of which had its own *raison d'être*. He noticed that on some, for example, detailed tutorials on various aspects of hacking appeared, accompanied by access codes to restricted data bases. It became clear to Maxfield that he had entered a world in which there was an orderly progression of hacking feats that lead to a lexicon of computer crime.

As Maxfield scanned the boards he began to establish a rapport with his targets. Through their messages, he learned that hackers, armed with computers and modems, had begun trespassing into private computer systems, including those belonging to corporations, foundations, universities and banks. Hacker gangs began to go 'carding', using valid credit-card numbers obtained from discarded carbons, accounts posted at video rental stores, or even by hacking credit-bureau computers. 'Trashing' was another trick. Hackers sifted through trash to find thrown away computer passwords and code words and confidential company phone directories. Corporate trash, Maxfield learned, is a hacker's treasure chest.

One day, Maxfield found a four-part tutorial on credit-card fraud posted on an exclusive east coast BBS dedicated to advanced hacking. Its creator posted the warning, 'You MUST have a fluent tongue and a semi-deep voice (skip this part if your voice is still cracking – refer back when you get a real one).'

Maxfield was having a field-day. When he started, he counted between 400 and 500 hackers on the boards. Within two years, their numbers would increase by a factor of ten. 'The hackers form little cliques and gangs, so I went after the top ones. I didn't bother with the little kids who didn't know anything because they weren't really a threat,' says Maxfield. 'In the process, I had to talk to them all. By setting up the sting operation, they came to me. I had to do a lot of analysis and decide who was who and who was the bad guy and who was the casual kid who liked some software now and then and didn't pay for his phone calls. No one was going to prosecute that person, but

the person who was deleting files in some government system –
he was a threat and he had to be identified and dealt with.'

At the beginning, Maxfield says, 'We had no intention of
arresting anybody. We were strictly doing intelligence gathering.
The FBI had really no background to the nature and extent of
the electronic underground. So we spent probably the first six
months just gathering information.'

Soon after Maxfield began working undercover, in November
1982, one of the bulletin-board operators decided to have a
piracy party and invited all of the users to his house for a huge
software swap. Maxfield, who had become a member of the
bulletin board, was invited. He left a message with the system
operator (sysop) asking if he could bring a friend. The sysop
said, 'Oh sure, the more the merrier.'

Maxfield's friend was an FBI agent. Both of them were
operating undercover. They parked a quarter of a mile away
and set up a camera on a tripod in the parking lot of a nearby
high school. With a powerful telephoto lens they began taking
photographs of teenage hackers emerging from their parents'
cars, lugging their computers into the sysop's house.

'It was just like on TV,' recalls Maxfield. 'You're sitting there
with binoculars watching the bad guys drive up in their cars.
You take a picture of the licence plate and call it in on the
radio to find out who the car belongs to and then, as they get
out the car, you take their picture.' When Maxfield and the
agent finally arrived at the party they were led to a recreation
room. 'There must have been about twenty computers and
forty people. The room was jammed. Everybody was copying
software like crazy. In that afternoon, over $100,000 worth of
illegal software changed hands.'

The BBS computer and its modem were surrounded in a
corner by a group of hackers trying to break into a university's
mainframe. The FBI agent, who looked like he was a student
dressed in a T-shirt and jeans, walked over and made friends
with a college professor who had brought some equipment

from his university to the copy party. The professor ran off duplicates of copyright software and gave it to the FBI agent. 'Meanwhile,' says Maxfield, 'I spoke with some pirates and I mentioned that I was one of the original inventors of the blue box. And this guy jumps up and announces it to the whole room. All of these hackers converged on me. Well, at about that moment, the doorbell rang and one of the hackers said, "Oh my God, I hope that's not the FBI!" I looked over at the agent and I couldn't keep a straight face.'

The party was useful. It provided Maxfield with introductions to hackers, while his notoriety as Cable Pair spread. After the new year he began noticing an influx of names appearing on the bulletin boards. Teenagers who had received computers for Christmas began testing their data-communication skills. The Hacker, a 14 year old from Detroit, stood above the rest. The Hacker's parents had given him a modem for Christmas, and with it he and his $250 Atari 400 travelled through computer systems all over the US. The Hacker became co-system operator of a BBS called the Secret Service. It was the creation of a 12-year-old hacker in Los Angeles by the name of Megabyte. The Secret Service BBS had a hidden section requiring a special access code.

BBS access numbers are as closely guarded as secret formulas. Some are posted on underground boards, but to gain access to their hidden sections is extremely difficult. Computers at the Department of Defense, like hundreds of businesses, give an indication when you've reached them. But with some BBSs one is required to know a password in order just to find out what BBS is on the other end of the modem. Once engaged with a system, a user is required to give his real name, phone number, address, occupation and interests. The sysop will then call and give a secondary password, provided the caller has passed scrutiny.

Maxfield monitored Megabyte and the Hacker, carefully making notes of the stolen long-distance carrier codes hidden in the secret section of their BBS. He fed the information to the FBI, and to MCI and US Sprint, the long-distance telephone companies whose codes had been stolen and posted. On a Friday morning in May 1983, investigators from the Los Angeles Police Department, armed with a search-warrant and joined by representatives from Pacific Telephone (the local phone company) and Sprint, walked into Megabyte's house and 'cleaned his bedroom for him', says Maxfield. Megabyte was charged with 146 counts of wire fraud and placed on probation.

Maxfield, meanwhile, had become good friends with the Hacker, who he also knew as Eric Stajda, freshman at DeLaSalle Collegiate High School in Detroit. 'He seemed to be the one to watch,' says Maxfield. 'He had been talking about wanting to be on defence systems. He was special,' says Maxfield. 'He was on the boards all of the time. He was on dozens of them. Once he learned how to phone phreak, it was a full-time occupation.'

Maxfield, who had met Eric through the Secret Service BBS, called him the day after Megabyte's bust.

'Eric, aren't you afraid?' asked Maxfield.

'I'm not worried,' he said. 'I live 2,000 miles away. I'll just change my handle.'

Overnight, the Hacker became the Wizard of Arpanet and a founding member (and eventual leader) of the Inner Circle gang. The Inner Circle communicated through the Security Land BBS, an élite, Beverly Hills-based bulletin board created by a hacker called Napoleon Bonaparte. The Wizard's new title reflected Stajda's dedication to cracking defence systems within the Advance Research Projects Agency Network, or Arpanet, for short.

Regarded as one of the most vital data networks in America, Arpanet links the Pentagon with 300 mainframe computers and 50,000 users at universities, defence contractors, the Pentagon and other Department of Defense locations for the exchange of classified and non-classified information. 'It might be nothing more than annual budget information,' says Maxfield, 'or it could be very sensitive and classified, like the results of some kind of missile guidance-system development project.'

Normally if a hacker wanted to break into Arpanet, he would find out a password. Unless they are very facile, you don't guess passwords. You steal them. 'So what would happen is this,' explains Maxfield. 'You might have a hacker who is an airman in the Air Force, or he has a friend in the military or a government official or someone who has access to where the computers are and, by one means or another, he obtains a password.'

The Wizard continued making inroads into the Arpanet's system. One day, he managed to break into the Pentagon. 'The Wizard had found a way to get a dial tone from inside the Pentagon,' explains Maxfield. 'He had heard from somebody that there was an 800 number you could call and if you knew what to do you, you would get a Pentagon dial tone. The number belonged to the Defense Department,' says Maxfield. 'At that point you could dial anywhere the Pentagon could dial, at the Pentagon's expense. These included all the defence circuits on the Pentagon's private network, just like in the movie *War Games*. You could access Department of Defense computers, anything, provided you knew the phone numbers and the passwords.

'Well, my phone rang one day and it was the Wizard, and he says, "Cable Pair, listen to this!" The next thing I know, he three-way connects me with a general in the Pentagon and he's talking to the general . . .

'The Wizard pretended he was another general somewhere. Of course, because he had a very young sounding voice, the conversation degenerated very rapidly. The name he chose was totally bogus and I kept wanting to break in on the conversation and say, "Eric, hang up!" I couldn't even hang up because then it would be obvious that somebody else was on the line, so I just had to hold the phone and, finally, the general hung up his phone and that was the end of the call.'

With the Wizard as their founding leader, the Inner Circle gang began targeting other defence areas. 'One night they tried to order a red alert at NORAD, the North American Air Defense Command headquarters. There was a hacker who was the son of a British diplomat and he had access to various secret codes. For example, all high-ranking members of government are assigned a code-name. At the time, George Bush, Vice-President of the United States, was known as Timber Wolf. So, if you called up a certain unlisted telephone number that the hackers had found out, which rang at the White House switchboard, and said, "I want to speak to Timber Wolf," you were connected to George Bush, no questions asked, no matter where he was.

'So they were calling up NORAD and ordering Red Alerts: "This is Timber Wolf, I've got a code three . . ." They never really got anywhere with it, but the point was, it got everybody in an uproar. Needless to say, the Secret Service was not pleased, nor was the State Department when they learned who was the source of the codes. All of the codes had to be changed. The diplomat's son, who had diplomatic immunity, had to be persuaded not to do this any more,' says Maxfield.

'They also found a way to bill telephone conference calls, 59-way conference calls, to the White House switchboard. So they were giving President Reagan big phone bills for their phone-phreak conferences. It was just an incredible, wide-open scene. The Inner Circle was already doing the stuff that was in *War Games* before the movie came out. Afterwards, there was a tremendous explosion of activity.'

War Games, the movie about two teenage hackers who penetrate government defence computers and nearly start a nuclear war, produced an eager new crop of hackers. For the normally introverted teens, their technical prowess could be measured by a kind of modem machismo. At the time, Donn Parker, a computer and data security consultant at SRI International, a California-based non-profit research institute, commented, 'The malicious hacker problem is continuing to increase drastically and is getting far more serious. The lowering costs of equipment, the attraction for new kids coming into it as a rite of passage, points to an increasing vulnerability of American business to the hacker problem.'¹ Parker's expertise ironically landed him the job of technical consultation to *War Games*.

By 1983, within months of the movie's release, Infocorp, a marketing research concern in Cupertino, California, reported that there were 600,000 computers at use in homes in the United States, a six-fold increase since 1980. Infocorp's president estimated that 120,000 to 180,000 of the computers were equipped with modems, the required instrument hackers use to gain access to bulletin boards and other computers.

Meanwhile, in his undercover role, Cable Pair had become an adviser to the Inner Circle, and maintained a number two position on their secret bulletin board. What the hackers didn't know was that with every encounter they had with him he gathered evidence to bust them. He monitored their calls with dial number recorders, so that he could determine where they were calling and what systems they were breaking into. Maxfield even got to know them personally, inviting hackers to his office at the height of the post-*War Games* frenzy. Kids travelled over 600 miles, from as far away as Washington, DC, to come and meet the veteran hacker and phone phreak, and to play with his equipment.

Most of the Inner Circle turned up: the Stainless Steel Rat, PBX Super Switch, Myth, System Lord, Mr Binary, the Rodent and, of course, their leader, the Wizard of Arpanet. Maxfield told them that he worked as a telephone-equipment repairman.

A couple of weeks after the get-together, Maxfield examined the messages on the Inner Circle's BBS and sensed a growing hostility between the Wizard of Arpanet and Mandrake the Magician, a hacker in New York. By now, the Pentagon trick was old hat. The Inner Circle had moved into the major leagues. A San Diego Inner Circle member, known as the Cracker, discovered the access code to Telemail, a network service operated by the GTE Telenet Communications Corporation in Vienna, Virginia. Companies subscribing to Telemail paid, besides the price of a phone call, a minimum monthly fee of $500, and $14 an hour for use during business hours. The Telemail network links more than 1,200 commercial computers, including firms on the Fortune 500 list of the biggest American industrial companies. It also has a fair share of government accounts.

Mandrake the Magician, like the Wizard of Arpanet, was an Inner Circle system operator. In the manner of victors dividing up spoils, they divided Telemail's major accounts between them. One day, the Wizard was in a bad mood. He called up Mandrake's mother in Scarsdale, New York and swore at her. Then he superimposed his user ID over Mandrake's and took the Magician's accounts, including the one belonging to the National Aeronautics and Space Administration (NASA). The Wizard left electronic cartoons and 'Kilroy was here' messages for Mandrake and NASA agency employees to find.

Mandrake guessed the Wizard's password and proceeded to delete the Wizard's accounts (including NASA's), instantly destroying all of the electronic mail messages they held.

Incensed, the Wizard retaliated by wiping out Mandrake's Coca-Cola account. They waged their battle throughout the month of May 1983. Companies lost mail, had it rifled through or received shocking messages. One of the hackers' gimmicks provided cheap entertainment. They would send insulting messages signed by one executive to another and immediately fire offensive replies to the supposed originator.

Telemail had four different groups invading it. Besides the Inner Circle, there were the friends of the Inner Circle, Phalse (Phreakers, Hackers and Laundromat Service Employees) and random system abusers.

By June, Maxfield had identified the hackers. At that point,

Cable Pair was asked if he wanted a Telemail account to play with. 'The Wizard,' he says, 'offered me a piece of NASA.'

In the early part of the summer of 1983, according to Maxfield, GTE Telemail called up the FBI and told them someone had just destroyed their system. The FBI rang Maxfield. 'They said, "Who's hacking Telemail?" I said, "Well, it's the Wizard and it's Mandrake the Magician and this guy and that guy." I gave them about twelve names. And so then they set up the trap-and-trace, and dial number recorders.'

In the end, the intruders had caused so much turmoil among the users of the Telemail network that the Telenet Corporation had to shut down the service. Hackers had changed the passwords of paying subscribers so they were unable to leave or collect messages. They found other ways of blocking subscribers from using the service and deleted information from corporate accounts. Investigators estimated the company suffered approximately $500,000 in lost time and repairs.

In mid October 1983, the FBI conducted simultaneous raids on the Telemail hackers. They hit the Wizard's home in Detroit, Napoleon Bonaparte's in Beverly Hills and issued search-warrants on hacker homes in Tucson, Arizona; Oklahoma City; New York City and upstate New York; and San Diego. In all, computer equipment was seized from fifteen youths from coast to coast.

The Wizard of Arpanet became a minor celebrity. He even boasted, 'Hackers from all around the country were calling up and comparing the number of FBI agents who raided them. I had about nine,' said the Wizard. 'One guy in California only had three.'[2]

Ultimately, the Cracker in San Diego and three other adults plead guilty to violation of Federal felony wire-fraud statutes, while six others would plead guilty to various misdemeanour charges. The juveniles, such as the Wizard, were not charged with crimes since computer intrusion was not yet regarded as a crime.

When he was busted, Napoleon Bonaparte (Bryan Green, a 17 year old at Beverly Hills High School) did not name names but said he knew of someone who had been 'bragging about deleting mass quantities of data'.

'It was intentional,' said Napoleon Bonaparte. 'It's not like he slipped and fell on his keyboard and, the next thing he knew, NASA was gone.'

A spokesman for NASA said that since the break-ins, the system has been changed completely, including the passwords. He told the *New York Times*, 'It's much more complicated to get into the system.' (In September 1987, a group of West German hackers, belonging to the Chaos computer club, broke into the international computer network of NASA and rummaged freely through the data for at least three months before they were discovered.)

Maxfield's work continued. A hacker called the Iceman, leader of the Black Triangle, supplied a tutorial on conducting credit-card fraud on the World of Cryton BBS. Eventually, six high-school students 'purchased' thousands of dollars worth of computer-related equipment which was sent to a mailbox rental service in Waukesha, Wisconsin. The Secret Service, having been informed by Maxfield of the group, installed a video camera to monitor pick-ups from the box.

Maxfield had learned about the case through scanning the bulletin boards and forwarded information to the police. 'I've reported crimes to victims who didn't even know about it,' he says. Normally, a victim, having seen unaccounted charges on his credit card or telephone bill, files a complaint with a law-enforcement authority or contacts Maxfield through his company, Boardscan. If the victim is a computer operator, Maxfield analyses what data has been changed or destroyed and if the hackers left anything in the way of electronic fingerprints. He writes everything down in an activity log.

'My role is to identify the perpetrator. Once the suspect is identified, we obtain a court order to put a dial number recorder on the suspect's telephone,' says Maxfield. 'It's similar to a house being robbed . . . you interview all of the neighbours.' Only in this case, the 'neighbours' are hackers signing on to the BBSs.

Maxfield has a network of twenty-five well-placed informants who make enquiries for him on BBSs all over the world. He is as tireless as his targets, who log on at all hours. 'It's a giant Dungeons and Dragon's game,' he says, referring to the addictive computer fantasy. 'If I can't catch hackers, I get really frustrated. I kill monsters or Klingons.'

Once the suspect is identified and Maxfield has sufficient evidence, a 24-hour search-warrant is issued. 'We hope to catch him in the act by monitoring his calls to the victim,' he says. The hacker is not arrested at the search-warrant stage, but the police obtain his logs, diaries, address books, long-distance codes and his computer. The next step is the analysis stage where Maxfield or police computer experts decode the evidence.

'Any good cop knows his local crooks like he knows his brothers,' says Maxfield. 'I know the hackers in the same way. I read their messages and I probably know them better than their parents, yet I don't know what they look like.'

Soon after his undercover work began, Maxfield noticed some new twists in the hacking game. The anonymous marauding instincts of criminal hackers gave rise to even greater thrills than simply cash rewards. A sense of anarchy prevailed. On a bulletin board in Phoenix, Arizona, hackers posted a recipe for thermite, an explosive chemical compound. Imahacker in Detroit posted recipes for pipebombs and poisons. 'Make sure you wear gloves,' he advised. 'Death can occur within sixty seconds of contact. You could get sick just touching this stuff. So be very, very careful.'

'Now this was a 14-year-old boy,' says Maxfield. 'An all As student in school, he had never been in trouble before in his life.'

On a board Maxfield monitored, called Black September,

formulas for nitro-glycerine and plastic explosives shared the same data base as files on the Russian Embassy. Information on wire tapping and bugging was also available. The Black September gang: Brain Tumour, Surf Monster, Mr Mastodon, Dial Tone, the Rogue and Lord Shadow, created a step-by-step log-on procedure for breaking into TRW to attain credit histories. This BBS became one of the many which featured the credit histories of Ronald Reagan, Colonel Oliver North and Admiral Poindexter.

Hackers flexed their muscles in other ways. Extortion became commonplace. 'Hackers would obtain all the passwords to a computer system, and maintain complete control of the computer by remote,' says Maxfield. 'They would threaten to shut down an entire operation if ransom money was not paid or they would simply demand a free account on a machine and say, "Or else I'm going to destroy every other operating account."'

More alarming were disgruntled data-processing employees who began posting anonymous messages on BBSs, requesting hackers to plant logic bombs, worms and viruses into their company's operating systems. A logic bomb is a programming code embedded into the system that usually instructs a computer to perform acts that can be both damaging and dangerous. A fired employee may have a hacker insert a logic bomb to modify the payroll system so that when his name is deleted, it will delete all other employees from the system. Worms, on the other hand, unobtrusively absorb the memory of a computer. Virus programs instruct the host machine to summon stored files and copies itself on to the files. The computer's memory soon becomes a mass of confusion.

There were times when the requests from angry employees were daunting. Mr Slippery, 12, never considered his hacking to be that special until one day he received a mysterious call from a stranger. The man offered Mr Slippery money to destroy a bank's records. 'At that point in time, I realised that it would be an incredible way to launder money. If I was real smart I would move out of the whole thing, because that was an obvious indication of organised crime to me.'[3] Mr Slippery turned him down.

At the height of the hacking fervour that followed the release of *War Games*, Geoffrey Goodfellow, a reformed hacker working at the SRI research institute in California, said, 'If companies try to thwart the attacks on their mainframes by plugging the holes in their security armour, they run the risk of antagonizing the intruders and escalating the intensity of their own next raids.'[4]

One hacker was told that the security of the San Francisco-based United States Leasing's system was too tight. The hacker replied, 'No security is too tight.' To prove his point, the hacker entered the system and caused $250,000 worth of damage through sabotage.

One of the classic hacker programs making the rounds of the Massachusetts Institute of Technology was the surreptitiously placed 'Cookie Monster' program. When someone working on a computer least expected it, the screen would suddenly flash the word 'cookie'. If the startled programmer didn't respond, the concealed cookie monster would go berserk, writing 'cookie' over and over, obliterating whatever was on the screen, leaving the final demand: 'Gimme cookie.' The only way to stop the monster was to feed it by typing in the word 'cookie'.

Maxfield discovered that hackers embody the cheerful indifference to conventional morality of their forerunners, the Yippie-inspired 'phone phreaks' of the early 1970s. In the hacker's handbook, property rights do not exist, nor does privacy. Imahacker, for instance, posted a message on his BBS: 'If you want to make a prank call to the President of the United States, well, here's the phone number to dial.'

'This was a direct line right to Reagan's desk in the Oval office and, believe me, this was the real number,' says Maxfield. 'He

31

even told them to use a payphone so that, if you got traced, you could run.'

With their adventurous amorality, phreakers encountered unexpected risks. Maxfield remembers when phone phreaks in the 1960s built blue boxes for the Mafia. 'Once they delivered the blue boxes, they were killed so they couldn't rat on their customers to the FBI,' he says. 'So the hackers are dangerous to themselves. They're also a danger to society. They have absolutely no thought for the ultimate consequences of their actions. They're only living in the here and now. They're so immersed in this fictional world inside the computers and networks that they really don't think about the consequences. They're extremely ego-centred and hacking in itself is extremely addictive because of this constant reinforcement and thrill. It's just like a drug addict who keeps taking stronger and stronger doses of a drug to attain better highs. They keep climbing to greater heights of audacity in their hacking.

'One night,' says Maxfield, 'they tried to connect the Pope with Queen Elizabeth and President Reagan. The Pope was asleep; the Queen's secretary refused the call and Reagan was not in the White House.'

Two of the telephone numbers came from the son of the British diplomat. The diplomat's son posted others on his BBS including the password to the reservation system of the Holiday Inn in Cambodia, the British VD hotline, Dial-an-Atheist, earthquake reports and the British Stock Exchange report.

While the diplomat's son eventually got caught, a hacker named Mad Marvin from Phoenix, Arizona, picked up where he left off. 'Call the embassy of the USSR in Tokyo, Japan,' he wrote on his BBS, as he proceeded to list all of the names of the staff and their direct lines. Scattered among the list were a number of KGB operatives. Right after this message was posted on several boards, the sysop of the World of Cryton BBS and about fifteen other hackers set up a long-distance conference call and dialled the Russian embassy in Tokyo and spent three hours on the phone talking to the Soviet science and technology attaché and the military and air attaché. 'They were offering their hacking and phreaking services to the KGB,' said Maxfield. 'Luckily I had an informant that was a part of the gang and I was able to report this to the Defense Department.' Soon after he did, Mad Marvin disappeared from the hacker boards.

'It shows you the extent that they'll go to when they're thrill seeking,' says Maxfield. 'What could be more of a thrill than, "Let's call the KGB"? I mean, we're talking sedition and treason but they are kids in a totally unsupervised, unstructured, uncontrolled environment.'

Hacking is perfect for spying, says Maxfield, because it's such a clandestine activity to start with. Hackers camouflage their calls by using 'network weaving', a technique using numerous links that make calls virtually untraceable. Joe, a phone phreak in Texas, leaves a tangled trail behind him whenever he phreaks a call. He has perfect phone pitch and is able to phreak his calls by whistling the numbered tone signals of his blue box. He is so good that he has been able to use the technique to dial direct to Moscow, talking at length to English-speaking disc jockeys on Radio Moscow.

Joe is one of Maxfield's informants, part of his electronic network of spies that have helped him track down criminal hackers in North America, England, Sweden, Denmark, the Netherlands, West Germany, Italy, Argentina, South America, Australia and Japan. But for his work on the celebrated 414 case, Maxfield did not use any informants.

The leader of the 414 gang was a 17-year-old, all-American type, Neal Patrick. He joined a Boy Scout Explorer troop headed by Dennis Bayne, a system-engineering manager at IBM. As Neal and his friends learned more about computers, they began trading information. Soon they decided to form an exclusive computer group. They called themselves the 414 gang because 414 happened to be the three-digit area code for their hometown, Milwaukee, Wisconsin.

'They had a secret bulletin board,' recalls Maxfield. 'In fact, it was so secret, you never saw it advertised. It was strictly an invitation-only type system. I found out about it by intercepting a message on the sting board (the hacking and phreaking section he created for the FBI sting operation). I took a chance and sent a message to the leader of the gang explaining what phreaking tutorial services I could offer members and asking permission for the password to the bulletin board. I pretended that someone "in the know" had actually told me about the secret bulletin board.'

Patrick sent a message to Cable Pair welcoming him as a member of the board. 'From that point on it was all down hill. We began reading all their messages about the computers they were getting into.'

In the beginning, the 414s stumbled across a BBS in New York called OSUNY – Ohio Scientific Users of New York. The OSUNY BBS was a treasure trove of secret messages and codes posted by users who shared access numbers to MCI and Sprint long-distance telephone services. The users also gave instructions in ways to avoid having unauthorised phone calls traced. The 414s also posted a variety of data network numbers, such as subscribers to Telemail, and added 'How To' tips for gaining access to major computer systems around the country.

Working independently, and mostly at night, members of the 414 gang accessed computers on GTE's Telenet network. The way a given computer answered back indicated what sort of machine it was. Since each computer had its own format for permitting access, that narrowed the range of possible passwords.

At times, there was hardly any challenge at all: hackers on the OSUNY or other BBSs to which the 414 gang had access had already posted the passwords. But even guessing them took little effort. Many companies never bothered to change their sample passwords supplied by their computer manufacturer.

By using his father's TRS-80 Model II computer and an automatic redial modem, Neal Patrick could break into a system using passwords such as 'system', 'demo' or 'test'. Patrick pointed out that one of the 414s broke into New York's Sloan-Kettering cancer centre computer by using the name 'test' and the password 'test'. By doing so, they gained privileged-user status by using the help menu and typing 'set process/priv=all'.

When a 414 member used his $1,200 Apple II to gain access to the Sloan-Kettering computer on 3 June 1983, it crashed. The computer was used to bill other hospitals for computer services and to monitor doses of radiation given to patients at Sloan-Kettering. In all, the 414 gang made some eighty intrusions on the computer.

When the 414s broke into the Los Alamos National Laboratory in New Mexico (where nuclear missiles are made and tested), they were a heartbeat away from accessing information relating to the design of nuclear weapons. The 414s gained unauthorised access to a data base shared by subcontractors, academics doing research, and employees of Department of Energy contractors. The electronic break in at Los Alamos that led to the detection of the 414 gang took place on 28 June 1983, less than a month after the Sloan-Kettering crash.

At around the same time as the Los Alamos activity, personnel of the Security Pacific Bank in Los Angeles noticed unauthorised access into a computer's system being used by the bank for program development. It was at this time that the bank decided to keep 414 leader, Neal Patrick on the line with a 'Super Star Trek' simulator.

It wasn't only the Star Trek simulation that foiled the 414 gang. 'Hackers are creatures of the night,' says Maxfield. 'They have the mistaken idea that it's safer to break in at midnight when no one is around. But if they did it during the day, they would be surrounded by legitimate users and wouldn't be noticed.' In late July 1983, two FBI agents showed up at Neal Patrick's home. Search-warrants were served, based on suspicions that the gang had broken into sixty business and government computer systems in the United States and Canada.

The 414s both delighted and scared people. Their hacking provoked emotive responses from federal officials who wanted to put a stop to an epidemic of computer tampering. Said one shaken-up Pentagon spokesman: 'It's time to put the fear of God into these people.'

Neal Patrick, leader of the 414 gang and a junior at Rufus High School in Milwaukee, became an instant star, appearing on the cover of *Newsweek*, being interviewed on the Phil Donahue television show and guesting on the *Today Show*. The media fell in love with the hackers who entered restricted systems. Patrick was invited to testify before a congressional committee studying computer security. Within two months, the first federal computer-crime law was passed.

The capture of the 414 gang marked the beginning of the end for Maxfield. By December 1983, he had worked for eighteen months undercover. While neither the 414s nor the Inner Circle realised who had prompted their demise, Maxfield's days as an FBI informant were numbered.

The Phalse gang specialised in hacking IBM voice-mail systems. IBM had introduced voice mail for their own internal use. Voice mail or Audio Distribution Systems (ADS) enable users with touch-tone phones to send voice messages back and forth to each other. For the Phalse gang it was an irresistible toy. They could eavesdrop on others and use the system to communicate with each other.

Maxfield had followed the gang for several months, tracking them on systems in Paris, Rome, Canada – wherever IBM had a voice-mail network. Because wherever one existed, the Phalse gang had gained control of it through knowing the passwords.

The leader of the Phalse gang, Eric Corley, gave Maxfield's alias, Cable Pair, an account. 'I was a member of the gang,' says Maxfield. 'They were using one particular voice-mail system as a super, secret, hidden, private bulletin board and using the system's facilities they had broken into to exchange information about committing further crimes.

'Some of these guys were keeping score. "I destroyed five systems last week, how many did you destroy?" They would just chortle every time they ripped somebody off. I got so angry. There were thousands of these hackers who essentially had a free hand to do anything that they wanted to do and they were doing it.

'I had been undercover for almost one and a half years and I was feeling the strain,' recalls Maxfield. 'It was also very frustrating because all these crimes were being committed and the FBI's approach was to gather intelligence. In other words, they were not allowed to tell the victims or warn them. The victims had to come to the FBI. That's the way it was. The FBI is not like a local police department. Their primary mission is intelligence gathering.'

The Phalse gang had penetrated IBM's computer network, taking over forty-six accounts. 'This system was being raped and pillaged and my contact at the Bureau said, "I'm sorry, but we can't do anything about it until they discover it and call us." It was totally frustrating.

'Finally, I just broke . . . I wanted to get these guys. They were just destroying the system. They had complete control over it and the victim wasn't even aware of what was going on. They would have found out eventually, but, by that time, there would have been major damage. My idea was prevention, stop them before they get started.'

Maxfield, out of frustration and anger, sent a warning message to the console operator. 'What I didn't know was that the hackers had control over the operator's account. I sent the message on a weekend, which was a mistake. I should have waited until someone was there. The operator eventually received my warning, but the hackers intercepted it first. It basically said, "Call the FBI." But it came from my account, which had been given to me by the leader of Phalse, so the hackers knew that the warning came from me. In other words,' says Maxfield, 'I broke my cover.'

Immediately following the interception of Maxfield's message, the leader of the Phalse gang called the FBI and successfully impersonated an executive of IBM and said to the FBI agent on the phone, 'What's going on? I got a message saying there's hackers in our computer and I should call you.'

The agent, according to Maxfield, did not verify the identity of the person he was speaking with by requesting the telephone number of the caller and ringing him back. In fact, says Maxfield, 'He spilled the whole story of the investigation and my role as an informant to what he thought was the security director of IBM when, in fact, it was the leader of Phalse.'

Eric Corley successfully impersonated the IBM ADS systems controller and spoke at great length with the FBI agent, asking, for instance, how informants become members of hacker gangs.

'These people [hackers] are very hungry for technical avenues through which they can communicate,' said the agent. 'You feed them a little bit of bait and a lot of times they'll go for it. You enter into a dialogue with them and they end up taking you for a ride.' Corley tape recorded the conversation he had with the FBI agent and published a verbatim manuscript of it in the first volume of 2600, the monthly magazine for phreakers and hackers.

The agent, not realising he was talking to a hacker, spoke of Maxfield's role as an informant for the FBI: 'We are kind of unique in that we do not have any other source available in any other part of the country that could supply us with information like this.'

On Monday, when IBM's real ADS system controller

responded to Maxfield's warning, the agent rang Maxfield. 'What's going on? I think we've been had. I just got a call from the ADS controller at IBM.'

Then the agent told him about the first phone call.

'Oh shit,' said Maxfield. 'My cover is blown.'

The agent in charge of the investigation was suspended without pay for thirty days. 'He was sent to FBI purgatory,' says Maxfield.

From the beginning while he was an informant for the FBI, Maxfield sensed that there was 'a concern that I might go native. When the cover was blown, I think there was a feeling that perhaps I had changed sides and it was a deliberate set-up to embarrass the FBI. I think the initial reaction of the FBI was, "that son of a bitch Maxfield set us up."

'I was more concerned at first with the hackers calling in death threats on the phone but also I was waiting for the FBI hit squad to come and wipe me out. . . . Paranoia struck. You're under attack, you're under great stress, your cover's in ruins, you know the FBI is extremely angry at you even though it wasn't totally your fault.'

John Maxfield, from an outsider's point of view, had played both sides against the middle, a deadly consequence of being an over-exposed informant. His story is not far from the realities of spies and agents who make their living by keeping secrets.

Maxfield describes what happened next by literally quoting chapter and verse from the FBI manual: 'Chapter 3, paragraph 19, subsection 5, which deals with informants, says that if your informant's cover is blown, you deny his existence.'

Cable Pair was on his own.

'The hackers knew who I was, because I'd met some of them personally. I had even invited them to come to my office. It was a very frightening time for about the first month or so. I would get threats like they were going to break every bone in my body, they were going to bomb my house, rape my wife, kidnap the kids and poison my dog.

'You see, we had no experience. Nothing to base it on; so it was a very scary time. You know . . . are these guys going to come around? I mean, I fully expected to have my office fire bombed. I thought somebody was going to accost me in the street; pull out a gun and shoot me. You know, I fully expected that to happen. It never happened . . . that's not to say it couldn't still happen.

'They want to put me out of business. I could be murdered by hackers in the next couple of months. As an ex-hacker, I understand. They know I know all of them. I know their identities. I have 7,000 of them logged on my computer. They laugh at the FBI, Secret Service, MCI, Sprint, but they don't laugh at me. I was one of them. I'm a real hacker and they're not. It's a matter of professional jealousy. Most of them have no real technical skill. They're wimps and nerds, but they live in a world in which they are gods.

'I force them to recognise themselves for what they are. I'm the one who rips off their masks. I deliberately go out of my way to draw their fire. I'm gunning for the Glitch so he will slip up and I'll get him. How do you find out where they are without exposing yourself?'

Maxfield was pilloried in the first issue of 2600, and he received plenty of electronic hate mail. According to the hackers, he is a traitor. They do not fear him so much as despise him.

'The hackers thought they made a big score by pulling off my mask,' he says. 'To them, it was like pulling off the mask of Darth Vader.'

Within a short period, Maxfield began receiving offers of support from hackers who wanted to change sides and work for him as informants. 'They saw it as an opportunity to get out before it was too late,' he says.

Donn Parker, senior management consultant at SRI, spoke with Maxfield after his cover was blown and encouraged him to continue in private practice. Parker has written five books on the topic of computer crime and is regarded as one of the world's leading authorities on the subject. Parker believes John Maxfield is 'a legend in his own time. I think his work is very valuable. He's probably the most knowledgeable person I know on the subject of hackers. He's gained a great deal of respect from the law-enforcement community and has helped solve many cases.'

'Maxfield,' says Parker, 'is an enigma. He is simultaneously trusted and regarded with suspicion by the criminal-justice system, the commercial computer user and hackers. One thing is obvious: he is as fascinated by chasing them as they are addicted to hacking.'

Besides acting as a consultant to a broad spectrum of clients, including banks and government agencies, Maxfield has a lot on his hands these days. The computer hackers are growing up to be computer criminals.

'These guys have graduated from *War Games* to the real underworld,' says Maxfield. 'For example, there is an orderly exchange of credit-card numbers out there. This is the organised crime of the future. There is virtually no exposure,' noting that a teenager with a $150 computer, a $50 modem and a telephone can sit in his bedroom and rob a bank 2,000 miles away. 'Who needs a gun? And there's no physical evidence. No fingerprints. No trail.'[5]

In the United Kingdom, the amount of money defrauded by computer criminals in an average case has risen from £31,000 in 1983 to £389,660 in 1988. The maximum single loss recorded among detected cases has also risen during the same period from £500,000 to £10 million.[6]

Total annual sterling losses caused by computer crime exceed some £40 million.[7] Banks, brokerages and investment firms suffered the most. Of the known cases, 25 per cent did not result in prosecution. Typically, only 15 per cent of all computer crime is reported. In some cases, employers felt the adverse publicity would damage the corporate image or the company's share price.

Estimates of computer fraud vary, but they are considered to be $3–5 billion annually for US businesses alone.[8] Computer fraud has obvious appeal. Experts at the FBI say only one out of 22,000 computer criminals is sent to prison. They estimate that only 1 per cent of all computer crime is detected, only 14 per cent of that is reported, and only 3 per cent of those cases ever result in jail sentences.[9] The average dollar amount in reported computer frauds is estimated by the FBI to be $600,000 versus an average of $23,000 using manual methods.[10] Still, the maximum sentence is one year and a $5,000 fine.

To this day, Maxfield's investigations have resulted in more prosecutions of computer hackers than anyone else in the field.

The biggest computer crime detected by Maxfield involved a hacker who broke into the Bell Telephone Laboratories and stole $1 million of proprietory software. Maxfield's intelligence gathering helped to identify the intruder as Shadow Hawk, a hacker living in Chicago.

As hackers like Shadow Hawk mature, they typically become successful, highly valued employees of corporations. Their career goals will be well-defined and they will continue to respond to technological challenges in an intellectual, clever and personal way. Unless action is taken during the next twenty years, many of the hacker vandals of the early 1980s will continue to manipulate computers and data bases but regard any thefts as 'borrowing', thus avoiding any difficult moral dilemmas.

Today's hackers, unless instilled with a code of ethics, will be tomorrow's computer criminals who will feel no guilt at stealing from huge, impersonal organisations. To their colleagues and superiors, computer criminals will seem completely trustworthy.

The computer technology they've learned to master at a young age will develop greatly during their lifetime, and, as they mature, so will the power of computers. What we've seen so far has been literally child's play. In the years to come, advanced technology will be in the hands of far more people. By scanning today's electronic bulletin boards, John Maxfield, in part, is tracking tomorrow's computer felons.

'I had the naive hope that I could stop it before it got started,' says Maxfield. 'But it's always gotten worse. One thing is certain, I'll never lack employment. The hackers will follow me to the ends of the earth to get their revenge and if I retire, it would be a victory for them. You gotta understand,' he says, 'I could walk away from all of this tomorrow and go back to fixing teletype machines and facsimile recorders and installing telephone equipment, but then the hackers would have won. It would be their victory. I really have no choice but to continue.'

The sun has set hours before Maxfield decides it's time to go home. He flicks off his computer terminal and grabs his jacket. As he heads out into the damp Detroit night, Maxfield walks past an autographed picture of James Doohan, the actor who played Scotty in *Star Trek*. Above Doohan's signature is the command: 'Warp speed, Captain Maxfield'.

Chasing fakes

'We're not peepers. We're not gumshoes. We don't chase errant wives. We are commercial investigators.'

WILLIAM THOMPSON, manager,
Commercial Trademark Services

A bright yellow paper lantern floats on a string above Lung Shan Temple on the outskirts of Taipei. In the temple courtyard, stone-carved dragons coil round thick pillars while gold serpents scale the upturned corners of its roof. Lung Shan means Dragon Mountain in Taiwanese and, banked against one of the temple walls, a mountain of joss sticks tucked into red packets are sold by a woman pushing the beads of an abacus.

Down the street, past the food stalls, the salamanders and the shoe makers, merchants with microphones shout at patrons to drink more snake venom to keep warm on a chilly autumn night. Neighbouring hustlers implore gathered listeners to try a bit of ground deer antler for what ails them.

A ginger-haired monkey, dressed in a yellow sweat shirt and denim overalls, scratches his head and ambles his way along a café counter. Looking bored, he issues a gaping yawn. The monkey glances at his hairy wrist as if to check how long before closing time. To find out, he would have to examine the rows of fake Cartiers, Rolexes and Piagets being sold along the infamous Snake Alley before him. Sandwiched between the shark-fin soup merchants and snake-juice emporiums are stalls selling some of the shiniest counterfeit watches in the Orient.

Like most street markets throughout Asia, Snake Alley is a world unto itself. Counterfeit goods are sold openly. The side-show of carnies hawking exotic potions merely veils the criminality of the exercise.

Product or commercial counterfeiting is the business of making inferior copies of originally designed and patented goods with the deliberate intention of deceiving consumers and stealing from the original producer. Commercial counterfeiting is always an infringement of a manufacturer's trademark and may also include an infringement of his copyrights, patents or designs.[1] The targets are usually prestigious brand names: they include companies like Dunlop, Hoffman LaRoche, ICI, Adidas, Kodak, Chanel, Bell Helicopters, Rolex, Dior, Louis Vuitton, Gucci and Levi Strauss, to name a few.

Product counterfeiting is an international problem and accounts for between 3 and 5 per cent of world trade, equal to $60 billion a year. A report submitted to the British government in February 1986 stated that copyright piracy could be costing British firms in excess of £1 billion a year in lost sales.[2] The British computer industry alone is said to lose £150 million a year through copyright and patent infringements.

The US International Trade Commission estimates that the cost of counterfeiting to American industry is rising by $6–8 billion a year. As for those shiny watches on Snake Alley, the Swiss watchmakers' trade association, *Fédération Horologère Suisse*, claim that over 9 million fake watches are manufactured every year at a loss to the legitimate industry of $55 million.

Counterfeiting does more than gouge away at company profits. Its cost can also be measured in human life. In 1986, the American Medical Association (AMA) had evidence of at least twelve deaths due to counterfeit drugs. This total excludes fatalities in Third World countries where dangerous fake pharmaceuticals often flood the market.

In a 'museum' at Commercial Trademark Services (CTS), a Hong Kong-based firm specialising in the detection and prosecution of product counterfeiting, the exhibits include fake eye-drops that can blind, worthless and dangerous 'antibiotics' and ointments that can scar and disfigure. Fourteen aeroplane crashes and at least two deaths have been traced to counterfeit aviation parts. Hundreds of heart pumps have been recalled due to dangerous fake components.

CTS works closely with Hong Kong Customs and Excise officers who have earned an international reputation for their anti-counterfeiting operations. But despite the fact that HK$56 million worth of fakes were seized in Hong Kong in 1987, the number of fakes that slipped through the net is thought to be many times that figure.

The equation is simple enough. According to CTS founder Anthony Gurka, a veteran of over 1,000 raids on counterfeit operations in Asia, 'A demand will always be made for a successful product or trademark. If markets can not receive sufficient supplies of the legitimate product, then counterfeits will fill that vacuum.'

Covering an area from Peking to Singapore, CTS employs 200 investigators and researchers, including 20 undercover street detectives. Tired of misconceptions about his chosen profession, William Thompson, manager of CTS's Taipei office, explains, 'We're not peepers. We're not gumshoes. We don't chase errant wives. We are commercial investigators.'

Since 1969 their quarry have been counterfeiters who make near-perfect copies of almost anything produced in the West: toys, clothes, athletic gear, computers, pharmaceuticals, automotive parts and luxury goods of every description. The Far East is considered to be the major counterfeiting centre in the world today and CTS's client list includes not only many of the world's most famous name manufacturers, but small outfits whose products have proved cheap to reproduce.

Companies hit by counterfeiting have sometimes made the mistake of evaluating the Asian market solely from a sales point of view, overlooking the tremendous capacity the region has for manufacturing. Seventy per cent of all licensed merchandise, for example, is already made in Asia.

Unlike the original manufacturer, a counterfeiter has an exceptionally low overhead. His factory can be a kitchen, rather than an industrial park. Thanks to the originator's experimentation, all research and development is provided. With the help of pre-paid advertising, so too is consumer demand. Never mind taxes, either. Counterfeiting is part of the huge iceberg of the black economy. What has been seized is only the tip of it.

The ludicrously low fines and penalties meted out for counterfeiting in most Asian countries has proven, at best, simply part of the cost of doing business and, at worst, an incentive to steal and defraud. By pursuing counterfeiting as a means of revenue, the manufacturing base of a nation can all too easily rest on imitation, delaying any meaningful technological advancement.

Copyright, patent and trademark laws vary with every country and those laws, even while this book was being written, were changing throughout the world. The most significant impact on the copyright regulations in Third World countries has been the threat from the United States that the import privileges enjoyed through the Generalised System of Preferences (GSP) will be revoked if the countries receiving GSP continue to counterfeit American technology and intellectual property in the form of words, music and film.

Solving the problem is not easy. Once a gold Rolex watch is found to be a fake, for instance, it must be traced back to a factory and eventually the factory will be raided. Usually police do not have sufficient time or manpower to dedicate to product counterfeiting investigations. To solve the problem, targeted companies have begun to take trademark and patent laws into their own hands. Hiring private commercial investigation firms, such as CTS, is one answer.

Detectives at CTS work on the front lines, gathering evidence

48

for legal shoot-outs. 'Many lawyers have remarked that they are the gun and we are the ammunition,' says Gurka. Over the last 20 years, CTS has produced evidence for over 1,000 clients. At any given moment, investigators scattered throughout Asia are at work on up to 170 separate cases – each with its own twist; its own cast of characters.

An undercover investigator shares with a counterfeiter a mutual fear of discovery. The tension is played out face to face. It's a drama of detection filled with danger and, at times, farce.

In his Hong Kong office on a humid August afternoon, over stacks of files marked 'Urgent', Steve Chan, CTS operations manager and veteran detective, is telling a story. His forceful personality makes an impact. So, too, does his compact, muscular build. Beneath his bluff exterior, Chan can be thoroughly calculating.

To create his totally fabricated, yet never questioned credentials, Chan has had to become a versatile actor. When confronting counterfeiters, he is the ultimate con man.

While sampans and junks jockey for position in the harbour, ten flights below his office, Chan is talking, of all things, about Tiger Balm. To describe Tiger Balm is, they say, to capture the sensation of snow evaporating by fire. The powerful analgesic with a pungent menthol scent has found an important niche in the homeopathic practices of Asian cultures ever since it was created by an old Chinese herbalist in Burma in the 1870s. The balm, colourfully packaged in little jars, is used instead of aspirin, nasal decongestants, lip salves, insect-bite lotions and other curatives. Stroll into any office building from Taipei to Kuala Lumpur and some over-taxed secretary will be gently rubbing a dab of Tiger Balm on her temples to chase away a headache or smearing some of the powerful analgesic on a minor cut. The only drawback to using Tiger Balm is that the stuff smells so strong that whatever the secretary might touch after using it will have a menthol scent.

One day, when Chan was in his local drugstore, he picked up a jar of Tiger Balm and noticed something unusual about its design. His instincts told him it was a fake. After some friendly exchanges with the sales girl, he was able to determine when the manager would be out of the store. Chan returned after the manager left and persuaded the girl to give him the identity of the supplier.

He returned to his office and contacted the Haw Par Corporation in Singapore, makers of Tiger Balm. The manufacturer, aware of the potential damages of counterfeiting, spends millions of dollars each year to protect its world famous 'leaping tiger' trademark. CTS was quickly commissioned to terminate the production of the fake balm.

The first thing Chan did after receiving the name of the supplier was to put the man under surveillance. He followed him on his route to various shops all over Hong Kong and discovered that he lived in a fourteen-storey block of flats, eight flats to a floor.

Chan, after some thought, took the elevator to the top and worked his way down, sniffing doorknobs until he hit one which reeked of menthol. Chan knocked on the door and, when the distributor appeared, made the excuse that he had gone to the wrong apartment. He apologised and left with a clear picture in his mind of the man and evidence of counterfeit Tiger Balm inside his flat.

After conferring with the attorney handling the case for Tiger Balm, Chan was told that he would have to get evidence of the crime being enacted. This was not as easy as it sounded. Through continued surveillance, CTS learned that the counterfeit balm was being manufactured in a shack north of Hong Kong in the New Territories, just a few miles from the Chinese border.

Despite being a Mandarin-speaking Chinese, Chan knew he would stand out in the tiny village in which the balm was being made. In an area inhabited by peasants and the odd chicken, he would be an obvious outsider. Chan needed to go undercover, but he could never pretend to be a native in a village in which everyone was so well acquainted. When he had developed his undercover routine, Chan smiled. It was just crazy enough that it might work. He met with the CTS immediate stand-by crew and plotted his strategy.

One bright morning, Chan and his team loaded a large van with video cameras, lights, monitors, microphones and electronic equipment. They left CTS headquarters in Causeway Bay on Hong Kong island and crossed the harbour through a tunnel to the mainland.

While the van nosed its way down the narrow streets of Kowloon, the investigators rehearsed their roles. After a while, the scenery changed and the grim slabs of concrete housing projects and worn-out factories gave way to the open fields and rice paddies of the New Territories.

As they approached their destination, the team was well prepared. Chan and his colleague, Derek Lam, would be movie stars on location. The rest of the team would be extras and technicians. They would tell locals that for the film they were making they needed to capture a flavour of the New Territories and wanted to include rural scenes.

The sudden appearance of actors, extras and technicians with sophisticated equipment was designed to create a colourful distraction. While Chan and Lam drew the attention of an elderly couple who had unwittingly leased a nearby shack to the manufacturer of fake Tiger Balm, an inconspicuous cameraman wandered over to the shack. Luckily, the counterfeiter was at work. The couple invited Chan and Lam into their home. As the woman prepared tea, the man stared at Lam in wonder. Sporting sunglasses, a scarf, gold medallions and jewels, Lam resembled Sammy Davis.

While neighbours gathered round the 'stars', the CTS cameraman nonchalantly began to take footage of the counterfeiter in action. Through an opening in the wooden door, he was afforded a full view of the counterfeiter filling jars with fake Tiger

Balm. In the foreground was a stack of forged labels. For several minutes he filmed the man and his modest warehouse. When he had finished, the cameraman walked over to the crowd and gave a thumb's up sign. Following his cue, the entourage suddenly announced that they had to go to another location and bade the couple farewell.

In the attorney's office back in Hong Kong, the following day, Chan learned that the evidence was solid enough to prosecute the maker of the fake Tiger Balm. Within the week, police raided the warehouse and put the man out of business.

Chan plays his various roles with gusto. In his office there are photographs of counterfeiters with their arms round him, smiling for the camera. Chan's talents have helped CTS seize millions of pounds worth of fakes over the years. He describes his impressive track record by saying only that he is good at observing details. Chan's experience has taught him over the years what to look for. Inevitably, they are the things counterfeiters forget to think about, like emptying the garbage.

Recently, Chan had been posing as a buyer of counterfeit Seiko watches and gradually acquired various components of a fake Seiko from a supplier. To solve the crime, Chan needed to find out where the factory was. After he placed an order for forty fake Seikos, CTS put surveillance on the distributor.

One night, Chan retraced the distributor's route to a warehouse. When no one was looking, he systematically went through the trash bins, sifting carefully through all the refuse until his fingers touched a tiny metal winder. He examined it closely and spotted the Seiko hallmark. He put it in his pocket and rode his motorcycle back to CTS headquarters in Causeway Bay. In his office, he carefully compared it to a genuine winder and determined that it was a fake. In doing so, he confirmed the location of the counterfeiting factory.

'Later we played another trick and ordered a big quantity – several hundred,' says Chan. 'We were in touch with this subject six times and, step by step, eventually the guy gave us not only the complete watch but sold us the mould he was using to manufacture the fakes as well.' Even more solid evidence was the contract he signed with the counterfeiter for a massive order of the watches in the name of Chan's 'uncle' in Indonesia. 'While the delivery was being made for our goods,' says Chan, 'we had already arranged for customs to arrest the guy with the mould and watches.'

Chan told the counterfeiters, 'OK, wait for me while I go down to the bank to collect my uncle's cash.' Within minutes, customs officers, armed with Anton Pillar orders (allowing for the search and seizure of evidence on grounds of suspicion), conducted simultaneous raids on the factory and five other locations Chan had reported to them. All locations were positive. Thousands of watches were being seized as Chan returned to the factory with the cash. 'What's the problem?' he asked the counterfeiter. 'Is it a robbery? What's going on?' The counterfeiters never realised Chan's role in their demise. To them he was merely a client who would need to take his business elsewhere.

There is often a grudging mutual respect between the investigator and his target, but Chan, who has earned the nickname 'Mad Dog' among his peers, says, 'I don't think they are clever, because they are still learning. We are both still learning how to cheat each other.' But the practice of catching a counterfeiter is hardly a game. 'I am not pretending,' he says. 'That is only my technique. If I am not using that method, how can I go hunting the counterfeit maker?'

Chan's working wardrobe contains outfits from coolie's rags to tailored executive business suits. If he is posing as a big businessman on a stop-over from Tokyo, for instance, Chan makes a point of buying a copy of *Asahi Shimbun* from his local newsagents to tuck inside his brief-case *en route* to his meeting.

'The aim is to understand the man's character,' says Chan. 'Before attempting to get information from him, I must have information about him. First of all, I observe his age and learn

53

something about his travel patterns.' By doing so, Chan is able to fortify his own role as an international businessman, relaying stories from his various trips. To impress prospective counterfeiting partners, Chan spins stories that leave the impression of a sophisticated executive. 'The general knowledge helps to convince them that I am a well-travelled businessman,' he says. 'You should always support your pretext with a very good story.'

Chan did some business a while ago in Korea when the local people were not allowed to smoke foreign tobacco. 'When I went down there, I brought a lot of cigarettes and brandy. An investigator has to learn about the people of every country he visits. You need continually to increase your knowledge, to improve your technique.'

CTS clients greatly depend on Chan and his colleagues. But it is not only work for targeted companies that keeps them occupied. Chan and Co. have also worked for big banks and corporations in Hong Kong, the venerable 'Hongs', as debt collectors. The investigator has also unravelled a complicated insurance claim involving the death of a closet morphine addict.

Chan's flexibility allows him to be at home in any situation on land or sea. One day he was assigned to track down a counterfeit shipment of a well-known brand of cassette tape. The vessel, a lighter carrying 180,000 tapes in 26 containers, was making its way down from the People's Republic of China (PRC) to Hong Kong. After successfully getting past the tight security of Whampoa dock, he reached the captain of the ship. Chan posed as an inspector for the consignee to check what was delaying the cargo. A swift inventory of the containers confirmed, through their numbers, that it was the cargo CTS was after. He was also able to confirm when the ship would be leaving the PRC.

Chan's ruse worked so well that the captain invited him to play mah-jong with him and his crew and to stay on board until they reached Hong Kong. But Chan had more important things on his mind. He asked the captain how long it would take them to sail to Hong Kong as well as vital information about radio contact. When he left the ship, Chan took the last ferry that evening back to Hong Kong. He would maintain observation on the mountain top of Green Island, at the mouth of the Hong Kong harbour.

The next morning at 6.00 a.m., the lighter appeared but, legally, it was too soon to impound the ship. The manufacturer of the fake cargo would be breaking the law only when the lighter entered a jurisdiction in which counterfeiting of such goods is a criminal act. Chan began to panic. He had to keep in contact with the vessel and it was sailing right past him.

'I needed to concentrate on that lighter but I was the only person on the mountain top. I had to follow it but I had no boat, no sampan, nothing!' Chan spotted a dockyard nearby and began to shout for help. The workers ignored him and he began to shout even louder. A fisherman in a small steam-boat heard Chan and stopped. 'I told him I was working with the Customs and Excise department. I said, "I want to hire your boat. I'll pay you any amount of money, it doesn't matter."'

Chan hopped on board. The fisherman gunned his engines and took off in hot pursuit of the lighter. Chan contacted the ship by radio and instructed its captain to bring it in to Hong Kong harbour. The chase ended at the waterfront dock of Tsimshatsui in Kowloon. Once the cargo was unloaded, customs officers descended and made arrests. Before a camera, Chan took his bow next to the unloaded contraband. The photograph is more than a snapshot. It is a stage credit for Chan's successful portrayal of a new character.

Chan is a consummate undercover man and I learned a great deal from him. But adventure cannot be fully imparted. It must be experienced. The best way to understand what it was like to be on the front lines of fraud was to go undercover myself.

In the middle of the typhoon season of 1987, I travelled from Hong Kong to Taipei and Bangkok posing as a buyer of counterfeit handbags, computer chips and Louis Vuitton leather goods. I met counterfeiters, factory owners and salesmen who never knew I was working undercover, gathering evidence to prosecute them. In every case, the person I investigated had taken a popular design, trademarked logo or field of intellectual property that was not their own, produced exact copies of it and sold it for a fraction of the price of the original.

The man on the street would probably never know the items were fakes until something went wrong: a 'designer' brief-case unhinging in the middle of a busy intersection; a fake computer crashing and erasing a data base. My temporary clients in these situations were the manufacturers of the genuine items. They were anxious to recoup lost market shares and restore reputations tarnished by identical but inferior fakes. Louis Vuitton, the French maker of luxury luggage, for example, spends $1.5 million a year to stop the manufacture of counterfeits. Computer firms have fought back as well. In an effort to protect patented software and computers, Apple has been waging war on counterfeiters since 1981.

In the case of Katherine Sapphire, a successful designer of luxury handbags, the person responsible for the fakes was a former employee, a girl of 27, named Eva Wong, who left her job after a disagreement over her salary.

Over the years, Sapphire's Hong Kong-based firm had secured large accounts in America and Europe. Her elegantly designed evening handbags are made of silk, lamé and intricate bead-work. Sapphire's factory on Cheung Chau, a nearby fishing island, was filling orders at an ever increasing speed.

Shortly after Wong departed, big clients of Katherine Sapphire's rang the designer and told her that her former employee was offering buyers the same goods at a substantial discount. It was Eva Wong's lack of initiative in approaching Sapphire's existing clients that proved her greatest mistake.

Early one September morning I met Mark Payne, a manager at CTS, and Derek Lam, who was to be my 'Hong Kong associate', in Sapphire's Kowloon design studio. Sapphire, a New Yorker who had lived in Hong Kong for many years, showed us her product range and described the designs Wong had claimed were her own in an effort to woo Sapphire's clients away. Sapphire wanted us to find out how far Wong had progressed in stealing her designs and her business. She had a hunch that Wong had persuaded the owner of the factory producing her handbags to manufacture identical ones for Wong. To find out, Derek Lam and I, as Wong's prospective clients, would arrange a visit to the factory.

During the four years she worked for Sapphire, Wong acquired a great deal of knowledge about the business, such as the various ranges, styles, pricing, and so on. She began to model herself, both in terms of business acumen and appearance, after Sapphire. By the time she had left, Wong had gradually transformed herself to look like the New York designer. Her waist-length hair was cut to her shoulders; she wore the same horn-rimmed glasses as Sapphire and her wardrobe matched the designer's. In many ways, Wong had become a clone of Sapphire. The move to make counterfeits of the designer's products was the final step.

Unlike counterfeiters who start out cold, Wong had contacts. She had worked with buyers and was aware of levels of demand. When Sapphire spoke about Wong's departure and the acrimony between them, I realised that Sapphire was on the verge of losing not only her creations but also a business she had nurtured for a decade. I immediately got the impression that whatever had caused the rift, it was significant enough for Wong to take everything she could from Sapphire, to the degree of claiming all that was her employer's as her own. What we were getting into was not just your ordinary faked goods scam, but the bitterness of a vengeful protégée against her mentor. We were dealing with an *ingénue* counterfeiter of considerable clout. Four years ago, Eva Wong was a secretary. Today, with the convenience of Sapphire's trademarked designs and her factory, Wong was able to title herself as designer and company president.

At the handbag factory on Cheung Chau island where Wong had great influence over the work force, the fakes were being constructed next to the originals. The only difference was that Wong's company name, Seafire, instead of Sapphire's appeared on the label.

In preparation for my meeting with Eva Wong, I talked at length with Derek Lam about the textile industry in Hong Kong. There was too much to understand in such a short period of time. I quizzed myself on the roles of suppliers, manufacturers, factory inspections and pricing. We set out guidelines on our target price, delivery requirements and designs. Finally, I had to choose what to wear. I'd never met a fashion buyer. After a wardrobe shake-down, I decided on a turquoise silk suit.

I met Derek Lam in the lobby of the Park Lane hotel. Over lunch with Mark Paine, also from CTS, the three of us planned our strategy.

'You look petrified,' said Paine. 'Relax.'

I didn't eat a bite of food. My outfit was all wrong. It seemed to trap moisture. I tried to think like a New York fashion buyer and developed a slight Brooklyn accent as we huddled, waiting for Wong's assistant to arrive. He would take us to her Seafire Industrial Company in Kwun Tong. Eventually a bellhop appeared carrying a small blackboard bearing my assumed name, Alex Jones. As he approached us, I took a deep breath and said, 'Here I am.' A moment later, we introduced ourselves to Wong's assistant, a man in his twenties. He escorted us outside to a waiting taxi.

For the next three hours, I was a New York fashion buyer, checking out prospective merchandise on my way to the annual Canton Fair. In his role as my assistant, Derek Lam had contacted Wong earlier to set up the appointment. In the taxi we chatted about jet lag and the weather. Wong's assistant offered his card. It was buff-coloured, professionally printed and bore his name in both Western and Chinese script. He looked like the archetypal Hong Kong yuppie: tortoise-shell spectacles resting on the bridge of a perfect nose, a yellow polo-shirt tucked inside a buttoned-down Oxford.

When we arrived at our destination, we walked past cooked food stalls on the pavement and made our way through a large industrial complex. Floral displays with good-luck messages decorating the lobby attested to the recent opening of the building. As we stepped out of the elevator on the fifth floor, Eva Wong, dressed in black and white, horn-rimmed frames and swept-back hair, greeted us with a smile and a handshake. We were the first clients to visit her in person. The other five had placed telephone or written orders. She was, despite this, considerably more experienced at her game than I was at mine.

My only brush with the fashion business was strictly at the retail end. What I knew about women's handbags was that they were simply never big enough. More than understanding the pricing structure of beaded satin handbags, I wanted to examine the personality of a counterfeiter. Eva Wong didn't look like a crook, in fact her face could have appeared on the cover of *Vogue*. I had memorised the questions I was supposed to ask. If I kept the show rolling, with the added skills and experience of Derek Lam, there would not be any trouble.

When the door was closed to the small 'sample room' that doubled as a conference area, leaving the three of us alone, the adrenalin began to flow. Within a short period, we were all puffing on cigarettes. Habit accounted for Derek; panic for Wong and I. I explained that we required a large shipment of handbags within a matter of weeks. We were gearing up for the Christmas season and we wanted to know if Eva could deliver them on time.

Our real job was to find out how she sold her products to clients and to learn what designs she presented as her own. Derek asked if he could photograph the handbags on display. Wong, flattered, agreed. All but three out of twenty were exact copies of Sapphire's. She brought out a bundle of photos depicting the rest of her inventory. Each had a coded sticker on them but the codes bore no relation to Wong's system of inventory. Instead, they matched Sapphire's.

Wong had all the accoutrements of a serious businesswoman. She had surrounded herself with trusted employees. The two people we had passed on the way to the sample room taking inventory were none other than her mother and brother. Generally, counterfeit manufacturers are required to produce their goods incognito: at night behind locked doors in secret hideaways. Like Wong, most counterfeiters usually only hire relatives and trusted friends.

Wong was a young star on the rise. Already she was filling orders for buyers in France, America and Canada. She told us she even had her own factory, on Cheung Chau. In all, she painted a rosy picture of a young company, newly registered and on the move. In fact, an initial check by CTS of Seafire Industrial Company through the companies' registrar in Hong Kong showed 'no such business'.

Wong was very candid with us. She detailed current orders her company was fulfilling, to the point of describing individual volumes and pricing. For the Japanese market, Wong would attach a 15 per cent mark-up to the handbags. She assured us that we would get a good bargain. It turned out to be a straight 30 per cent less than Sapphire's prices. Her business naïvety came through when she had to formulate the price list of an inventory that was clearly not her own. The arrogance with which she claimed the bags were her creations was matched by the sincere gratitude she showed us for our shallow compliments. It was as if Wong had fooled herself before trying to fool anyone else.

The next day, Derek Lam and I took a ferry ride with Wong to the factory in Cheung Chau. The weather was hot and humid, the harbour, choppy. On the island, strips of fish were hanging out to dry. Narrow streets provided thoroughfares for dogs, roosters and the occasional tourist. When we arrived at the factory, a three-storey house, Wong proudly showed us her work force cutting and gluing together handbags. In fact, they were Sapphire's employees.

As we arrived in another building where more bags were being made, a man approached Wong to tell her that a group of people were presently catching a ferry from Hong Kong and would be at the factory within minutes. Wong appeared quite concerned at this and insisted that we finalise our business and catch the next ferry due to depart in a quarter of an hour. The sense of urgency was very real. Sapphire's factory inspector was on his way. Had he arrived while Wong was there, her credibility in front of Derek and I would have been severely damaged.

On the ferry ride back to Hong Kong, my cover was nearly blown. Wong asked me a series of questions about prominent buyers for department store chains in America. Finally, she asked, 'What stores do you buy for?'

My heartbeat quickened. I took a sip of water and tried desperately to recall the names of American fashion chains. I remembered preparing for the question but my anxiety chased away the answer.

'The Limited,' I said, hoping it would do the trick.

'Oh really?' queried Wong. 'I believe someone else is the buyer for the Limited.'

Pause.

'I took over their position two weeks ago,' I explained. 'This season has brought with it tremendous turnover.'

'It's been chaos,' said Lam.

'Say, I like that jade bracelet you're wearing,' I said. 'Where did you get it?'

Wong explained that the jade came from a Hong Kong shop. 'It's for protection against *fung shui*, you know, bad spirits.'

With that, we moved on to a topic close to the Chinese heart: superstition.

'I would say you're a snake,' said Wong.

'I beg your pardon?'

'You were born during the Year of the Snake in the Chinese calendar. Am I right?'

'. . . Er, yes! That's amazing!' I said, hoping to humour her.

'I knew it,' Wong said smugly.

I would have admitted to being an Ox, even a Pig, if it kept her from grilling me about the rag trade. When we hopped off the ferry on to Hong Kong island, tentative plans were made between Wong and Lam for their next meeting. All further interaction would be through Derek Lam, my Hong Kong associate, since Alex Jones was heading back to New York after visiting the Canton Fair.

Back in Hong Kong, I was glad to be myself again. 'Alex Jones' was never very real to me, but to Eva Wong my alias remained very real indeed. She sent Alex Jones a charming letter of thanks, beneath a bold Seafire Industrial Company letter-head. If I was not investigating her, I would have been touched by the enclosed books on the Chinese horoscope, one devoted to those born during the Year of the Snake. I also would have been impressed with her generosity in enclosing a Chinese lantern to use during the Mid-Autumn Festival. Instead, I felt sad to be the wiser of a business transaction that was fuelled by delusion. I wanted to shed my alias quickly. Eva Wong's livelihood, on the other hand, depended on deception. It was easy for me to drop my disguise. Not so easy for Eva.

In the early morning hours of 5 December 1987, Eva Wong's firm was raided. Waiting outside the Seafire Industrial Company to greet her was a Hong Kong solicitor bearing a writ against her signed by a magistrate the day before. Had she bothered to read that morning's paper she would have seen that an injunction had been taken out against her firm by Katherine Sapphire's solicitors. The solicitor also carried an Anton Pillar order, a civil search-warrant that permits the holder to seize evidence, in this case, boxes of handbags.

Simultaneously, a raid was made at the Cheung Chau factory where the manager admitted illegally making handbags of Sapphire's designs under Wong's Seafire label. A settlement was reached out of court, with Wong reimbursing Sapphire for revenues lost. Despite the setback, Eva Wong remains undaunted. CTS informed me several months after the raid that she wanted to schedule another sales presentation with Alex Jones.

It is conceivable that if a company, such as Katherine Sapphire's, suffered bankruptcy at the hands of the counterfeiters, the fakes, not the originals, would continue to roll off the assembly lines. They would be sold in prime tourist locations throughout Asia to visitors more concerned with bargaining than worrying about a designer's balance sheet.

Most counterfeits are sold by hawkers in the carnival settings of street markets, such as Hong Kong's Temple Street. At one end of the mile-long market, a sizzling, steaming, open-air food hall is a blur of shirtless men sweating over scores of clay pots resting on fiery kilns, each one containing boiling sharks fin, chicken feet or sea-blubber stew. The potent aroma of 100-year-old eggs and overripe cabbage wafts over the 200-odd stalls. In one corner, finches hop from bamboo cages to select fortunes wrapped in shiny brown paper. The products, from jeans to radios, gleaming under bright lights, are displayed in cramped open-air tents. Shoppers squeeze past the stalls to the distant strains of live Cantonese opera.

Nearby, a performance of another kind is taking place. Sandwiched between stalls, glossy photographs of Louis Vuitton handbags and Rolex watches are displayed on the collapsible stands. Young merchants plead with tourists to take a look at the gold watches that could be theirs for only US$28. When a sale is agreed, a young boy scurries off through the market's maze to retrieve the fake from an adjacent safe house.

The clandestine nature of Temple Street's counterfeit sellers is the latest twist in what used to be a roaring trade. Police raids have brought it to controllable levels. Hong Kong's high-profile Customs Bureau regularly wins kudos for its efforts in the war against fakes. Elsewhere, the battle rages on.

Undercover in Taiwan, I learned how simple it is to steal some of the world's most valued intellectual property. In a Taipei electronics arcade, I posed as a foreign buyer of fake IBM BIOS chips capable of programming a computer to operate as an IBM. Within twenty-four hours I was told fifty chips could be delivered to me for US$10 a pair. If I was willing to wait another day, the price would drop to US$8. To elude the authorities when I left the country, the salesman suggested concealing the chips inside a pair of boots.

The last time we met in Hong Kong, a good friend and investigator with experience in battling counterfeiters in Thailand offered some advice before my trip to Bangkok. In the bar at the Hotel Furama, I jotted down some notes. Weeks later, as my plane began its descent over the Gulf of Siam, I glanced at his cryptic instructions: 'In Bangkok, smile a lot. Don't get pissed off. Don't go around alone. Everyone has guns. Don't trust anyone. 500,000 drug addicts. 800,000 whores.'

In Thailand I learned that sometimes the legwork of an undercover investigator takes on burlesque proportions. CTS investigator Geoffrey Hill, based in Bangkok, spends a fair share of his time in the famed Patphong district where dancing G-stringed women lend their own interpretation to 'live performance'. One evening the British investigator took me to his favourite club in the district. As we passed the bouncers at the door, 1960s rock music blasted out of huge speakers and a parade of girls wearing numbered tags danced on a stage.

Hill sat down and ordered a drink. He then asked the waitress a question. 'Where is No. 117?' A native of northern Thailand, No. 117 had travelled to Bangkok, like so many other young women, to find a job. She wound up at the night-club where she immediately became popular with tourists and locals alike. One night over drinks, Hill had suggested that she might consider working for him by supplying information about clients thought to be involved in counterfeiting. She accepted and became one of two informants used by CTS in the Patphong area.

The waitress, wearing a bright yellow bikini, told Hill that No. 117 was 'busy'. Hill stirred his drink and looked as thoughtful as you can in a strip-joint. While it might be stretching the definition to call a stripper an 'intelligence expert', as Hill does, she gathers critical information from targets CTS could normally never reach. 'In a place like Bangkok,' says Hill, 'if you don't have contacts, you're stuffed. We need them at every level.'

The Bangkok bureau of CTS, like those scattered throughout Asia, has adapted to its host environment. Hill and his colleague, James Nichols, are the only foreign investigators in a buzzing office of native Thais. Beautiful sprays of orchids are placed before small shrines in the secretarial pool that is segregated by dark-green leafy palms. Buddhist monks in saffron robes had blessed the office during a two-year anniversary celebration and left behind strands of white string that surround a room containing, like the boardroom in Hong Kong, a variety of counterfeit goods.

Market surveillance is a continual task for Bangkok commercial investigators. To discover which shops sell counterfeits, I merely had to act like a tourist. My companion for Bangkok market surveillance was a soft-spoken Thai housewife. Kohrinee Wansurak's identity is well disguised. She works as a double undercover agent for CTS. 'No one but my husband knows what I do,' she says, adding: 'If I told my parents or my family they would be afraid for me, and if they told anyone I would be in serious danger.' A distant relative of Wansurak's is part of a counterfeiting syndicate. And, like criminal syndicates anywhere, its members are merciless with informants.

As Wansurak and I combed the shops for fakes, I began to see why Thailand had gained its reputation for enchanting ambiguity. Like classical Thai dancing, there is a graceful formula to be followed in negotiation and this I learned the hard way when Wansurak and I, following a long day of market surveillance for Louis Vuitton, entered a leather-goods emporium in the hope of discovering whether their factory was producing Louis Vuitton fakes. Our aim was to find out if they could fill an order for counterfeit Louis Vuitton writing pads – 'to be handed to our clients at Christmas' – and, in so doing, allow us to view their factory operations.

Both of us slipped off our shoes and climbed the stairs to the manager's living quarters and office. He wore a plaid shirt and had an easy swagger. Full of guarantees about attaining low-priced bolts of high-grade, fake Louis Vuitton fabric, the manager assured us that it was as good as the legitimate brown and gold material with the distinctive 'L.V.' initials. He was very glad we had come to him. When I asked to see the factory, he grew silent and frowned.

Over the course of our negotiations, he spoke directly to Wansurak in Thai. After much convincing, he acquiesced and an appointment was set up for us to see his factory the next day. He had told Wansurak that I was making him a little nervous with direct requests to view his operations, and with reason. The man had been raided only a year before and paid severe fines for producing fake Gucci, Cartier and Louis Vuitton leather goods.

The fines he paid were not to the prosecuting firms but to the police. Corruption exists in Bangkok to the extent that the destruction of seized goods, usually by bonfire, is carefully monitored by agents acting for the legitimate manufacturers. It is estimated that 10–20 per cent of seized counterfeit items are taken by police for personal use. 'Most people tend to be sympathetic with vendors,' says Boonma Tejavanija, a Thai attorney specialising in trademark law. 'The fact that we have to explain to the police the problems counterfeiting creates has to be our biggest task,' says Tejavanija, adding: 'To them, copyright infringement presents no major problem.'

Very few copyright cases go to court in Thailand, the simple reason being that the prosecution is never sure what they will get. In a land where commercial intelligence gathering must be done covertly or not at all, firms like CTS must go through a byzantine process to curtail the illegal manufacturing of products. They are first required to secure a power of attorney from the targeted firm. Only then are they legally empowered to be a representative or agent of the trademark holder. Following a formal complaint of infringement to the police, a raid is conducted by police with search-warrants. From that stage on, it is entirely a criminal action. Arrests are made and, normally, settlements are handled out of court. The goods are confiscated and, in those cases that reach the courtroom, the counterfeits are often resold by the judiciary.

A representative of Gucci in Bangkok has learned that any prosecution victories in the war on fakes are not worth disclosing. A newspaper account of the burning of fake Gucci handbags incited a pro-Thai industry backlash. 'Their feeling was: "Why should we give money to foreigners?"' says the local representative, adding: 'It's a situation we have to deal with very carefully. We no longer publish our victories in the local press.'

For the targeted companies and the detectives who fight counterfeiters from Asia to Europe, the job is a fascinating contest.

'It's the ability to deceive, to lie, to cheat and do it with enthusiasm,' says Keith French, a senior investigator with London-based Carratu International (CI), founded by ex-Scotland Yard Fraud Squad detective Vincent Carratu in 1963. From its offices in the UK, France and South Africa, CI has developed a clientele of over 1,000 firms, including the top names in luxury products, pharmaceuticals and designer goods.

When French first began working on counterfeiting cases, he went to Italy to track down the makers of fake Cartier watches. In terms of appearances, French was well suited for the assignment. His olive skin, salt-and-pepper hair and blue eyes make French look more Mediterranean than English. On his journey, French never found the watches. What he discovered instead were excellent Italian counterfeits of Cartier's leather wallets. Cartier, hearing of French's discovery, commissioned him to investigate the source of the leather goods.

French was concerned about the potential role of the Mafia within the counterfeit leather-goods syndicate. Lately the counterfeiting market had broadened within Italy to include everything from sink plugs to Bugattis. Counterfeiting had become one of the safest and most convenient means of laundering Mafia funds. Investigators at CI had become aware of the role of organised crime in counterfeiting when a Mafia *capo* scheduled a meeting with an undercover investigator in a bank vault. The mafioso told the CI agent, 'You can't shoot me in here because they've got cameras. You can't listen to me with a recorder, either. I'm safe here. It's the only place I will conduct business without my bodyguards.'

Like the investigator in the bank vault, French had to pretend he was a buyer of counterfeits. He had initiated his market survey of the fake Cartier watches in Milan and followed the trail through Tuscany. When he reached Florence, French booked a room at the Regency hotel. Early the next morning he ventured through the open-air markets. It was in a shop, just down the road from Piazza San Lorenzo, that French first noticed the counterfeit wallets. He waited until the manager had left for lunch and began talking with a sales clerk. After some persuasion, mostly in the form of L.20,000, she gave French the name of the factory supplying the wallets.

French approached the factory on foot. He could not see much from the street, so he entered through the front and asked to see the manager. Speaking in Italian, French introduced himself as a British buyer of leather goods and over the course of their first meeting, French let it be known that he was interested in seeing what they could do with designer products, particularly Cartier leather goods.

After the preliminaries, the manager gave French a tour of the factory. The view from the street had given no clue to its true dimensions. There were three floors and in the basement thirty women worked at a bank of sewing machines that turned large rolls of leather into wallets, key-rings, handbags and other accessories. The factory's size meant that French would need time to uncover how extensive the operation was. He wanted to be exposed to every aspect of the organisation: to inspect satellite factories, learn about the suppliers and gain knowledge of the firm's export capacity. To lend credibility to himself and legitimise his motives, French's first objective was to place an order. From experience, French understood that the more an investigator knows about the operation, the more foolproof the eventual raid. While there is no set script of priorities to follow, it is imperative that an investigator gets to know the person in charge.

Some top counterfeiters, like the mafioso in the bank vault, will go to great lengths to vet a potential buyer. In the case of the Italian factory owner, he had other methods of checking out his potential associates. His secret was to get to know a person by engaging him in social events. French was invited to several parties and boat trips. As time went on, he was drawn into a deeper involvement in the company.

French relayed information about the factory back to Cartier and continued to get closer to the heart of the operation. The factory owner liked him. He said he hated dealing with British businessmen because he could never trust them, but French was 'a gentleman' and he looked forward to having a long business relationship with him. The Italian invited French to his villa. One evening after brandies, the man brought out a collection of pistols and, to French's horror, began shooting at the ceiling. After the smoke had cleared, French noticed bullet holes where his host had fired his guns for previous guests. Over nights and days that totalled three months, French gradually gained the trust of the counterfeiter.

When he felt the time was right, French placed an order for several hundred fake Cartier wallets. To secure the deal, he gave the counterfeiter L.5 million as a partial payment. As his negotiations concluded, French put into action plans to raid the Italian's factories. The hopeful seizure of fakes would culminate in the arrest of the counterfeiter and his cohorts. One of French's conditions before placing the order was a personal inspection of the factories.

His plan was simple. While moving from one factory to another, a convoy of unmarked police cars would follow him. After French left one factory and moved on to the next, the police would make their raids. Before his factory tour, French waited patiently on the steps of the Regency for the Italian to show up in his van.

Earlier in the week at the hotel, French had been introduced to a group of tourists. On the evening before the raids, French shared a long and friendly dinner with an Australian surgeon and his wife, an American naval captain, a wealthy British businessman and a pair of German women in their eighties. As he sat in the lounge of the hotel and sipped his coffee, French told them that he was a leather-goods buyer from Britain.

The next morning, standing on the hotel steps, French looked at his watch and began to get anxious. Something was wrong. The Italian, who was to pick him up for the factories tour, was already an hour late. As French looked across the street he could see plain-clothes policemen whispering conspicuously into walkie-talkies. French began to panic. He let another half-hour pass. More than anything, he feared the operation would fail. He also did not want to lose face in front of the ranks of Italian financial police who had been commandeered for the raids.

The president of Cartier Italy had been a journalist earlier in his career and he had developed a very good relationship with the Italian press and television networks. The president had made arrangements for the counterfeiter's arrest to be televised.

At half-past ten, the Italian counterfeiter pulled up to the kerb. As he emerged from his van to greet French, police sirens began to blare. While television cameras rolled, uniformed police officers cordoned off the area and members of the Italian financial police surrounded the counterfeiter and French. When the authorities opened the van they discovered 5,000 counterfeit leather items. Earlier the Italian had conducted his own inspection of the factories. The police who were following him decided to raid them in succession after he had departed.

A police colonel, aware of French's position, came over to him and quietly asked the investigator if he would like to be handcuffed to the counterfeiter in the police car. French said that he would in order to keep up the pretence of being a buyer as long as possible and gain further information.

'So they handcuffed me to this other guy,' says French, 'and put me into the police car in front of the hotel. I looked back towards the hotel and standing on the steps staring at me in disbelief were the hotel staff, the Australian doctor and his wife, the American submarine commander and the German women I had shared a wonderful meal with the night before.'

To add to his embarrassment, footage of French, handcuffed to the counterfeiter, appeared on Italian national television that night.

Other CI investigators have found themselves in perhaps less public but hardly less compromising situations. One slightly paranoid counterfeiter, who controlled a large chunk of the Asian market for fakes, arranged a meeting with a CI investigator in a sauna in Singapore. When he entered the sauna, the counterfeiter, telling him that he did not want any surprises, ordered him to remove his towel.

Dealing with the unpredictable is an inherent part of a product-counterfeiting investigator's job. One day Vincent Carratu's son Paul, working undercover, found himself negotiating the purchase of a Chinook helicopter. 'I walked away from it thinking, "What the bloody hell am I going to do with a helicopter?" You end up in the most ridiculous situations!'

During one case, in which he spent nine months undercover, Vincent Carratu, the founder of CI, became very attached to the criminals he was shadowing. 'I felt very sorry to think that I would have to pull the rug from under them and get them caught. It's difficult when you do that. While I was able to surface through embassies to contact my family, they were watching me like a hawk. They weren't sure of me – not until later. I had to be very careful. It is difficult and you find living a lie isn't easy. It's not everyone's cup of tea.

'First of all,' says Carratu, 'you have to be very much an extrovert, so that you can talk to people, relax with people. You have to be a bit of an actor, a bit of a ham so that you can act it out.'

Carratu, at 60, is an ingenious master of disguise. His appearance changes frequently, made to measure for each case he handles. Carratu's moustache comes and goes, as does his plummy accent, which is often substituted for the various dialects, drawls and twangs that emerge in English, French and Italian. He is the kind of seasoned undercover man criminals confide in and apologise to for getting him into trouble. In order to gain further knowledge of counterfeit operations for clients, Carratu has been arrested some thirty times with his subjects. Rarely do they realise that, were it not for Carratu, they would never have wound up behind bars in the first place.

Carratu travels the world eight months of the year tracking down counterfeiters for his clients. Despite its dangers, the business has rewards. In London Carratu drives a chocolate-brown Rolls Royce. His worldly charm and disguises have endeared him to many a criminal. After a Carratu-instigated raid in Antwerp, the criminals with whom he shared a cell after the bust promised to make it up to him. As Carratu was the only man they trusted, the counterfeiters asked him to deliver messages to their wives and families.

Carratu's first case as a private eye involved nine months of undercover work in order to track down makers of fake Gillette razors in the Middle East. Carratu's assumed role as a member of a criminal syndicate was a success. At one point during the case, he was approached by Al Capone's legendary right-hand man, Meyer Lansky. For fifty years Lansky had masterminded the Mafia's gambling operations.

Following a poolside chat at the Saint George hotel in Beirut, where Carratu arranged to have a waiter take a picture of him, Lansky produced a forged US California State bond. He was looking to Carratu to help him flood the market with millions of dollars worth of the valuable certificates.

Carratu contacted the FBI, who at first did not believe Lansky had left Israel. The federal agents also refused to believe that the old man in the photo with a little white poodle on his lap was Meyer Lansky. After checking out Carratu's story, the agents returned and took a lengthy statement from him. Eventually, Lansky was extradited to the US. In the midst of a protracted legal battle in Miami, Lansky, caught in the legalities of his final crime, died of cardiac arrest. Carratu, meanwhile, continued his undercover job. The organisers of the counterfeiting syndicate trusted Carratu enough to invite him to their 'Gillette' razor factory in the Golan Heights. Soon afterwards the manufacturing plant was raided, permitting Carratu to finally surface after nearly a year undercover. The duration of the Gillette case was especially trying for Carratu. In another he would come face to face with the investigator's worst nightmare.

Recently, Carratu was handling a case for Paco Rabanne, the cologne and perfume manufacturers. When he flew to Brazil, it was not his intention to go undercover.

'I went over as a consultant to find out from the lawyers why counterfeit cologne kept turning up all over the place,' he says. 'They had no idea what they were up against.' The lawyers gave Carratu the name of the counterfeiter, Gilberto Joa. When Carratu arrived in São Paulo, he took a room at the Maksud hotel and contacted the local chamber of commerce to find out what he could about Joa. He learned that the counterfeiter had a large manufacturing plant and was well connected with government officials.

Employing a strategy that has worked for him many times before, Carratu placed an ad stating that he was interested in purchasing large quantities of perfume and cologne bottles. In conversation with prospective suppliers, Carratu made it known that he was interested in designer packaging and that he would pay the top price for perfect copies, especially of Paco Rabanne. He said that he was very disappointed with what was available on the market.

Carratu presented himself as an expert. Because his under-cover identity was a South African businessman, it made sense. In his sanctions-ridden surrogate homeland, many things were counterfeit, but he wanted to crack the market with flawless copies – ones that may cost a little extra than the usual fakes but would be virtually undetectable. Carratu's aim was to be invited into an operation rather than push his way forward. 'It's always better to be asked to join several times before agreeing to take part,' he says. 'That way, you're always above suspicion.'

Joa responded to the ad and met Carratu at his hotel. Over drinks Carratu was very derisory towards available counterfeit cologne packaging, saying that it was all clumsy and amateurish. 'It's nothing but rubbish,' he said, adding that his trip to São Paulo had been a waste of time. Joa opened his brief-case and

74

showed Carratu a perfect imitation of a bottle of Paco Rabanne cologne.

'Now you're getting there,' said Carratu. 'This is more like it.' Carratu said that he was still doubtful that any counterfeiter could deliver the volume that would make a joint venture worthwhile. At that point Joa explained that he was the owner of the factory that had manufactured the cologne bottle. Carratu described other operations that he had been involved in. All of which were extraordinary in some way. Joa, after a few more drinks, began to feel honoured to be in Carratu's presence. He was eager to impress him.

Carratu was interested in discovering more about the export system the company had and how it was able to penetrate European markets and invade New York, Texas and Florida.

'Tomorrow I'll show you my factory,' said the man.

As they approached the road leading to the factory the following day, Carratu could see what looked like a castle wall surrounding the building. Inside the factory, Carratu counted seventy workers rapidly filling bottles and packaging them on several production lines. He nodded approvingly to Joa.

'From there on,' recalls Carratu, 'we were in business.'

Carratu stayed in São Paulo for a month and, after securing vital information about the firm's operations, he returned to London. A few weeks later, the Brazilian telephoned Carratu and asked him to come back to São Paulo because he had new information about potential markets and wanted a further meeting. Paco Rabanne, Carratu's client, urged him to go back. Suddenly, the sting operation was getting much more involved than Carratu had ever imagined it would. 'First of all I had no intention of getting in as undercover,' he says. 'I was purely there to find out why action wasn't being taken. And what happened was that I suddenly found myself getting in deep. Whether I liked it or not, I was going undercover. I thought, "Well, São Paulo is so far away from Europe, nobody will know me out there." I thought I would be all right, so I got very involved with the man and his company.'

When Carratu returned to Brazil, he stayed with Joa for a month in the counterfeiter's villa. On his arrival, Joa took him into town to meet the rest of his team. In an eighth-floor office, Carratu was introduced to Joa's bank manager, his accountant, his lawyer and the financial director. After they had all taken their places round a large boardroom table, Carratu was asked to sign on with the firm as the export director.

The financial director, whose office they sat in, rested his coffee cup on a saucer and turned to Carratu. 'Before we talk business,' he said, 'I'd like to ask your opinion about something.'

'Fine,' said Carratu. 'Fire away.'

The man contacted his secretary on the intercom and asked her in Portuguese to bring in a copy of *Time* magazine. A lengthy article about Carratu, with a photograph, had recently run in the publication and Carratu began to get nervous. When the man's secretary asked which issue he wanted, the financial director became irritated and told her harshly it was the one on his desk. Carratu rapidly thought about finding a means of escape.

'I couldn't jump out the window,' says Carratu. 'The situation seemed ridiculous. I kept thinking: "How do I answer for this?"'

The secretary came in with the magazine. It was folded over and Carratu could not see the cover. The man grabbed it from the secretary and, throwing the magazine in front of Carratu, said, 'What do you think about *that*?'

'And there it was,' says Carratu, 'a big article headed: "Is it safe to do business with South Africa?"'

Relieved, Carratu suddenly remembered his undercover role and began to speak at great length on the topic of South African import restrictions. 'I probably talked far more than I should have done, but it was very close.'

A month later, the company and factory were closed down. Because of the volume of perfect fakes manufactured by the Brazilians that had flooded the world market, Paco Rabanne was forced to redesign its trademarked logo. Following his close call, Vincent Carratu began taking a more managerial role at CI.

Going undercover remains a double-edged sword for Carratu's colleague, Keith French.

'There are moments when you think, "What am I doing here? I could be earning twenty times as much on the other side,"' he says. 'But that's the short term. And when you're sober, you think, "Great, it could be good – but for how long?" What it comes down to is: I don't want to be forever looking over my shoulder. There's a fine line. That thin, red line and it's so very easy to go over. . . . If the deceit and the cheating continues over into your private life, then you're lost.'

– 3 –

The art of detection

'It amounted to an invitation to go with these two
strange men who were doing something highly illegal.
They wanted me, in the dead of night, to go with
them, dressed in my dark plimsolls and sweater and
show them where to dig.'

DOREEN STONEHAM, authenticator,
Research Laboratory for Archaeology
and the History of Art, Oxford

As he drove through the streets of Geneva, Mario, a Swiss-
Italian banker, placed a call to England. The woman the French
call 'Madame Oxford' picked up the receiver.

'I have a piece that needs testing,' he said. 'When can you
get here?' Before she replied, he added, 'I will pay your fare.'

'I've heard that one before,' she said.

'It's Etruscan. I visited the tomb myself.' There was a long
pause. '£300 in advance. Expenses on top,' he said. 'Please
come. I need your help.'

Doreen Stoneham glanced at her diary. 'I'm fully booked
during the week. It will have to be on the weekend.'

'No problem.'

On a Sunday in July 1988, Doreen Stoneham left her home
in Dorchester-on-Thames and flew to Milan where Mario
met her at the airport. A few minutes later, Mario's friend,
Frederico, another banker, arrived from Naples. After he had
passed through customs and immigration, the three of them
travelled in Mario's BMW through the Alps. As they neared

79

Geneva, Mario picked up his car phone and booked a table at a restaurant.

The weather was sunny and warm as the two bankers and Stoneham ate lunch in a garden overlooking Lake Lugano. She would be flying back to Heathrow in a matter of hours and so the Italians rapidly got down to business.

Mario and Frederico had acquired what they believed was a rare Etruscan treasure but they needed absolute proof before putting it on the market. Stoneham, an authenticator from the Research Laboratory for Archaeology and the History of Art at Oxford, was the only person they could trust to determine if it was fake or genuine. The locals in the small village near the tomb where the object was unearthed claimed it was a fifth-century sarcophagus figurine. Having purchased the stone effigy, Mario arranged to have it smuggled from Tuscany to Geneva, where he would go through the formalities of authentication. Once its estimated age was confirmed, its value on the open market would soar. Mario had paid some £500 for the piece, confident that it would reap ten times that under the hammer.

Stoneham, a blue-eyed brunette in her late forties, had been authenticating ceramic art since she began working at the Oxford lab in 1970. The range of her work was vast and included: ancient Han Dynasty pottery figurines of kneeling women, twelfth-century artefacts from Mali and Persian Am Lash ceramic bulls, sixth-century Japanese Haniwa tomb figures and Thai Buddhas. Many of the objects tested had been smuggled out of their country of origin and into the hands of dealers – such as a collection of Zapotec funerary urns from Mexico.

'A lot of the stuff I see, you can't ask people where they got it,' she says. 'The story is always the same. You know: "It's been around for many years . . ."'

The urgent request to fly off to Geneva to meet a dealer and take samples was nothing new to Stoneham. She had come prepared with sterilised sampling containers and a drill with a dental bit, the kind normally applied to a tooth during root-canal work. As usual, Stoneham was held up at airport security. Under an X-ray, her drill bears a striking resemblance to a gun. It was a delay for which she had planned. What she didn't know was the real reason she had been summoned to Switzerland.

There was, in fact, more to Mario's request than the mere testing of a smuggled sarcophagus. As afternoon sunlight played on the surface of the lake, he touched the corners of his mouth with his napkin and put it on the table. Mario looked steadily at Stoneham and said slowly and quietly, 'Frederico has just discovered a tomb.'

'Really,' said Stoneham. 'How did you know where to dig?'

Outside of Cerbeteri, where Mario grew up, a huge Etruscan metropolis was buried. 'You can tell just by looking at the lay of the land. My father did it before me and his father before him,' said Frederico. He added that everyone in his village robs tombs just for the sheer fun of it. 'The only trick is getting the goods across the border.'

To do that, Mario had employed a furniture-moving company to smuggle the goods across the Italian border. Doreen was familiar with the situation. She had frequently flown to France in order to sample artefacts, because dealers did not wish to break laws prohibiting the removal of rare artefacts from the country. One day, French customs officers turned up in Stoneham's office to determine if she had been involved in an elaborate smuggling operation. Realising that she had only removed samples in order to authenticate the age of the antiquities, the officers did not pursue their enquiry.

Over lunch in Lugano, she listened carefully as Frederico explained how he recently had dug down about a metre and came across the roof of a tomb. He continued digging in earnest. 'I came to the door and it had bronze rings on it. I cleared a path and the door opened, like the door of my garage. I went inside and there was a skeleton.' Beyond the remains, a collection of artefacts was covered in dust. Frederico methodically stripped

81

the tomb of its contents. As he left, he noticed there were two paths going up to the door.

'We are sure the other path leads to another tomb,' Mario told Stoneham. 'The real reason we wanted you to come here today is we'd like you to come back with us for a week to tell us where to dig to find another tomb. We want you to verify whether or not the objects we unearth are genuine.'

Stoneham thought it over. She had reckoned Mario and Frederico were members of the Mafia, but later found out they were privately robbing the tombs for themselves and acting as a fence for other thieves. The two bankers had broken away from a gang of tomb robbers who were now pursuing them. Rival gangs, including the Mafia, threatened to kill them for encroaching on their territory. The local police were launching their own attack.

Despite the risks, Stoneham knew it was a rare moment. She took a sip of wine and became pensive. For the first time, she was being offered a piece of the action.

'It amounted to an invitation to go with these two strange men who were doing something highly illegal,' she recalls. 'They wanted me, in the dead of night, to go with them, dressed in my dark plimsolls and sweater and show them where to dig. All I could imagine was some show-down of sorts with three different sets of guns. I found it all so hilarious. I'd love to have gone, though I don't know what would have happened. . . . I would have probably gone simply out of curiosity.'

Following their lunch in Lugano, Mario took her and Frederico to his house. 'He took us to his cellar,' recalls Stoneham. 'Outside there was a dog chain and a huge bone. The door was padlocked and had a spy hole. He opened it and the room was festooned with perfectly genuine tomb pieces.'

Once inside, Mario explained, 'My friends who sold me the sarcophagus said they found the arm first. Here,' he said, 'take a look.'

The arm belonged to the terracotta effigy of a man from the

ancient country of Etruria, who walked the roads of what is now western Italy some 2,500 years ago.

Stoneham was not impressed.

'Oh, it's perfectly OK,' Mario assured her.

'He explained that his friends had grovelled around for about a square metre and all the fragments they found fitted magically into one,' she says. 'Without a piece missing, they glued it together and began looking for a buyer. . . .

'But you can always tell when something's been broken deliberately,' says Stoneham. 'Let's take a Greek or a Roman bust. Inevitably, it will be damaged. If you go into a museum and there's a genuine marble piece, they never have noses unless they're put on with plastic. If something has deliberately been broken to make it look genuine, not one single part is ever lost. You can just stick the whole lot together even if it's meant to be an ancient vase and it's found in pieces.'

Mario's Etruscan treasure was in perfect condition, with several 'natural' breaks. If the tomb robbers had to break it further, it was only for an easier passage to Geneva. He trusted his sources and was quite proud of the fact he was high on their list of respected buyers. To them, by working as a banker across the border, Mario was a valuable Swiss connection who could move the smuggled goods easily from Geneva. The deal could never be made from Tuscany. Italian authorities would see to that.

'They came to me first,' said Mario, 'because they thought I would like it. We arranged to get it here. And now,' he said, looking at Stoneham, 'we will get your certificate that proves it's authentic.'

Stoneham took out her drill and began to take samples of the sarcophagus figurine. As she did so, Mario thought aloud, 'I wonder where we could sell it. Which would be the better museums? Or should we take it on the open market?'

Stoneham concentrated on her work, carefully collecting the dust from the stone coffin and putting it into simple vials. By the time she made her final drilling, she knew the bankers had been had.

'There are certain features that never happen, that you see time and time again in fakes,' she says. 'It was a much smaller size than the average and that's an indication that it's a fake. Normally these Etruscan sarcophagi would be about life-size, about 6 feet long. If it's made in a different material from the normal material, that indicates it's a fake. All sorts of little things. And this was much smaller. It had been broken very carefully and put together.

'There is the shadiest of shady stories to tell somebody very naïve, which they had swallowed, hook, line and sinker,' says Stoneham. 'It was the way it was being sold. I mean, that thing was so important that if you had genuinely found it, you might be careful about smuggling it out because the reputable museums would not want to touch it and if you've got problems, you've got to invent solutions.' Mario and Frederico's solution was simple enough. Like so many dealers before them who handled fake or stolen goods, they would need to invent an acceptable provenance for their 'treasure'. To strengthen the object's fraudulent history, its endorsement by a respected authority was vital.

Stoneham's spirit of adventure is tempered by prudence and, in the end, she did not join Mario and Frederico on their moonlit tomb-robbing excursion. Instead, she quietly returned to her work at the Oxford laboratory.

Doreen Stoneham does not seek adventure; it is thrust upon her. She lives a double life in which the tedium of sampling and authentication is counterbalanced by the cutthroat dramas of the art world. By testing questionable 'artefacts', Stoneham encounters their equally dubious owners, some of whom will stop at nothing to attain an Oxford certificate of authenticity. The certificate's value is best described by the French who say that with a certificate from the Oxford laboratory, a dealer can double, at the very least, the price of an artefact and sell it twice as quickly. Increasingly, the Oxford certificate of authentication has become a condition of sale – a testimony to the faith buyers place in scientific proof versus art dealers' expertise. These days glossy advertisements in prestigious art magazines not only include details of objects, but also state if they have undergone testing at the Oxford lab. Desperate dealers whose art has failed the Oxford test have attempted forging the certificate of authenticity in an effort to complete a deal.

Auction houses rely heavily on the Oxford lab certificate. 'It has a lot of clout,' says Robert Kliner, a specialist in Chinese ceramic art and deputy director of Sotheby's. 'Oxford offers the only test that is universally accepted.' The laboratory's certificate not only 'adds an air of authenticity' to a piece, but also, according to Kliner, it makes it easier to sell. 'It's very valuable. Once people know it's genuine, they will pay a proper price for the object.'

Sotheby's, as with many auction houses who use the lab, send unglazed pottery or unusual artefacts with questionable provenances to Stoneham. Kliner submits an object for authentication when its owner refuses to accept Kliner's assessment that the piece is not genuine. 'It makes my job easier,' he says. 'It's the final line of defence.'

When dealers who have grown attached to their collections are told their favourite piece is a forgery, Stoneham is frequently the target of their wrath. 'Part of it is convincing themselves they haven't been done,' she says. 'They've paid a lot of money for something that has no financial value. They are upset, angry and, above all, humiliated.'

For dealers, authenticity is a high-stakes game, fraught with feelings of either great relief or angry betrayal. 'There is always a reaction,' says Stoneham. The Oxford test can reduce a dealer's 'priceless antiquity' to a worthless forgery overnight. At the same time, dubious examples of art are often vindicated in the lab on Keble Road. A porcelain Chizhou vase with debated authenticity submitted by Christie's, turned out to be genuine. The accompanying certificate from Oxford helped to increase its sale price from £30,000 to £90,000.

Gratitude for positive results comes in a variety of forms. In one case, a French dealer's reputation was at stake. His client, a member of a very wealthy and powerful Swiss banking family, decided to have the object he had sold them tested at the Oxford lab. Several days after the test, which proved it was authentic, a crate of pink champagne appeared in Stoneham's office. A north London dealer specialising in African tribal art felt so vindicated by his certificate from Oxford that he sent Stoneham a bouquet of roses. Dealers who know their goods are fakes, but want the certificate of authenticity anyway, have offered subtle bribes to Stoneham, such as an all-expenses-paid trip to Thailand. Others with less panache will simply tell her the object is genuine, and demand the certificate. For Stoneham, the certificate has become as much a litmus test for dealers' characters as a means of authenticating.

'There are dealers I have a tremendous admiration for and of whom I'm very fond. They tend to be the big dealers who have been in the field a long time. They deal in expensive objects and they've got their act together. They have a good eye and I've learned a lot from them. But there is a type of very small and very petty dealer who is in it for the money. They don't know their material. They're in it for the gain and their greed blinds them, making them an easy target for forgers flogging "bargains",' says Stoneham. 'If I find a thing fake, reputable dealers tend to destroy the object or return it, but disreputable ones can't get rid of the artefact fast enough. They don't want the truth,' she says. 'But they want a genuine report, enabling a quick sale.'

When one dealer received a certificate that disproved the stated age of firing of his Persian artefact, he decided to take the matter into his own hands. His simple attempt at forging a certificate was unsuccessful, but he was on the right track. The primary difference between the Oxford certificates is colour: red ink for fake, black for authentic. The dealer mistakenly believed his problems were solved by simply changing the colour of his red form by photocopying it. As with art, only originals of the certificate are viewed as legitimate.

The Japanese, however, generally have more faith in themselves than in any certificate, black or red, from Oxford. In Japan, art dealers must undergo a ten-year apprenticeship. Legend has it, according to oriental-art dealer Richard Marchant, that while 'most people in the west believe in the test, people in the east believe the least.' While the testing procedure has become a formality for his clients, Marchant says it's easier to sell a piece that has been tested. 'More and more people these days will only buy subject to a certificate of authenticity.' But, the Japanese dealers who visit his shop are not especially interested if a ceramic piece fails the test, if, in their opinion, the object is genuine.

Perhaps a bit like the Japanese, Stoneham, in the twenty years she has authenticated art, has developed a somewhat jaded attitude towards the world of art. The impact proven authenticity makes on a reserve price at an auction can be huge. The drive for profit by auction houses, says Stoneham, often obscures their desire for proven goods. 'They don't want the truth,' she says. 'They have vested interests.' Stoneham has also found that archaeologists, keen to prove their expertise, are more interested in fortifying academic credentials than learning if their discovered artefacts are indeed genuine.

Twenty per cent of the lab's business is derived from auction houses and 5 per cent from private collectors. The rest comes from dealers. Roughly 1,000–1,500 objects are tested every year, each test costing about £150. In 1987, the laboratory made £153,000 profit, all of which went back into Oxford University, which funds 30 per cent of the laboratory. The rest of the funding is comprised of private and government grants.

Over the years, Michael Hughes, Christie's oriental-art expert, has seen the demand for Stoneham's services rise. 'The test is absolutely invaluable,' he says. 'It's the only one people believe in totally as a guarantee of authenticity.' Hughes, well aware of the pressures unscrupulous dealers are capable of applying, suggests that while Stoneham is afforded a glimpse into the sublime aspects of the art world, her work exposes her to its darkest elements. Says Hughes, 'She is sitting in a nest of vipers.'

For the authenticator and the forger, art is a field full of intrigue and ambiguity. For instance, when Michelangelo faked and substituted the work of his teacher, Ghirlandaio, was it forgery or flattery? Did Modigliani sign the paintings of his friends to bemuse his patrons or to perform an act of charity? Salvador Dali applied his signature to scores of empty canvases. Was it his idea of a surrealistic joke? We may never know the answers, but history has taught us that for every forgery there is both money to be made and a mystery to be solved.

More than the unravelling of a mystery was at stake in the case of Turkish 'antiquities' unearthed in the late 1960s from an obscure cemetery near the Aegean on the outskirts of Hacilar. The artefacts were double-headed ceramic vases depicting large-breasted, big-buttocked fertility goddesses with inlaid eyes of volcanic glass and granite. A number of leading museums, including the British Museum and Oxford's Ashmolean, purchased a varied collection of Hacilar artefacts on the London art market. By doing so, they simultaneously put their reputations on the line and fostered a market for forgeries.

Based on earlier findings in the area, the curators assumed that the objects dated back to the fifth millennium, BC. As more of the ceramic goddesses began to appear on the market, each exhibiting features never before seen on prehistoric pottery, doubts were raised about the authenticity of the vases. After a period of uncertainty, the keeper of the Ashmolean approached

Dr Martin Aitken, deputy director of the Oxford Research Laboratory for Archaeology and the History of Art, and asked him to resolve the doubts surrounding the vases. Aitken seized the opportunity to apply a newly developed method of dating antiquities, known as Thermoluminescence, or TL.

As its name suggests, TL is the glow of light that occurs when a substance is heated. It represents the release of energy which has been stored as trapped electrons within the crystal lattice of a mineral. This energy is acquired by absorption from nuclear (or ionising) radiation, which is ever present in the air and soil. In terracotta, and indeed, in all types of ceramics, there are minerals that accumulate TL. When originally fired in the potter's kiln, an artefact heated above 500°C sets the thermoluminescent 'clock' back to zero. From that moment, the object ages in its new form and begins to absorb radio activity. At the same time, its TL content increases.[1]

The process of TL dating is a means of judging the age of an object by how much radiation it has absorbed since it was originally fired. In order to arrive at the date of original manufacture, a sample taken from the object is heated to over 500°C. A glow curve carefully monitors the dose of radiation the object has received since it was originally fired. Next, the sample is exposed to radioactive isotopes, strontium 90 and curium to calculate the total dose of radiation the object has absorbed since archaeological time. An alpha counter determines the annual radiation absorption rate of the object. To determine its age, the archaeological dose is divided by the annual rate of absorption.

TL testing was independently developed by scientists George Kennedy in California and professor Norbert Grogler at the University of Berne. Pre-existing ways of detecting forgeries relied on subjective analysis. The TL test provided scientific evidence and specific time periods of manufacture – an invaluable method of detecting modern forgeries. The Hacilar tests opened the door for the authentication of other clay artefacts, including ceramics, porcelain, and the clay core of bronzes. From the outset, Dr Aitken realised the test would have a somewhat dramatic effect: 'There's always been a sense of adventure involved with the test, for one is detecting fraud.' When the Hacilar goddesses purchased by the British Museum and the Ashmolean were tested, it was discovered they were not prehistoric artefacts, but recently fired forgeries. Out of the seventy Hacilar-style pieces tested, fifty turned out to be fakes.

The news of the technique used to unveil the celebrated forgeries spread quickly in the art world and soon Aitken and his colleague Stuart Fleming found themselves deluged with requests for authentication. Private collectors and museum curators, auction houses and dealers began hedging their bets on acquisitions and allowed their art to be drilled and sampled, tested and pronounced genuine or fake. Eventually, the Vatican would commission the lab to test the authenticity of the Shroud of Turin. When the shroud was shown to be a fake in October 1988, Professor Edward Theodore (Teddy) Hall, then the director of the research laboratory, explained the occurrence by saying, 'There was a multi-million-pound business in making forgeries during the fourteenth century. Someone just got a bit of linen, faked it up and flogged it.'[2]

The lab had not been created as a commercial venture, and yet, despite on-going TL research, it was evolving into one. Fleming and Aitken had other interests and hardly the devotion required to pursue commercial sampling of antiquities. They decided it was time to hire an assistant.

At home in June 1970, Doreen Stoneham remembers paging through the *Oxford Times*, when she spotted the ad for an assistant in the Research Laboratory for Archaeology and the History of Art. Stoneham had received a degree in physics from Bristol University in 1962 and in the eight years since, she had married an atomic scientist, briefly taught A-level physics and raised two daughters. Fleming, who had just received his Ph.D.

in physics at Oxford, needed someone to take samples and to operate the TL testing equipment. The equipment's state-of-the-art sophistication required handling by someone with a science background. Stoneham sailed through her interviews and was hired. When she began working at the lab, there were several methods for calculating the age of ceramic artefacts, but one that had just been developed by David Zimmerman was the fine-grain method. Clients welcomed the small sample technique that did not mar the aesthetic appeal of their treasures.

At £100-plus per object, the test was not cheap. But then again, if the object was found to be genuine, the fee was a bargain. The TL test soon became a definitive means of detecting a porcelain object, for example, as a priceless Ming vase or an immaculate forgery. As more artefacts were submitted for lab tests, a statistical pattern became apparent. Despite the fact that many pieces submitted were, to begin with, already under a cloud, 50 per cent of all the pieces of art submitted to the Oxford lab since 1970 have been proven forgeries.

In 1979 Fleming left Oxford to become director of the museum laboratory at the University of Pennsylvania, so after nine years on the job, Stoneham took over. Among collectors, her work had already gained recognition. In Paris they had begun referring to her as 'Madame Oxford'.

In her laboratory clothes – an A-line skirt, blouse, cardigan and sandals – Stoneham is overdressed compared with the women she now employs as assistants. In a lab that must remain in darkness, lit only by a red photographic light, personal appearances are of little importance. The only piece of 'jewellery' fastened on to their T-shirts are blue plastic sensors that absorb radioactivity emitted by the lab's isotopes. The blue discs are the kind hospital X-ray technicians wear and they are read monthly as a means of monitoring levels of radioactive exposure to the alpha and beta rays. Having potentially lethal isotopes down the hall from her office is one of the many inherent risks of Stoneham's occupation. Being stopped by airport security is another.

Ever since her drill was mistaken for a gun, Stoneham has scattered twenty of them in central locations from Paris to Hong Kong. While she has trained several people in the fine art of sample drilling, including pottery experts at Sotheby's and Christie's, it's a vulnerable method. Pottery samples are easily contaminated by grains of soil that can add centuries on to the calculated age of an object. Likewise, when faced with a pastiche, a deceptive driller may sample the only truly ancient part of an artefact and purposefully omit to sample the rest. Taking a sample of an art object that has historic importance can be a tense experience. 'You get arms and legs dropping off,' says Stoneham. 'But inevitably, you find a form of glue underneath, and fortunately, you realise: "I didn't do it."'

One day a rather pompous dealer came into the research laboratory at Oxford. 'We have to work in a dark-room because the daylight affects the TL result,' she says. 'We use red photographic lights, and he obviously didn't like it. He was telling me how valuable his stuff was and what a fine example of a T'ang dynasty horse he had that was over 1,000 years old. Just then he lifted it up and smashed the legs off because he missed the table top. Oh God! The horrified silence.'

By 1988, dealers were paying £150 a shot for Stoneham's calculations. It had become a kind of gentleman's lottery. If the TL test proved an object genuine, and the result was considered 'consistent with the suggested period of manufacture', the impact made on its value was dramatic – a bit like hitting a jackpot. A T'ang dynasty ceramic horse, proven by the Oxford lab to have been originally fired in the sixth century, garnered £250,000 in a sale at Christie's in December 1985. Its twentieth-century impostor changed hands for a fraction of the price.

The only drawback with the TL method is that the test calculates an object's age to within a 20 per cent period of accuracy. So if an object were tested and found to be 2,000 years old, for example, it will have been manufactured some time between 1,800 and 2,200 years ago. The dates of some pieces remain a mystery. In 10 per cent of the samples, the mineral composition prevents any meaningful reading to be given.

Stoneham describes her work not as detection so much as witchcraft. 'TL is a very dirty science. Medicine is a dirty science. We're not working with pure substances. A scientist doing TL takes a pure sample of quartz with no defects and he'll report loads of papers on how quartz reacts to certain things and all the defects responsible,' she says. 'That's great. But when we have a pot, my quartz is mixed in with loads of other things all giving their own little 6 cents' worth to me.'

Due to the volume of testing the lab does, Stoneham is continually picking up new clues. 'I learn something every week,' she says. 'It takes about ten hours to run a test, but in fact within minutes you can get indications. There are certain things I can tell, like Mandarin Chinese Han ware. I can tell within minutes if it's going to be wrong.'

Forgers of ceramic antiquities, like copiers of any form of art, become criminals when they deliberately sell or present their reproductions as originals of other artists. Christine Insley Green, former director of antiquities at Christie's and now consultant to the auction house, says that forgeries come in waves. In the case of the Hacilar goddesses snapped up by the British Museum and the Ashmolean, for example, once the forgers realised there was a market for their work, they proceeded to flood it. Dealers, auction houses and museums who had become unwitting victims of the fakery were among the first to receive conclusive results from the Oxford lab. For those who had invested heavily into worthless clumps of modern clay, deciding what to do with the forged Hacilar artefacts became problematic. Today, dealers (more so than museums) have several options if their discover their *objet d'art* is a fake.

A private collector and millionaire in Geneva who spoke only on condition that his name be withheld, says, 'If he's very rich, very full of himself and fancies himself to be a connoisseur, he might swallow the loss and not mention it.' The alternative, he says, is to adopt the attitude, 'If it fooled me, it will fool someone else,' and wait for the opportunity to trade it – without mentioning, of course, that it is a forgery.

Dealers are not the only victims of artistic deception. Stoneham admits losing sleep over pastiches, which she regards as her nemesis. Clever restorers will combine old and new fragments, making the authentication process akin to solving a complex crime. 'I regard what I do as detective work,' she says. 'I'm seeing fraud as it's being done. If I have the piece in my hands, I examine it very carefully and draw my own conclusions. When I see the hint of a crack that has been carefully smoothed over or that the style or something doesn't look right, I will take a sample from all parts of the item if I feel that it could possibly be a pastiche.'

Stoneham has learned that when it comes to the detection of art fraud, more than mere instincts count. If it is not unscrupulous dealers she must continually be on guard against, Stoneham is particularly watchful of restorers. In the early days of TL testing, so as to avoid damaging the piece, samples would be taken from an inconspicuous place such as an object's feet. 'There was a restorer in Zurich who had an entire bookshelf filled with hundreds of genuine feet, waiting to be affixed to fake vases,' says Stoneham.

'Restorers are our worst enemies and best friends,' she says. 'I should be wary of them, simply because the biggest problem we face in forgery is the pastiche. They marry maybe two genuine parts that don't belong to make something really quite extraordinary, which can be sold for a good price,' she says. 'They can restore so cleverly that you can't see that 90 per cent is newly added material. There is certainly one restorer doing that,' says Stoneham. 'He's even carving parts of T'ang horses. He just has a box of genuine bits of pottery from other pieces and he adds those to his carved tails and legs.'

Stoneham has come across novel examples of restoration. She once witnessed the submerging of a kiln-fired 'antiquity'. As it became drenched, the object swelled and disintegrated in a watery swirl down the drain. There was the time when a ceramic Persian bull, an antiquity with a selling price of £20,000, had been tested as genuine. The restorer had cleverly glued together bowls and cups from the correct period and then plastered over them to create the shape of a bull. 'While every part was genuine,' she says, 'it must have been in a thousand fragments.'

The value of a fragment can grow exponentially, if correctly parlayed. Switzerland's lax laws governing the sale of antiquities are an open invitation to smugglers, particularly the Italians, who, like Mario and Frederico, bring Etruscan treasures across the border. Once an object has arrived in Switzerland, the owner may send a genuine Etruscan pottery fragment to her. 'They'll say, "This is part of a vase we're restoring. Please send us the certificate."' In one case, she says, 'They sent a photograph showing this fragment *in situ* in what is now officially called an Etruscan vase, but apart from that fragment, the whole of the vase was fake,' she says.

Shortly after the Shah had fled Iran, and in the wake of the revolution that touched his supporters around the world in 1979–80, Stoneham received a call from an Iranian gentleman who had found refuge in Hungerford. 'He had just managed, by the skin of his teeth, to get his possessions out of Iran,' she says, adding he claimed to be the archaeological adviser to the Shah's wife. The Iranian had a collection of Persian artefacts he had managed to smuggle out of Teheran and he wanted Stoneham to provide proof that they were genuine so that he could sell them in his Mayfair gallery.

When she arrived, the items were being laid out in rows. There were over 100 pieces, including fine ceramic chariots, bulls with long horns and antlered deer. All with shiny red and green glazes, the objects dated back to the eighth century, BC. The atmosphere was tense while Stoneham drilled into the ceramic artwork. The phone rang and following a lengthy conversation in Farsi, the man said, 'That was the Shah's wife.' As he warmed up to Stoneham, the Iranian explained that he had become a kind of nomad, ever since his wife and children were blown up in his house in Paris. He said he had to keep moving to avoid anti-Shah terrorists and therefore lived in three cities. In his Hungerford mansion, Stoneham moved from one object to the next, quietly drilling into the ancient ceramic art.

She finished her sampling and double-checked the labels on her plastic containers. The man led her to a large oak-studded door. Following his harrowing tales of being chased by terrorists, says Stoneham, 'He opened the door and pushed me through it. I didn't even know where I was going.' But she made it back to Oxford and conducted detailed TL tests on the Persian artefacts. The dealer received the results of the tests and shortly thereafter, he sold one of his ceramic bulls to another Iranian.

While she was in Hungerford, Stoneham had taken a sample from the bull's chest and it had turned out to be genuine. The man he sold it to, however, didn't like the look of the bull's back and asked her to test it for him. 'I didn't know where this piece had come from. He simply said, "I've got a bull, please test the back,"' she says. 'I took a sample from the back and it came out fake.' When Stoneham told the buyer the bull was indeed a fake, the Iranian, who had paid dearly for what he thought was an eighth-century BC Persian artefact, was furious. He immediately contacted the dealer and complained bitterly that the piece was a modern forgery.

At that point, the Iranian dealer who had initially asked Stoneham to test his collection, felt thoroughly betrayed by her and refused to pay the laboratory's invoice of some £800. Stoneham did not understand why he was not paying, nor did she realise that she had tested the same object twice. The bull was a pastiche, and while she was fooled the first time, in the final analysis it was a proven fake. No amount of persuasion would bring in the money from the Hungerford dealer. Finally, the director of the lab, Edward 'Teddy' Hall, took matters into his own hands.

'Teddy is a well-known collector himself and he cuts a lot of style,' says Stoneham. 'Sadly, he was going to lose the money. So he got his butler, and his very old, handmade, convertible Mercedes. It's the only one of its kind in the country. His wife put on her mink coat and the butler drove them in full style straight down to Mayfair. Teddy and his wife went into the shop and Teddy had already looked in the window and sussed out which piece was the most expensive – the one whose real value was equal to our bill.

'He said to the Iranian owner from Hungerford, "I'm a collector, you might have heard of me. I'm a great collector of pottery." I don't know what the owner's response was, but he was obviously very impressed. Teddy said, pointing to the bowl in the window, "Now, I do rather like that little piece. Do you think I could take it home, just to examine it and decide whether it fits in?"

'"Oh yes, sir, yes, sir," said the dealer. Teddy took it home and then he wrote a letter:

Dear Mr . . .,
You will remember me, I came in and admired your wonderful pieces. I took home a bowl and it is the centre-piece of our dining table. Last night I had a dinner party and among our guests was our deputy director, Professor Aitken.

He said, 'What a lovely piece you have in the middle of the table.' And I said, 'Oh yes, isn't it beautiful, I'm thinking of buying it. I got it from Mr . . .' The deputy director said, 'Oh, that's strange, I think he owes us a lot of money.' I said, 'Oh, I couldn't possibly believe it from you.'

So I'm just writing to say that I know you must have overlooked any bill. We would be delighted if you could pay this.

PS I'm just holding on to the bowl a little bit longer to study it, if you don't mind.

'The dealer was on the phone the next day and he *screamed*!' says Stoneham. 'He reckoned the reason he wasn't paying us was because "that bitch", yours truly, had ratted on him by telling the result of one of his pieces to one of his Iranian clients. I said to Teddy, "This is news to me."'

It slowly dawned on Stoneham that the dealer's reaction stemmed from the negative test results on the ceramic bull.

'The man rang up and Teddy said we still have the piece,' she recalls. The man replied, 'I'm coming around to shoot you.' Eventually lawyers were called in, says Stoneham. The dealer paid up and the bowl was returned.

One of the most sensational frauds in the world of art involved another Iranian and clearly illustrates the professional perils involved in the detection of forgeries. In a field plagued with deceit and intrigue, authenticators of art apply expertise to arrive at truth. In a court room, under cross-examination, that expertise is easily undermined and often made to look like vague and subjective opinion.

No museum curator, dealer or authenticator relishes being an expert witness under such court-room scrutiny, especially in a criminal trial in which the authenticity of $18.5 million worth of Persian antiquities is at stake. 'You can look like a buffoon,' says Marcus Linnell, director of client financial services at Sotheby's. 'Everyone in this field knows it. The feeling is: "There but for the grace of God go I."'

When Pieter Meyers, head of conservation at the Los Angeles

Museum of Art, received a call from Cyrus Vance, Sr., the Assistant District Attorney of New York, he was not the least bit surprised. In fact, he had been expecting it. What Cy Vance wanted to know was whether or not Meyers would become involved in a case that would require him to give expert testimony on silver and gold Persian artefacts.

In order to prosecute successfully, Vance needed to know if a London-based Iranian dealer by the name of Houshang Mahboubian, who had a gallery in Mayfair, had attempted an $18.5-million insurance swindle against Lloyd's of London. He was preparing a case against Mahboubian based on evidence that he staged the theft of his own art collection. In 1986 the Manhattan robbery squad arrested burglars in a storage warehouse attempting to steal two crates containing forty boxes of hammered gold-and-silver Sassanian art.

The collection covered a broad range. One box was said to hold 'gold-and-agate necklace, ring, earring and bracelet, first millennium BC', and to have an insured value of $20,000. A pair of gold lion heads, dating from the ninth or tenth century BC, was cushioned in another box. But there were also big ticket items: a silver plate of the Achaemenid period, valued at $1 million; an inscribed gold plaque valued at $1.8 million, a Sassanian silver rhyton, or drinking horn, valued at $1 million; two rhytons valued at $2 million apiece; and an unusually large flat-bottomed gold bowl that had five bulls circling its side in relief and was valued at $3 million.[3] Police believed the men had been hired by Nedjatollah Sakhai, a New York art dealer, alleged to have been Mahboubian's partner in crime.

For his part, Meyers had examined and tested virtually every piece of Sassanian silver in the world: from collections in the L'Hermitage in Leningrad to galleries and museums throughout Europe and America. In the process he had revealed an entire collection of forgeries and had seen some of the most magnificent specimens of the Sassanian civilisation, which ruled Persia for four centuries. In one study he had carefully examined 300 silver objects, studying physical dimensions, shapes, thickness profiles, toolmarks, methods of manufacture, decorating techniques, and gilding methods. He made use of X-ray radiography, metallography and determined elemental compositions by neutron-activation analysis.

It was no surprise that Meyers had been picked to give testimony in the Mahboubian case. Despite his level of expertise, he was rather hesitant. It was his first court-room invitation. 'Almost everybody sometimes gets fooled by having to express an opinion that turns out to be wrong,' says Meyers. 'Every museum, no matter how good the curators are, does make mistakes and they all have forgeries in their collection.'

But Meyers was open to persuasion. 'I was interested because the objects could have been very significant. If they were authentic, for instance, they were easily the most important objects of the civilisation,' he says. 'There was a certain amount of curiosity.'

If nothing else, it would give him an opportunity to examine the state of the art of Sassanian forgeries. In his experience, the use of technology had previously helped to halt the making of fakes. One method in particular, the technique employed by Doreen Stoneham, had worked wonders. 'For a while there were a lot of forgeries in ceramics' he says, 'of Greek vases and Greek pottery, in particular. But with Thermoluminescence dating, it allowed us very clearly to distinguish forgeries from authentic Greek vases. It stopped the whole production of forgeries because, all of a sudden, the market collapsed . . . You have to keep abreast of the forgers,' he says. 'They know what they are doing.'

Vance and his team were operating on the assumption that if Mahboubian intended to bilk his insurers, Lloyd's of London, out of $18.5 million, it would make sense if the goods were fake to begin with. Once they had been stolen and the insurance policy redeemed, Mahboubian would need to get rid of the

Persian art since the chance that it could be traced back to him was too great. If the art was fake, however, he could sell it for scrap and still cash in on his insurance policy. Following the robbery, an anonymous caller with a Middle-Eastern accent urged police to take a closer look at the dazzling collection of artefacts.

Like Doreen Stoneham, Pieter Meyers has the benefit of scientific proof on his side when detecting forgeries. Meyer works from a spacious office and high-tech laboratory in the Los Angeles County Museum of Art. Meyers, a Dutchman with brown eyes, thinning hair and a moustache, is not especially gregarious. He is someone who is first a scientist – perhaps a man more at ease in a laboratory than at a cocktail party.

Meyers has developed an expertise through many years of research. His career has been fast-paced, marked by significant opportunities. Unlike Stoneham, his team of skilled restorers and analysts handle much of the work in his department. He carries the seniority of an administrative director with ease, relaxed in knowing that competent assistants will see projects through.

In contrast, Stoneham's career began after an eight-year hiatus from academia. She is not a scientific pioneer like Meyers, rather, she is a practitioner of a technique that in and of itself is not extremely difficult to master. The ability Stoneham has of detecting fakes comes from years of daily experience. Stoneham is a housewife thrust into the glamorous, if not shady world of art authentication. She looks after her samples in a fastidious and maternal way, underscoring the notion that she is perhaps an ordinary woman who frequently finds herself in extraordinary circumstances.

Meyer's expertise in the field of authenticity has developed from a background in radiochemistry and nuclear physics, a combined discipline in which he received his doctorate from the University of Amsterdam. While working on his Ph.D., Meyer applied nuclear-dating techniques to study works of art and archaeological materials. Today, Meyer's accent is a worldly amalgam reflecting his Dutch roots, a teaching stint in Cairo and research at the Brookhaven National Laboratory on Long Island.

During his research at Brookhaven, Meyers applied the relatively new technique, neutron-activated autoradiography, to the works of Rembrandt, Van Dyck and Vermeer. Autoradiography, the method of taking X-rays of paintings, clearly depicts the evolution of an artist's work. While it can be employed to detect a forgery by revealing previous layers of paint, it is a means of discovering how artists produced their masterpieces. As a result of the autoradiography testing, several paintings were found to be misattributed to the great masters. The museum was forced to acknowledge that the works were 'in the school of'.

It was an exciting time for Meyers and his method of authenticity testing began making a large impact on galleries, museums and private collections. Meyers became the head of the research laboratory at the Metropolitan Museum of Art in New York and continued to develop a personal interest in Sassanian silver. By the time he moved from the Met to the LA County Museum of Art, silver vessels of the Sassanian period (AD 226–651) had been the subject of a number of his technical investigations.

Cy Vance had asked Meyers to help him disprove the authenticity of some forty boxes of hammered gold-and-silver Sassanian art. Meyers was curious but reluctant. He had good reason. Art historians tend to avoid the sort of testimony Vance was after. The study of Persian antiquities is made up of a small, tight-knit group of scholars whose work is rarely placed in a public forum such as a court of law. Any serious discussion of forgeries can easily undermine the scholarship of a colleague.

Lawyers, even with minimal skill at cross-examination, can make an art historian look vague or silly. When testimony based on aesthetic opinion rather than objective test results is offered, the credibility of the expert becomes the focal point. The expert, rather than the art, is placed under a microscope. Added to the tension is the risk of potential lawsuits. After listening to an expert call a piece a fake, its owner may have it appraised by someone else and sue the expert for publicly lowering its value and injuring the owner's reputation. Mahboubian's brother, Mehdi, had already filed a $34-million suit against Sotheby's for allegedly putting him on a black list and limiting his opportunities to sell his art.

Although much work has been done on the dating techniques of ancient metals and their characteristics, there is no test that can calculate positively the exact age of a gold object, in the way TL testing determines the age of a piece of clay pottery. By attempting to prove Mahboubian's art was fake, Cy Vance had entered a field in which authenticity was difficult to pin down. As a result, forgery in 'ancient' gold artefacts was rife. Curators of major museums had admitted they had been taken in by skilled copiers of near Eastern ancient objects.

There were other things to worry about. Mahboubian had a notarised report included in the customs documents attached to the shipment of silver-and-gold objects. Drafted by Professor Wilfred Lambert of the University of Birmingham in the UK, it read: 'I cannot imagine that there is at the present moment a finer collection of ancient Iranian art, judged from craftsman-ship and artistic perfection, in private hands. While it is hard to pick out particular items, some of the . . . artefacts of this collection are as fine as any known to me in the world.'[4]

Lambert described one object, a silver plate, as a depiction of King Hormisd I on horseback, shooting wild boars. He claimed it dated back to the third century AD, when the Sassanian dynasty ruled Persia. Lambert called it 'an outstanding specimen of its kind, certainly from the royal workshops'. As Meyers arrived in New York, one museum director said his task of authenticating Sassanian silver-and-gold objects would be 'like walking into quicksand'.[5] Systematically, he studied each piece, utilising an X-ray machine provided by the Manhattan police bomb squad, and Meyers came to several conclusions about the collection, including the King Hormisd piece. He testified the plate had been cast, a technique not used during the Sassanian period. Moreover, his scientific tests showed the plate contained less than 0.001 per cent gold. In his experience, the gold content of Sassanian silver is always about 0.5 per cent. Meyers also believed the 15 per cent copper content in the object was too high and the 0.33 per cent bismuth too low to be genuine.

Meanwhile, the defence did some checking on Lambert and learned that he is an expert in Mesopotamian languages. Lambert had joined Birmingham University's faculty of ancient history and archaeology in 1965, and almost exclusively had studied cuneiform writing. Once he had studied Sassanian objects, he began offering authentication on them in 1970. While he told the court that Sotheby's and Christie's were among those who consulted him, a spokesman at Sotheby's clarified the point by saying, 'We use him to translate ancient cuneiform inscriptions and consult him on western Asiatic cylinder seals.'[6]

None the less, after Lambert authenticated the collection, Mahboubian submitted Lambert's findings and a statement from a Paris appraiser to Lloyd's of London. After seeing Lambert's authenticity report, Lloyd's took an inventory of the collection, confirming that the artefacts existed and were in the condition stated in the reports. The manifest for the two crates containing some forty boxes of objects described a collection of ancient Persian artefacts in gold or silver, mainly dating from the Achaemenid period (from 559–330 BC) and the Sassanian period. Lloyd's assigned an insured value to each object and wrote Mahboubian $23 million worth of insurance. Four and a half million dollars covered some jewellery in the collection that was later split off for shipment to the Metropolitan Museum of Art. The rest of the collection found its way to the continent and was later shipped from Zurich to New York.

In his opening statement, Vance pointed out to the jury that in 1983 Mahboubian had tried unsuccessfully to sell his collection to the Getty Museum in Malibu, California. Vance offered a single reason. 'The collection,' he said, 'is comprised mostly of fakes.' Saying it was one thing, proving it before a dispassionate jury was another.

Patrick Wall, Mahboubian's lawyer, had done his homework.

'He read, I think, every publication I have written and questioned all kinds of details in this book on Sassanian silver I co-authored,' recalls Meyers. 'He brought up things I didn't even know were in it.' Meyers didn't think he would have to be on the witness stand for more than an hour. He was there the better part of two days.

Wall had a field day with the two other expert witnesses, also brought in to testify the collection was fake. At the end of the day, they only offered opinions on a group of artefacts that admittedly included probable genuine pieces. The forgeries, if indeed there were any, were very good. They were not, in the words of one observer, the sort of 'obvious phonies found in the souvenir stand just down the road from the pyramid'.[7]

Harmer Johnson, a private appraiser and former head of the department of ancient and tribal art for the New York branch of Sotheby's, also testified. While discussing some of Mahboubian's Sassanian objects, he said, 'They are not blatant fakes. They are not the sort of plates that one would pick up and in five seconds say, "Oh my God, it's an outrageous forgery."'[8]

What Johnson pointed out, in so many words, was that the authenticity of the objects was debatable. Joined by Arthur Houghton, the acting director of the Getty Museum's department of antiquities, the experts' testimony came across as connoisseurship: opinions on an object's artistic quality, style of craftsmanship and the overall impression created by the object. They were the kinds of opinions that, rather than closing off debate, provoked attack.

Houghton, who had turned down the collection for the Getty, remarked that one of the reasons he believed they were modern forgeries was they appeared to have been cast instead of hammered. This prompted Wall to ask Houghton to recite captions from museum catalogues and bulletins describing scores of Sassanian objects as having been cast.

Johnson, a bearded Englishman, had joined Sotheby's as a porter and gained his knowledge of antiquities not from academic training, he told the court, but from 'years and years and years of touch and seeing and handling material . . . a gradual, almost unconscious building up of knowledge rather than my saying to you, "Yes, I became an authority on 4 March 1985," or anything like that.' While he spoke at considerable length about the fineness of line, the smoothness of edge, he said that often a first impression would override the opinion of someone who had spent a lifetime handling ancient objects. 'Well, it looks right or it looks wrong.'

Johnson contended that the problem with most of Mahboubian's collection was that they simply weren't good enough to be authentic. The workmanship was crude and not crisp enough, he said. Johnson pointed out that the heads of lions attached to one bracelet looked like the heads of pussy-cats. He held up a gold plaque decorated with a reclining stag that suggested 'a sort of Walt Disney expression'. 'A genuine piece might look funny or might look whimsical or grim or sad, but it never looks stupid.'9

It was the perfect bait. Wall, full of the righteousness of a good cross-examiner, wanted to know, why not? Wasn't it possible some average Achaemenid could have ordered a bracelet for his wife from a goldsmith, knowing she, unlike Johnson, actually preferred lions with the faces like pussy-cats? Does an artefact from the Sassanian period have to be immaculately crafted in order for it to be a genuine artefact? 'Doesn't schlock art survive?' Wall asked.

Johnson became defensive. 'We're talking about essentially

royal art. This is not material that the average man in the street 2,500 years ago was eating cereal off of.'

'Are you able to say with a reasonable degree of certainty,' countered Wall, 'that those pieces were not done by someone in that period?'[10]

Pieter Meyers, Vance's third and final expert witness, had reasons to be nervous, but, then again, so did Wall. Walking into the court room, Meyers knew that in Iran, where it was presumed the objects had been forged, 'there are whole factories where these things are faked'.

The defence attorney's repartee lost a bit of its sparkle during his cross-examination of Meyers. Meyers, it turned out, also had a problem with the recumbent stag plaque. It was not that the stag looked stupid; it had traces of cadmium, something ancient goldsmiths had never heard of. Meyers spoke about the applications of neutron-activation analysis and described how Sassanian silver objects contain a gold content significantly higher than the silver plates in Mahboubian's collection. Having X-rayed the objects, he had learned that the objects had been cast and not hammered. 'This technique of manufacture was not in use by the Sassanian silversmith,' said Meyers. 'At one point it was published as being a technique, and obviously this has not only confused for a while the serious scholar but also the faker, who assumed that he was using the right Sassanian silversmith's technique.'[11] Meyers pointed out later that the fact he could apply science to authenticity mattered hugely. 'It's the only thing that makes me feel secure because I'm not an art historian. If I didn't have the technical evidence, I shouldn't be able to open my mouth except to say I like something or not, but that's not scholarship.'

In his summation, Vance pointed out that a striking pattern had emerged from the testimony of all three experts. In each case that an object of Mahboubian's was insured for more than $1 million, the unanimous verdict was that it was a fake. The jury deliberated into the night, and the next afternoon the foreman, a Transit Authority employee, announced that Nedjatollah Sakhai and Houshang Malboubian were guilty on all counts. Mahboubian was sentenced to between one and three years for conspiring with Nedjatollah Sakhai to defraud Lloyd's of London out of $18.5 million by staging a phoney robbery. Sakhai received a sentence of two to six years.

Today, Mahboubian is free, pending appeal of the case and can be located in his Mayfair gallery, not far from Grosvenor Square. He has switched lawyers and is presently represented by Alan Dershowitz, famed defence attorney and professor at Harvard law school. Mahboubian had nothing to say to the court, but later announced that he would write a scholarly article that would refute the testimony of Meyers and the other experts. His collection remains in the Manhattan Robbery Squad's most secure holding room, nestled between pornographic videos and seized narcotics.

As a result of the case, a flurry of museums made public confessions that they indeed had fakes in their collections. A widely known Egyptian statue of a cat in the Metropolitan Museum of Art was 'in all probability', a spokesman admitted, 'a modern forgery'. The Dallas Museum of Art also came out of the closet, telling everyone that its most famous pre-Colombian ceramic sculptures were fakes.

Such candour was unique for curators, but then every authenticity case has potential impact on the art world. Doreen Stoneham's verdict in a matter of illegally imported African art into Canada created a whole new twist in what was already a sensational case. When Stoneham flew to Canada in the early 1980s, she was greeted at the airport by the Royal Canadian Mounted Police and escorted to their security holding rooms. Two Manhattan dealers had brought a Nigerian Nok head from the fifth century BC worth $650,000 into Canada without an export licence from Nigeria.

The dealers, Benjamin Heller and Isaaka Zango, were charged

with illegally importing the Nigerian relic to Calgary in December 1981, with police charging that they violated Canadian treaty obligations to the United Nations Educational, Scientific and Cultural Organisation (UNESCO). When Stoneham's test indicated the terracotta kneeling figure was fake, it exponentially raised the level of controversy surrounding the case, which has yet to be resolved.

About the same time, Stoneham was called back again to Canada to verify the ages of several terracotta models of figures found in the Medici Chapel in Florence. Thought to be the original models used by Michelangelo for lifesize marble statues, the objects were kept in a bank vault. Stoneham took samples as the owners and their solicitor looked on. While tests could never prove they were by Michelangelo, the results indicated that the models were from the Italian Renaissance period. On the strength of her report, the terracottas were sold for an undisclosed amount, said to be in the region of $30 million.

When the stakes are this high, it is easy to understand what Stoneham is talking about when she describes the 'tremendous thrill' of discovering if something is real or fake. 'It gives you a sense of power, because you can back up your statement,' she says. 'It is an ego thing as well. I like the truth and I like things to be logical. I don't like airy-fairy statements.' Stoneham says that TL testing is an excellent tool for detection. 'I like facts to be substantiated and this is a way of substantiating them. It is important. It's not life-saving, but I still like lies to be detected which is really what forgery is.' She hastens to add, 'I'm not gloating. It's a job for me. Something isn't right; something's wrong, I do my job. That's it. I'm just glad to have got the truth.'

Stoneham is fully aware that she lives in two worlds. 'I am in a field which is an expensive, glamorous world where people live in the West End, they live on the Left Bank, they live in Manhattan. They are used to a lot of style and good meals and a decent standard of living, and I must admit, I revel in that. But, I'm always itching to get back to the lab. There is a sense of mystery and suspense every time you push the button of the TL set. You never know what's going to come out at the other end . . .'

4

Adventures in the pirate trade

'I looked through the keyhole and saw six soldiers with
automatic guns who said they had a warrant for my
arrest.'

CHARLES MORGAN, senior vice-president and
head of Universal Studios' anti-piracy unit

In his wide-lapelled ivory suit, Isaac Zafrani cruised around
Panama City in a Cadillac that matched the colour of the
thick gold chains around his neck. His shoes were regularly
polished by hired hands. He kept wads of banknotes in his
pocket and at the right place and time Zafrani would peel
off a few and put them in the palms of waiters, associates
and potential friends.

Zafrani, whose Sephardic roots lend him a Middle-Eastern
appearance, had the entrepreneurial zeal to create an empire
that would one day cover most of Latin America and cross
the borders of Europe and the United States. In a place where
money can buy a man influence, Zafrani was always looking
for a bargain. 'Everything is for sale in Panama. Everything
is for sale everywhere. Only here,' he would say, rubbing his
fingers together, 'it's cheaper.'

One day, Zafrani realised how he could make a fortune.
The robust sales of video cassette recorders (VCRs) had caught
his interest and Zafrani realised Latin Americans and people
around the world who had purchased the machines would soon

require a stock of videos to keep them entertained. Zafrani's idea was simple: he would become their central supplier and cultivate a stock of inexpensive popular video movies.

Zafrani worked in Colon, a city whose roots go back to the mid-1800s when it became the half-way point for prospectors sailing from east to west during the California gold-rush. Later, the opening of the Panama Canal secured Colon's perpetual boom-town atmosphere. Amidst the thriving trading depots, nightclubs, bars and gambling houses, Zafrani's export clothing firm, Panafashion, began to transform itself. In a matter of weeks, it became the headquarters of his new enterprise: Star Video. With its creation, Zafrani would make an important move into international trade.

Zafrani capitalised on the location of his Colon headquarters. He sold video cassettes of popular films in bulk, to freighters travelling through the duty-free zone of the Panama Canal. He opened a Star Video store in Panama City and leased a large concession for his videos in Panama's Tocumen international airport, the primary hub to all Central and South American countries.

Tocumen, like the Panama Canal, is a thoroughfare that links Latin America to the rest of the world. By opening up a Star Video shop at the busy airport, Zafrani began further to invade the world video market. The well-lit store was stocked with bright pink-and-orange packaged cassettes featuring original artwork. The low-priced videos, at $12 a cassette, sold quickly.

Viewers from Miami to Tierra del Fuego soon were watching Zafrani's products. In a short period of time, Star Video had flooded the markets of Bogota, Colombia, and Caracas, Venezuela. Flushed with revenues, Zafrani began making shipments to America. To test the European market, Zafrani opened an office in Frankfurt, West Germany. For Latin America, Zafrani hired a team of salesmen/distributors who often embodied the spirit of the videos they sold. His man in Caracas, for instance, sported western shirts, cowboy boots and tight-fitting rodeo jeans as he pitched videos to Venezuelans hooked on spaghetti westerns.

Everything seemed to be going well for Zafrani. Everything, apart from a nasty labour dispute. Each day a group of unpaid textile employees paraded around Zafrani's Panafashion factory holding placards. The sight of striking workers was so unusual in Panama that it generated interest, if only due to the vivid contrast made between the workers without pay cheques and Zafrani, behind the wheel of a gold Cadillac.

Zafrani's ego was not stung by the lengthy strike, in fact, with the money he made from Star Video, he began to acquire all the trappings of a Hollywood studio mogul. He even acquired a yacht. What kept Zafrani from being the Samuel Goldwyn of Latin America was the simple fact that the movies he sold did not belong to him.

Isaac Zafrani, in two years time, had become the most powerful video pirate in the world. By selling fraudulent copies of first-run films, Zafrani, more than any other single operation world-wide, posed the greatest threat to legitimate video and theatrical interests. By 1984, his estimated profits were in the region of $20 million. Markets created by Hollywood studios and their distributors had vanished as a result of the Panamanian pirate king who produced an average 1.5 million videos a year.

Zafrani's business relied on the trade of illicit videos he obtained from connections in the Orient and Middle East. The momentum of his operation was fuelled by 300 'slave' video recorders that duplicated an impressive library of masters culled from the last ten years of major American film releases. The slaves, working non-stop, seven days a week, generated a daily output of between 3,000 and 5,000 Panafashion 'Star Video' cassettes. Unlike the backlots of Hollywood from where his prized bootlegs came, Zafrani's 'studio' bore minimal overhead. It was located above a hardware store.

Tony Blanco, a successful film distributor in Caracas, Venezuela, had some time to kill during a layover at Tocumen airport in Panama and wandered into the Star Video shop. Blanco was stunned by the wide selection of current films, some of which had not yet been released in Venezuela. He had never met Zafrani, but he knew that whoever was behind the operation had excellent black-market connections, a sizeable manufacturing plant and, judging by how fast the videos were selling, a fat bank account. He bought a couple of cassettes and boarded a plane home to Caracas. After sampling the videos, Blanco realised that if he did not do something quickly, ticket sales to his cinemas would drop as customers stayed home to watch Zafrani's pirated tapes.

Zafrani had sent solicitation letters throughout Latin America introducing himself and his company along with a voluminous title list of low-priced Star Videos. The store owners responded favourably and yet another facet of Zafrani's business grew. Star Videos had begun to appear in Venezuelan stores that normally sold camera film, televisions and stereos. Blanco could not stand by and see his business ruined by someone who was breaking all the rules. He placed a call to Hollywood. The man he wanted to talk to was Charles Morgan, senior vice-president of MCA Inc.'s Universal Studios unit.

While many US film executives complain bitterly about video piracy – a problem that costs them over $1 billion a year in lost revenues world-wide – few have acted as aggressively as Charles Morgan to stop it. Morgan, an attorney specialising in copyright law, has earned the reputation of a tough pirate chaser who has waged successful battles, whether in Fiji, London or the Yucatan. Fluent in Spanish and well-versed in the steamy politics of South America, Morgan moves easily in Latin circles.

After graduating from UCLA, Morgan studied economic development on a Fulbright fellowship in Santiago, Chile. Earlier in his career, Morgan was associated with a law firm in Mexico City. He is someone who has gained the respect of movie executives and pirates alike.

Not far from the queues of tourists waiting to visit Universal Studios, Morgan's office is located in a sleek black building a block from the Hollywood freeway. Down the road, Nudie's Rodeo Tailors sells $3,500 green polyester and rhinestone cowboy outfits. For $270, you can walk out of the store in a pair of lizard-skin boots. Zafrani, in all his flamboyance, would be at home among the gold-lamé 'Elvis' suits and pearl-handled pistols. He was a pirate who liked having impact. When Morgan became involved in the case he heard that Zafrani had married a much younger woman named Jacqueline. One day gazing towards the harbour Zafrani mused, 'Look at that yacht and my wife, Jacqueline. Am I not another Onassis?'

If Zafrani could pretend to be Onassis, Charles Morgan would get a lot of mileage out of a Gregory Peck/Lee Marvin impersonation. As adversaries, Morgan and Zafrani are total opposites. Where there is flamboyance with the Panamanian, there is measured style with the American. The hot-tempered Zafrani works above a hardware store. Charles Morgan has four secretaries and an office with original art, including a Warholesque portrait of himself. Zafrani's features are stout, over-jewelled. Morgan is tall and lanky; impeccably dressed. His personality is best captured in a pair of intense, hazel eyes that can level looks, like lowered howitzers, beneath angular brows. Morgan has been given the nickname, *cara de lapida* (tombstone face) by adversaries who have encountered his determined efforts to thwart raiders of studio films. Zafrani stays up all night, out on the town or plotting his next business move. Morgan, by contrast, could be up until day-break, calming his nightmare-prone 3-year-old son. Zafrani is an outcast of the Sephardic Jewish community in Panama. Morgan lives two blocks away from his childhood elementary school and is the son of Harry Morgan – the veteran actor who co-starred in both the *M*A*S*H* and *Dragnet* television series.

When Tony Blanco called from Caracas, he explained the situation to Morgan by telling him that, among other studio productions, Universal films were being pirated by Star Video. 'They're hitting the beaches in Caracas,' said Blanco. 'If you don't stop the concession at the Panama airport, it will invade territories you really do care about.'

'I first went to Venezuela,' remembers Morgan. 'I had a meeting with Blanco and some other people and they took me to a store that had Zafrani's merchandise. I picked up a Star Video cassette and just kind of on a whim I asked the proprietor if he was aware that these cassettes infringed copyrights. The guy said, "No, I didn't. Is there some place I could contact you?" I gave him the number to Blanco's office and a day later Zafrani's Venezuelan distributor showed up. He was the last guy on earth you'd want representing your titles legitimately.' Despite the man's pseudo-cowboy appearance, Morgan learned a lot about Zafrani's operation from him.

A large shipment of Zafrani's cassettes arrived in Caracas and Morgan intercepted it at the airport. At that point, he had no trouble convincing Universal's executives that they had a serious problem on their hands. Joined by Michael Hueser, an investigator with the Motion Picture Association of America (MPAA), Morgan headed for Panama. He learned that Star Video thrived on volume selling. Zafrani purchased master prints of films from the Middle East and blank tapes for roughly $1.50 a unit from Korea. After making thousands of copies, he would then ship them in cargo containers.

'He didn't restrict himself to Latin America – he would ship them to Los Angeles, Miami, Asia, Mexico, anywhere,' recalls Hueser adding, 'it was a recurring nightmare. I'd go to Costa Rica and his videos would be selling on the street. I'd fly to Panama and they were in the airport. I'd come back to Mexico and I'd see them in shops all over the place.'

By the time Hueser and Morgan arrived in Panama to mount surveillance on his operations, Zafrani's 300 'slave' duplicating machines had recently spun out 5,000 Star Video cassettes of *Flashdance* and *Return of the Jedi*. In most of his business deals, Zafrani had taken the precaution of putting his assets in the names of relatives. 'He was ready for us,' recalls Heuser. 'It had lasted for five years. Zafrani had great power and influence and he thought he was unbeatable. But he knew his days were numbered.'

If Morgan was going to organise a raid, he needed to know where Zafrani's duplicating operation was based. While in Colon, Morgan and Heuser visited a Panafashion outlet. As they walked down the aisles viewing hundreds of videos, Heuser heard an unusual noise. He moved to where it seemed to be coming from and realised the whirring sound, rather like switched-on machinery, emanated from the floor above. He stood still, pretending to study a video cassette. Heuser began to hear footsteps coming from the same direction. He nudged Morgan and they both looked up at the ceiling. Quietly the two walked out of the store.

Once outside, Heuser said to Morgan that he thought the machine noise probably came from banks of video cassette recorders located upstairs. Over the next couple of days, Morgan and Heuser organised surveillance on the shop, checking the various exits for possible pick ups and deliveries of videos. It didn't take long before Heuser's hunch was confirmed. Star Video in fact were manufacturing pirate tapes around the clock in the spacious room above the store. Later that week, Morgan and Heuser identified an even bigger duplicating factory in Panama City located above a hardware store. Morgan and Heuser began to make plans for a raid.

Universal and other major studios whose product Zafrani had pirated provided the power of attorney to Panamanian lawyer, Dr Vincente Garibaldi, to enable him to orchestrate a search and seizure of the Panafashion outlets. Warrants were issued for the arrest of Isaac Zafrani and his lawyer, Carlos Richards, on a variety of charges related to trademark and copyright infringement. One of the most serious charges claimed Panafashion illegally copied and sold over 1,500 titles of major American motion pictures. Foreign sales alone surpassed 1,000 units a day. Widely available in Venezuela, Colombia, Central America and the Caribbean at an average price of $25, Panafashion offered perhaps the best selection of videos available in Latin America, including titles such as *Tootsie*, *Superman III*, *Rocky III* and *Gandhi*.

With the help of the MPAA, the organisation to which Morgan's company, Universal Pictures belonged, Panamanian authorities were called in to administer criminal charges. Universal Pictures and Paramount Pictures prepared to conduct a simultaneous raid stemming from a civil case Morgan had prepared against Zafrani.

With everything in place, the team of police, investigators and lawyers staged what was to become the largest video-piracy raid in the history of the film industry on the largest illegal facilities in the western hemisphere. Panafashion's two factories, located in the free zone of Colon at the Atlantic entrance to the Panama Canal and Panama City, were simultaneously hit. Police filled a 40-ton container with seized cassettes and equipment. Zafrani had masters of virtually every major American motion picture released in the past ten years. Among the items seized were 4 shrink-wrap machines, 15,000 video cassettes, 308 'slave' duplicating units and 4 complete printing presses.

Zafrani was livid. 'We have rights, damn it!' he shouted at his son, who had telephoned him during the raid. Zafrani savagely scolded him for allowing Morgan and the authorities to seize his videos and duplicating machines. Zafrani's son, filled with anger, crashed the receiver down, walked over to Morgan and with fists raised, gave him a hard push. Despite the son's chiding, Morgan resisted. The fight for honour Zafrani and his son badly wanted, later became an armed confrontation. While relaxing in his hotel room at the Panama Hilton following the raid, Morgan was suddenly greeted by violent banging at the door. 'I looked through the keyhole,' recalls Morgan, 'and saw six soldiers with automatic guns who said they had a warrant for my arrest.' Zafrani had 'influenced' a local magistrate to sign an arrest-warrant on the strength that Morgan was attempting to flee the country. It was Friday afternoon and Morgan realised, if he were arrested, he would be spending the weekend in a Panamanian jail.

Morgan rang the hotel operator who had helped him place long-distance calls during his stay. 'I really got a problem here,' he said.

'You don't have to tell me,' she said. 'I know you've got a problem.' She placed a call for Morgan to the American Embassy. 'I got a guy on the phone who asked me if it had anything to do with drugs. . . . He was very frank and said the embassy could only notify my family and Universal after the soldiers had taken me wherever they were going to take me. The point was,' says Morgan, 'they would follow up after I was gone.'

The armed soldiers, members of General Noriega's *Fuerzas de Defensa*, the National Guard, stood outside Morgan's door while he made more calls. He phoned Heuser who was in the next room and Heuser contacted Vincente Garibaldi who represented Universal Pictures locally and other member firms of the MPAA. Garibaldi's brother happened to belong to the 14,000 member *Fuerza de Defensa*.

To gain extra time, Morgan ordered a meal. For the fifteen minutes it took for the soldiers to devour his dinner, Morgan had a respite from the threats and pounding at his door. After several hours, there was a loud commotion in the hallway. Garibaldi's brother had commandeered another group of soldiers and convinced the first group that an arrest should not be made. The strike of Zafrani's textile workers which had received a lot of public support was useful as a means of persuading the soldiers that Zafrani was an irrational man. When Morgan finally opened his door, there were no soldiers and no guns; just a stack of dirty dishes.

'More than anything else, I was concerned there might be

another attempt to arrest me,' recalls Morgan. 'We moved to the Marriott and Heuser arranged for a bodyguard to stand outside the door. When we heard a knock we knew he had arrived. A couple of hours later we peered through the hole and it looked like the lights in the hallway had gone out; that was the size of this guy. Heuser took him out for breakfast after he stood out there all night. He couldn't believe it. The guy had something like eight steaks.'

Panamanian justice was ultimately served in the case of Isaac Zafrani. After facing six criminal-theft charges for pirating copyrighted material, he was fined $100,000. According to news reports, he is now a reformed distributor of legitimate video cassettes. Morgan confirms this but adds that he is not aware of all of Zafrani's business activities. On a recent trip to Panama, Morgan and Zafrani lightly sparred with one another in the back of Zafrani's main store. Morgan stated flatly that the only way Zafrani stayed in business was by paying bribes. Zafrani basically told Morgan to mind his own business.

The Zafrani raid was important, but by no means easy. 'It was hard to convince the other (US) distributors it was worth the effort to pursue this thing in a territory like Panama. But piracy has to stop somewhere. The export capacity to the rest of the Spanish-speaking world had no limit.'[1]

Morgan's intrepid journeys on behalf of Universal Pictures have included meetings with Panama's General Manuel Antonio Noriega and former Panamanian president, Ardito Barletta. While on occasion Morgan represents other film companies, he works principally for MCA/Universal. His anti-piracy work began when MCA's powerful chairman, Lew Wasserman, grew impatient with the MPAA approach to solving the problem. Since then, Morgan has travelled around the world chasing pirates, spending two weeks out of every month on the road.

Despite finding himself in the midst of a global whirlwind, Morgan appears to be not the least bit harried. 'It helps to bring a lot of reading material,' he says. 'Piracy is just one of many problems or disasters the people I have to see deal with all the time.' Regardless, Morgan seems to get results. And, his work has not gone unnoticed. Sidney Sheinberg, MCA's president, commenting on Morgan, told the *Wall Street Journal*: 'He's our own Sherlock Holmes ... When you put Charley into a situation, he gets something done.'[2]

Morgan's involvement with piracy charts the development of the infringements of the medium itself. When he was hired to represent the foreign and domestic distribution rights of Universal's theatrical motion pictures in 1978 at the age of 34, the only piracy problem Morgan encountered were a small number of 35 mm. film duplicating cases. Censorship and scant diversional activity had prompted South Africans and people in Lebanon to become involved in the difficult and expensive process of copying the 35 mm. films.

One day in 1980 Henry Martin, Universal's head of theatrical distribution at the time, came into Morgan's office to tell him about a distributor in Fiji whose business was being taken over by pirates taping movies in New Zealand and Australia and showing them in Fijian hotels, bars and restaurants.

'To Hy Martin, it was simple. We had a distributor who needed to be protected and it wouldn't have made a whole lot of difference if the distributor was in Oklahoma City or Fiji.'

Morgan's first move was to go to the LA-county law library and photocopy Fiji's copyright act. The following morning he telephoned Fiji and spoke with the prosecutor handling the case. Morgan secured copyright certificates through the copyright office that made it clear that Universal owned the films being duplicated. When he finally reached Fiji, Morgan discovered to his amusement that his lawyer, the opposition lawyer and the judge, all had run off copies of his photocopied Fijian copyright act. He also learned in greater detail how the distributor of Universal films in Fiji was losing his audience to a manager of a logging business who supplied his workers with videos as a means of entertainment. The workers began selling the duplicates, or pirated versions of the tapes. The month-long investigation culminated in legal action taken against the manager who was sued for about $200,000, equal to the profits he had made from the pirated videos.

The first warning shots of the battle between the studios and pirates were heard in 1977 when Universal City Studios filed a law suit against Sony, claiming that the videotaping of broadcast transmissions by individuals for home use constituted a violation of the US Copyright Act. The lengthy case culminated in the 1984 Supreme Court decision against Universal.

Despite the doom and gloom the industry predicted with the advent of the VCR, the studios began to see opportunities in the limitless commercialism connected with it. Jane Fonda and her best-selling work-out video opened up the doors for a wide spectrum of entrepreneurs from the fields of fashion, music, business, religion as well as video-game inventors. With their purchase of the VCR, Americans began installing 'home entertainment centres' in their living rooms to accommodate stereos, televisions and their latest toy, the VCR. It didn't take long before studios, including Universal, saw the merits of transferring their 35 mm. films on to video. By 1988, the boom in VCR sales had placed some 30 million of the machines in American homes and another 61 million resident VCRs outside the United States.

The VCR has been a blessing in disguise for Hollywood's entertainment empires. In the last five years, the home video market has emerged as the single most important source of revenue for film companies. In 1981, approximately one million video cassette recorders were sold in America. In 1985, VCRs sold at the rate of nearly one million a month. For the first time, in 1986, the studios made more money from the sale of video cassettes than from cinema box-office receipts. There is little indication of a sluggish video market in the future. Industry analysts predict that video cassette sales will quadruple by 1995.

Ironically, the machine that has kept the industry in the black with unpredicted revenues, threatens to take it into the red. The VCR, by facilitating video piracy, has spawned one of the world's fastest growing white-collar crimes. Piracy, or the illegal duplication of films, is the latest form of copyright violation. It can be committed in a variety of ways. Pirates can duplicate new motion pictures before or immediately after they reach the theatres. Video retailers or their customers can copy videos and videos may be illegally shown in public without authorisation. Finally, pirates may intercept pay-television signals through satellite dishes.

It is estimated that 5–10 per cent of the cassettes on the shelves of America's 38,000 video outlets are illicit. From the movie industry's perspective, the most serious form of piracy is the theft or illegal borrowing of a 35 mm. or 16 mm. film print from a theatre, film depot, courier service or other industry-related facility, prior to its official release. Hollywood is especially prone to this illegal trade which involves the making of a relatively high-quality video-taped copy of a theatrical print. This 'master' is used for the duplication of unauthorised video cassettes. Unauthorised copies may also be made from master videotapes that have been stolen or 'borrowed' from insiders within the film industry. When such access is impossible, pirates have resorted to using handheld video cameras in cinemas to shoot illegal copies right off the screen.

These 'bootleg' videos can flood the US market or show up overseas before the film is even released in cinemas outside the US or before the film has been authorised for release to the domestic or foreign home video market. A perfect case study of this technique is Steven Speilberg's 1983 hit, *E.T.: The Extraterrestrial*, which was being smuggled illegally on cassette before it was officially released in cinemas. Despite the fact that it has yet to be legitimately released on video cassette in any country, *E.T.* is consistently the most popular video cassette in viewer polls taken throughout the world. In another example,

Poltergeist II: The Other Side was being publicly advertised in the Middle East before its legitimate US theatrical release date was even announced.

From the moment they are released, films have a limited lifespan. In order to extend the life of a film and maximise revenues in a series of different markets, movie studios circulate films according to a sequential release schedule. If it is an American film, a first exhibition in US theatres is followed by theatrical releases in the international markets. Domestic home video is the third market for the film, after which pay cable, and then, network television markets are exploited. The final market for the film is usually broadcast television syndication. International home-video distribution may trail the American domestic release of a film by six months or more. When piracy occurs at the beginning of any of these release cycles, such as when illegal copies are made from US theatrical prints, all downstream markets are negatively affected.

The production costs of typical Hollywood films averaged $18.1 million in 1986, plus another $7 million for prints and advertising. A major Hollywood studio typically releases 10–15 films each year. Each film is a new product that seeks to achieve success in various markets through the sequential distribution pattern. Each segment of that distribution chain is necessary to recoup a film's costs and to make a profit, part of which goes into new film development.

Two-thirds of American films never recoup their production, marketing and distribution costs. That leaves the remaining one-third to turn the profits that enable future films to be made. Film and video pirates do not have to bear the trial and error of such development costs. They concentrate their efforts on the 33 per cent of films that are successful and thus, the vital revenues which would otherwise flow back into the creative community go into the pockets of the pirates. Annual loss in potential revenues to the US motion-picture industry from world-wide film, signal and video-cassette piracy is estimated to be more than $1 billion – approximately one-quarter of the yearly box-office gross from all US cinemas.

Once a video enters the chain of piracy, it begins a global odyssey that can take it to South Africans living under strict cultural censorship or to isolated Pacific Islanders with limited sources of entertainment. As copies of illicit videos get passed along, from one pirate to another, mutations form. Inferior video cassettes originally filmed from the back of a cinema with a video camera (containing unedited audience laughter, the crinkling of sweet wrappers and silhouettes of movie-goers) will beget some eight generations of copies. Language barriers are overcome with homemade subtitles that translate the adventures of *Crocodile Dundee*, for example, into Arabic, Thai, Chinese and a host of other languages. Spontaneous editing occurs with pirating to suit local markets. *Rocky IV* became a twenty-minute fight film in Malaysia because audiences there weren't interested in the story.

There is recourse. The MPAA and its international counterpart, the MPEAA (Motion Picture Export Association of America), act as the voice and advocate of the American motion-picture and television industry. Founded in 1922 as a trade association for the American film industry, the MPAA has broadened its mandate over the years to reflect the diversity of an expanding industry. Today the association looks after producers and distributors of television, cable and home-video programming.

The MPAA's chief weapon against film and video pirates is its own Film and Video Security Office (FVSO), which comprises one of the largest private investigatory forces in the world. Close to 400 anti-piracy agents are employed by the FVSO, which began its operations in 1975. In the US, most FVSO investigators are former FBI agents, an old-boy convenience, as piracy cases in America call on the services of the FBI and federal prosecutors. Among the FVSO agents abroad, a decorated former chief of the Royal Hong Kong Police heads an FVSO office in the British colony, while in Europe, former Scotland Yard and French National Police investigators handle piracy cases.

The objectives of the FVSO include strengthening security within the film industry, assisting local governments in the investigation and prosecution of piracy cases, and providing technical support in criminal and civil litigation that follows investigations. FVSO agents also bolster existing copyright protection through legislative activity. A notable example of this is when the MPAA in England worked with the Federation Against Copyright Theft to change piracy penalties from £2,000 and two months in jail to unlimited fines and a maximum of two years' imprisonment.

The MPAA directly operates eighteen film FVSO posts throughout the world including: Sydney, Australia; Rio de Janeiro, Brazil; Montreal, Toronto and Vancouver, Canada; Bogota, Colombia; Rome, Italy; Auckland, New Zealand; Manila, the Philippines; Singapore; Johannesburg, South Africa; Taipei, Taiwan; London, England; Los Angeles and New York, the United States; and Caracas, Venezuela. In addition, MPAA regional counsel and investigators work as part of local umbrella anti-piracy organisations with national producers, distributors and retailers in more than forty countries. The MPAA anti-piracy programme operates in nearly sixty countries world-wide in one form or the other. Generally, where governments have not provided their own enforcement mechanisms, the film industry has stepped in to exercise self-help.

In a typical situation, the FVSO will get a call from a store owner complaining that his competitor down the street has a more expanded but highly suspicious library of tapes. Each complaint is routed to an agent handling that region who will contact the store owner within five days. Often the person who made the complaint in the first place assists in solving the case.

There have been results. In 1986, over 1,200 criminal and

civil investigations were initiated against film and video pirates in the US. Criminal convictions or guilty pleas were obtained in 44 cases. Damages and injunctions were obtained under civil litigation against an additional 58 individuals or establishments. Over 38,000 pirated video cassettes were seized in some 92 raids across the country. Additionally, 96 film prints were seized along with duplicating equipment, illegal packaging and other piracy tools. Hundreds of thousands of dollars in fines and several jail sentences were handed down that same year.

On a world-wide basis, over 3,800 police raids were mounted against pirate operations in 1988. Complaints alleging various acts of piracy fielded by the FVSO are now approaching the rate of 1,000 a year. The MPAA has a reward program in operation to help combat piracy. The MPAA offers up to a $5,000 reward for information leading to the arrest and conviction of any film or videotape pirate. As of 1987, more than $300,000 had already been disbursed under this program.

In May 1982 former president and veteran actor Ronald Reagan signed into law a bill increasing the penalties for piracy in America, making illegal duplication of a film a felony that now carries a penalty of a $250,000 fine and up to five years in prison. In doing so, President Reagan made US copyright infringement penalties among the toughest in the world.

Where copyright laws are weak or non-existent, successful charges have been brought against pirates under other statutes. Laws encompassing everything from receiving stolen goods, trademark violations, smuggling, and failure to pay customs duties have all been successfully used in film and video anti-piracy cases.

In order to bring criminal charges against a retailer selling pirated tapes, eight counterfeit tapes must be found. Investigators try to attain several times that number in order to strengthen their case. Most video-piracy cases are resolved in a straightforward fashion: MPAA lawyers draft a 'cease and desist' letter and give it to the pirate and that's usually the end of it.

Hollywood's domestic enforcement problems are dwarfed by MPAA missions overseas, where pirates often control half or more of the pre-recorded video-cassette market. In all Middle-Eastern countries with the exception of Israel, pirates control the cassette markets.

Unfortunately for the smaller, independent studios, there is no organised, well-funded body such as the MPAA and its security offices protecting their interests. In fact, pirates often target independent films first, before they are licensed and distributed in that territory. Most independent studios operate similarly to Paragon Arts International, a company specialising in low-budget films. Limited partnerships are sold through Paragon in a small market that allows a direct connection with investors. 'They want to roll the dice with us,' says Paragon producer Geoff Geoffray, 'and gamble that they will recoup their investment and make a profit. We count on video sales to cover our costs. Video revenues allow us to return the dice.'

The pirates, whether hitting the independents or the majors, mean business. 'For every imaginable way to view a film', says William Nix, director of the MPAA's Worldwide Anti-piracy Program, 'there is a corresponding form of piracy.' One sophis-ticated pirate, a projectionist in the New York City borough of Queens, was keeping the MPAA confused. For months, the MPAA could not understand how all new films were showing up in the East Coast video underground weeks before their theatrical release. The projectionist had built his own film chain, an elaborate device used to transfer 35mm. film prints on to videotape. Commenting on the situation at the time, Nix mused, 'We're not just fighting some video shop owner in Juarez who knocks off extra copies of "Gremlins" for his customers. We're being ripped off by pirates with millions of dollars in machine capital and international distribution networks that work overnight. Express mail should be so reliable.'[3]

'Our only competitive advantage used to be better quality,' says Charles Morgan, comparing pirated and legitimate videos. 'But with every passing month, the pirates offer better and better quality. I've picked up samples of pirated cassettes and played them at home and my 9-year-old son can't tell the difference. If I walk over to the TV it's "Daddy, don't touch that dial."'

What Charles Morgan is transfixed by is a movie that has weaved its way through a maze of pirates as sophisticated as James Bond and as ruthless as Dirty Harry. At the higher end of the scale, well-connected pirates do deals over drinks in Hollywood with industry insiders, while down the road, in Santa Monica, a pirate pulls out a gun and demands a print of the latest blockbuster from a shocked projectionist.

Film pirates have unlimited access to the industry they continually attack. A careless studio executive may leave a screening print lying on his desk overnight and it is gone by morning, for instance. There are three West Coast film laboratories where most film prints are made. Before having to wear newly issued pocketless lab coats and undergo security searches, technicians used to walk out surreptitiously with composite prints of films. Leaks can still occur in the projection rooms of the 22,000 cinemas across America as well as in the foreign-distribution networks. On occasion an actor, director or producer proudly lends a friend a pre-release video of the film he or she has just made, only to find out during an interview with a local FVSO investigator that the friend is a pirate and the unofficially released film has saturated the Asian market.

Each week, in the Los Angeles area alone, there are half a dozen incidents of piracy that involve film industry leaks of one kind or another. In 1985, the FVSO dealt with a particularly sensitive case involving leaks in the transfer of movies from the studios. FVSO investigators and Universal Studios representatives, whose films were being copied, determined that some of the cassettes, which had begun to turn up on the black market, were duplicates of executive screening prints. Because the prints lacked definitive markings, investigators could not trace where the leak was coming from.

Universal Studios eventually refined their markings of executive screening prints, and, like tracking down marked bank notes, the FVSO kept a record of where the prints were circulated and determined that the pirated cassettes had been made from a screening print delivered to CBS Television.

CBS, having conferred with the FBI and CBS security, agreed to mount surveillance on critical areas of the CBS facility. On 18 July 1985, CBS Television received a screening print for their executives of the new feature *Cocoon* from Universal Studios. A member of the CBS security force saw an employee of the Telecine department go to the projection booth, obtain the print and return to the Telecine department where he proceeded to place the print on a film chain and make a film-to-tape transfer. Later, the employee admitted that for the past three years or more, almost every new film coming to CBS had been film chained, and the cassettes made available to CBS employees. He mentioned in an interview that this process had been going on even before he was assigned to his department, and that the department supervisor was aware and approved of the film chaining. The FVSO was unable to interview the employee's supervisor because he suffered a heart attack at the time and was admitted to a local hospital.

The pirates selling the video-cassette copies of these films and others, William 'Buddy' Goldberg and Brian Lapan, were indicted and subsequently pleaded guilty to copyright infringement. Goldberg was placed on three years' probation, ordered to perform 300 hours of community service and to make restitution to the FVSO in the amount of $9,927. Brian Lapan was sentenced to three years' probation, fined $1,000, ordered to perform 100 hours of community service and ordered to make restitution to the FVSO in the amount of $5,205.

As in the CBS/Universal case, piracy of first-run theatrical films is usually accomplished by a pirate having contact with some facet of the motion-picture industry, where he is able to steal a film print or borrow one long enough to make a transfer from film to tape. The equipment needed to transfer film to videotape, known as a film chain, consists of a film projector, a prism apparatus, a video camera and a video recorder. The film image is merely projected through the prism into the video camera and recorded by means of a video recorder. Using this process, a master videotape is made which can then be used to make thousands of other copies.

Opportunities to pirate film occur at several points between distribution and exhibition. When a film is first released for theatrical exhibition, the producing company may order as many as 800 or more film prints from a designated film laboratory. These prints are then sent to regional film exchanges throughout the US. There are some thirty film exchanges which are jointly used by most of the motion-picture companies.

When film prints are received by a film exchange, they are stored there until orders are received from the producing company to send a print to a local cinema for exhibition. After exhibition, the film is returned to the exchange where it then may be sent out to another theatre. Generally speaking, film prints of full-length motion pictures, in either 16mm. or 35mm. format, are never sold to individuals or organisations.

Despite increased security measures by the motion-picture industry, there is always a chance that a dishonest employee in a film laboratory, freight company, film exchange, or cinema, will co-operate with a pirate to steal, or otherwise make available a film for duplication on to a video cassette. This type of piracy has the most adverse impact on distribution since a video pirate could obtain a video cassette of a movie even before it is released to cinemas and flood markets with illegal copies. This can be especially disastrous in some foreign countries where theatrical exhibition may not take place for several months after exhibition in the US.

The pirates involved in this type of operation usually work

from their home, their garage, or in some cases, a small video laboratory. Most of the time the private operation consists of no more than a dozen video recorders hooked up to produce multiple copies. A blank video cassette costs approximately $4 to $6 and the pirate can sell the finished product for anywhere from $50 to $100 or more.

Traditionally, one of the more bountiful areas for pirating is the Bel Air Circuit. Up until the mid-1970s, in the days before videos, it was customary that mid-level executives could borrow prints of films from another studio. The man at Paramount would call Warner Brothers and book a film for a party or private screening. Prints continually were 'lost', reappearing in other markets. Following several embarrassing situations involving prominent members of the film community, the newly opened FVSO drew up a program that severely restricted the borrowing of film prints to about half a dozen senior executives of each studio.

In terms of a public-relations exercise for the FVSO, the move was a disaster. The office had removed a prestigious form of social climbing. Studio executives with multi-million dollar homes, outfitted with screening rooms, in the posh Los Angeles suburb of Bel Air, now lacked a crucial means of entertaining friends. Feathers were ruffled. Tempers flared. Among the numerous complaints the MPAA fielded, John Wayne phoned up to say it was an outrage. The MPAA held its ground. It knew that with the development of video, piracy would soon take off in all directions.

Having started with antagonising film-industry chiefs, the FVSO began making more changes in the way the film industry operated. Investigators went to the source of film production and studied weaknesses in the system. They learned that after a day's shooting, a producer and director examine the 'rushes' and decide what to keep and what needs reshooting. As a film is gradually pieced together on separate sound and image tracks, a pirate cannot use it. Once filming of a movie is completed, the two tracks are taken to one of the labs, such as Technicolor, so that a composite print, uniting the image and sound tracks, can be made.

The composite film is often called an 'answer print' because it answers questions a director and producer might have about the film. After a private screening to discover what aspects of the film need to be improved, the lab or the studio scrap the answer print. In the old days, pirates would go through the trash at night and pick up complete prints. FVSO investigators suggested changes. Today, instead of junking the answer prints, labs and studios now send them to film-salvage companies which will chemically wash away all of the image, leaving the blank film which is then resold at a discount to film-makers. But even this process does not exclude pirates. The FVSO has found evidence that pirates have stolen films from the salvage companies.

One of the most desirable ways of pirating a film is to steal it when it is in video form: when it is being stored or edited for advertising trailers. The FVSO has obtained pirated video cassettes of movies a month or more before they even hit the dealers. This happened with *Karate Kid II* and a series of James Bond movies.

Pirates will stop at nothing to obtain fresh prints. Two thieves wearing clown masks held a projectionist at gunpoint in Santa Monica, California, and walked away with *Return of the Jedi*, the George Lucas sequel to *Star Wars*. The print was never recovered. Thousands of miles away at the Glenwood cinema in Kansas City, following the last screening of the day, another gunman took yet another print of *Return of the Jedi*. In this case, the FBI trapped and arrested the man and recovered the print. The gunman bragged that he would have pocketed $300,000 for the movie, plus $1 million from counterfeit videotapes. These incidents contributed to the total of six thefts of the *Star Wars* sequel from cinemas in the US, the UK and Canada.

Sometimes when films get stolen it's an inside-out job: inside the industry, outside Hollywood. The Fair Plain Cinema 5, a movie house in Benton Harbor, Michigan, had a special treat for its customers. In 1981, a few days before the début of *Raiders of the Lost Ark*, the cinema obtained a pre-release print of the film for a sneak preview. After the last showing, Dennis Johnson, the assistant manager of the cinema, left the theatre as if to go home. But after travelling several miles, Johnson made a U-turn and came back to the darkened cinema. He opened the projection booth, grabbed a film canister and sped off into the night.

Earlier, an anonymous caller had tipped off Paramount Pictures that Johnson was intending to use a copy of *Raiders* overnight to make duplicates of the film. Paramount had contacted the FVSO, who, in turn, got the FBI on the case. It just so happened that spare FBI agents working on another case were available on land and air to help. When Johnson drove by them, a team of twenty FBI agents waiting silently in the dark, in cars and in an airplane, began to tail him. After a 120-mile circuit around Lake Michigan, Johnson entered a warehouse in Elmhurst, Illinois, where his four partners were waiting to 'chain' the movie on to tape.

At the request of the FBI, a local magistrate quickly signed a search-warrant and the team of agents raided the warehouse and seized sixty-five illegal master videotapes that had been used to make duplicates of other films for America's Midwestern black market. For a mere $400, Johnson had sold access to the *Raiders* print for a fraction of the value he hoped to gain by selling pirate videos of the print.

While Johnson, described by the FBI as 'a loner who was into films', received the fairly lenient sentence of three years' probation and six months' community service, Paramount's security drive on *Raiders* kept illegal copies of the film off the streets for eighteen weeks, an unbeaten industry record.

Many US pirates deal only overseas and therefore, once the tapes have been shipped, it's very difficult to get evidence. Aided by extensive computer data bases that keep track of pirates and the release schedules of the films they steal, Richard Bloeser, director of the FVSO, and his team co-ordinate with FBI agents and federal prosecutors to stop the many forms of piracy that exist, ranging from back-to-back copying of cassettes in small retail outlets, to veritable factories of counterfeiting. FVSO investigators use high-resolution, wave-form and cross-pulse monitors that indicate the number of times a video has been copied and thus facilitate tracing.

With each generation of duplication, the more the quality of the video suffers. Pirates lose vertical-hold synchronisation, chroma levels and luminescence levels. Examining a pirated video is like conducting an autopsy after a homicide. The pirated video is very much like the corpse in a murder mystery. The perpetrator can only be found by clues, even if they appear in the form of small little dots at the bottom of a cross-pulse monitor. 'It helps if you have good eyesight,' says Bloeser, walking past a room of squinting detectives in front of a television in the Los Angeles FVSO headquarters.

For every safety precaution devised by the film industry, whether holographic labels, vacuum-formed packages, proprietary information on the tape itself, or even FBI warnings, pirates have found ways around the system. 'These are our children that are being bastardised,' says an industry insider who prefers anonymity. 'It hurts. We put millions of dollars into their development. The pirate doesn't give a shit about freight. He's paying less than $10 for the product. That's not even my cost. If it costs a pirate less to sell it than it cost you to make it, it's hard to compete.'

Pirates can afford to be discriminating. An undercover FVSO investigator, posing as a film-studio insider, established a working relationship with a video pirate based on the assumption that he would supply films for illegal duplication. After many weeks of persuasion on the part of the FVSO, one of the studios belonging to the MPAA offered a pre-released film to the operation. The pirate, presented with the fresh print, refused to touch it, saying it would never sell. 'We've picked up some real dogs,' says Bloeser, adding that pirates only go after films with guaranteed box-office appeal.

Bloeser was involved in the 1980 sting operation that led to what the FVSO calls the 'Second St Valentine's Day Massacre'. In one of the largest anti-piracy busts in the history of the movie industry, FBI agents arrested fifty-five organised-crime figures involved in pornography and video piracy. The organisation over the years had made profits on bogus copies of everything from *Bambi* to *The Exorcist* and had cost the film industry some $700 million a year in lost revenues. In a dramatic twist, one key suspect was so distraught by the raid that he died of a heart attack minutes after his arrest.

Another pirate conducted his business out of the boot of his Cadillac. Donald Ewald would travel each night from Downey to LA's San Fernando valley. He would cruise Ventura Boulevard and stop at a steak house where he would have a few drinks. He would bide his time until paged on the telephone by customers and then he would arrange a meeting with them in the parking lot. Lifting up the boot, he would reach down to select a copy of his latest pirated film. One of his regular clients was an undercover informant working for the FVSO. After several months of surveillance, the FBI filed a search-warrant for Ewald's home. 'He had turned his living room into a video library,' recalls Bloeser adding, 'he had a dozen machines set up with video cassettes all over. His den was his office and the walls were covered in wall-to-wall video cassette.' There were more than 700 illegally duplicated video cassettes in all, including 34 masters and 12 video recorders. During the case, the undercover FVSO informant had purchased a number of tapes including 26 copies of *E.T.*, 10 copies of *Raiders of the Lost Ark*, 10 copies of *Tron* and 8 copies of *The Empire Strikes Back*.

The most severe penalty meted out to a pirate for copyright infringement in the US was a $100,000 fine and a four-year prison sentence handed down to a man in Houston, Texas, who taped cable television broadcasts and sold them to operators of merchant ships, passenger liners and oil rigs.

Hollywood has fired its own shots against the pirates. When Warner Brothers released its Sylvester Stallone feature, *Cobra*, in 1986, it placed ads in *Variety*, the movie industry's leading trade magazine. The ads, a signal to potential pirates of the film said, 'Warning! Warner Bros. and *Cobra* declare war on video piracy.' The ads described how each print of the film carried a secret marking code that would enable pirated video cassettes of the film to be traced back to a single print and cinema out of more than 2,000 cinemas showing the movie. The system, known as CAP (coded anti-piracy), was first used on another Stallone movie, *Rocky IV*. At the time, movie executives received a fascinating lesson in the international operations of video piracy. The film was smuggled out of the US to Thailand where copies with local subtitles were sent to Malaysia and Singapore. From there, the pirated cassettes turned up in Jordan and then moved to Turkey where they were resubtitled in Turkish and sent on to Turkish workers in Germany.

The studios have also used Macrovision as another way of foiling pirates. Legitimate cassettes are encoded in such a manner that they cannot be successfully duplicated. Attempts at making homemade dubs from the Macrovision masters yield cassettes with very distorted sound and picture quality. Universal Pictures first used the system on *Back to the Future* with good results. But there are drawbacks. Macrovision will not have any effect on Beta tapes and for $300 to $400 pirates can buy a 'black box' that cancels its effectiveness entirely. CAP and Macrovision are exceptional examples of industry awareness and initiative in dealing with piracy. On a day-to-day level, Bloeser and his colleagues face a great deal more apathy.

'It's very difficult,' explains Bloeser. 'Most of them, they couldn't care less. It's a white-collar crime, a lot of people think it's a victimless crime, because they compare motion-picture studios to big insurance companies. It's no crime to rip off your insurance company, right? It's no crime to rip off the IRS, and so with the studios, it's the same thing: it's no crime to rip off Twentieth Century Fox or MGM. This is the way they feel. They feel these people are making millions of dollars and it's: "You're saying I can't make a copy of this cassette? What kind of blood-sucking monster are you?" Really. That's about the response. So, it is very difficult.

'It's like walking down the streets of New York and somebody comes up and says, "You wanna buy a gold watch?" The experienced individual knows he's going to get a rip off, probably. But even if he wasn't, he'd know it was stolen. So how many people really care that it's stolen? They think they're going to get a deal. Do they really care that it's stolen? And the same thing with a video cassette. If you went into a video store and the video-store owner said, "Hey, I can sell you this a lot cheaper than this one, but it's in a different box" Are you going to care that it's a pirate copy? Probably not.

'Of course, most of the stars don't really care. They get their money up front. They get paid for their theatrical performance. Maybe if they received royalties from cassette sales they would be more interested in piracy. It's quite simple. If you lose the market for something, then the studios aren't going to have money to make any more pictures. I mean if you can't sell a picture and can't make a profit on it, you're not going to make any more. Or certainly you're going to cut down on the number of pictures that you are able to make with the money that you do have. Instead of making pictures that cost $40 million, you're going to end up making pictures that cost a few hundred thousand that no one wants to see.'

Bloeser contends that the problem of video piracy could be solved with proper inventory control. Studios, he says, should avoid not only making extra copies of their films but also allowing employees to take them home at night. He says that leaving films overnight at the lab and having them sent over the next day is inviting trouble. 'It would be like Cartier and his diamond necklaces,' says Bloeser. 'He didn't just let employees take them home overnight. You've got to keep a tight rein on them. Fifteen million dollars is quite an investment.'

Stephen Clug (Cloog), vice-president of MPEAA, supervises Australasia from his base in Goldhill Square, Singapore. He estimates that American film studios are losing $350 million annually in the South East Asian region. It is here that the pirates are huge.

Clug has seen pirates at their most innovative, such as the time Thai pirates smuggled a film print into Singapore inside a cream jar to foil Customs. Such seizures, whether at the airport or in video retail shops, have changed the face of piracy in Singapore. With the help of recent legislation, the Singaporean video market has turned around. In 1983 what was 85 per cent pirate has now become 85 per cent legitimate.

Deeply tanned, short and balding, Clug wears safari shirts and holds a perpetual cigar below a gold Rolex. A native of Long Island, Clug has had a colourful career in the film business that began on the set of Cecil B. DeMille's *The Ten Commandments* where he supervised distribution to the Far East. Later, Clug worked for MGM in Central America, Puerto Rico, Paris and London. He is tough and abrasive but then he's dealt with some fairly menacing characters. In Paris during the late 1970s, one pirate he had caught tried to stop Clug from testifying against him by threatening, 'If I see your face in the courtroom, your wife is going to be a widow.'

The Paris experience was a new kind of boot camp for the former military-intelligence officer. In his current assignment, 'There are no docile sorts of pirates. It's bad, it's litigious. They will fight you to the core. Retaliation is a risk all investigators face in this region. Life in the Philippines, for instance, is very cheap. We try not to be too confrontational.' In May 1987, however, Clug was part of a team that raided a Filipino wholesaler of pirate videos who had a franchise network of 500 dealers.

Clug and his MPEAA associates around the world lobby governments to enact effective copyright laws and work with law-enforcement agencies, informing them of the problem of piracy. 'If the government and police aren't behind you,' says Clug, 'you're nowhere. Sometimes the biggest problem is the amount of corruption that goes on. We push for bilateral agreements to curb piracy and get rid of the loopholes, but it is a battle of wits between you and the pirates and,' he says, gesturing to the map on his wall, 'they're all over.'

A few hundred miles south, pirates Down Under thrive by plundering the underground market, taking $30 million in yearly profits with them. Unlike Indonesia, piracy of motion pictures is a criminal act in Australia and to prevent its occurrence Ray Stevenson, regional director of the MPAA's Australasian Film and Video Security Office (AFVSO) leads a team of dedicated investigators from his office located, suitably, on Hollywood Avenue, near Sydney's Bondi Junction.

The AFVSO, assisted by twenty federal and state police, tracked down a prospector from Wiluna, Western Australia, who had committed the unpatriotic offence of pirating *Crocodile Dundee*, the film starring Australian actor Paul Hogan. When Robert Ernest Winmill, 44, had attained an illicit copy of the movie at a Sydney hotel, it had not been released to the home-video market anywhere in the world. The AFVSO had been alerted by an informant that Winmill was selling *Crocodile Dundee* copies for A$60 each.

Investigators followed the prospector-turned-pirate's trail from Adelaide to Perth and gradually pieced together a picture of him from video retailers he had approached. By tracing his car-registration number, they eventually located him and raided his home in a Perth suburb. At the time of his arrest, Winmill had twenty copies of the pirated film that he had peddled across Australia. Back in Sydney, Stevenson and his team examined his tapes and discovered that they had come to the country through the usual process: originally pirated in America, shipped to Bahrain, where there are no copyright laws, and then once duplicated, distributed world-wide. Winmill's VCR was destroyed by the Court of Petty Sessions, Perth, and he was fined A$4,000.

Stevenson occasionally uses undercover agents, and one of his favourites is a man from the Northern beaches named Glenn. Glenn is 5' 10" and weighs 15 stone. His beer belly hangs over filthy jeans and he has smears of mortar on his T-shirt from the bricklaying job he pretends to be doing around the corner from the video outlets he visits in New South Wales. He has a cultivated limp and his straggly beard disappears into a mass of tangled curls that fall below his shoulders. Stevenson uses Glenn to survey video shops. Glenn's method is first to locate a building site in the area of the shop. Normally customers have to prove they live in the area but Glenn gets by, saying he's working at the nearby building site. So good is his act that Glenn has never been refused the opportunity to rent a video.

Once he selects a video, Glenn takes it to the Hollywood Avenue headquarters of the AFVSO where it is put through a battery of tests on various monitors to determine if it is a pirated film. If it is, Glenn returns to the shop to collect more evidence. The AFVSO must then prove the subsistence of copyright and that might mean going back to the States and getting the chain of title from the US to Australia.

The AFVSO tries to get four proven examples of copyright infringement and then they bring in the police who issue a search-warrant. The AFVSO raid the establishment and while Stevenson and his team are there, Glenn never appears in the final act. Through Glenn's low-key technique, the AFVSO has also been able to trace illicit videos to big-time pirates.

Glenn's biggest catch was Michael Ossedryver, proprietor of Ossie's Record Bar in Sydney who was eventually charged with twenty-four copyright offences relating to the hire, possession and distribution of counterfeit video cassette tapes and a further two charges relating to trademark offences. Ossedryver was fined a total of A$18,400 plus A$3,250 in court costs.

Glenn is but one of several undercover agents employed by the AVSO. 'The best we ever had was a lady who had three little kids. She was a fantastic liar,' says Stevenson. 'She could go in and keep a straight face, and say "Look here, I'm visiting my father who lives 'round the corner on such-and-such a street and he's not too well. I want to borrow a few tapes just to cheer him up." I remember one case she worked on while the fourth child was on the way. She was very, very pregnant. She had the tiny little tots trained so that they would go in with her and while she looked around for some tapes, they raced to the back of the shop. Of course, she had to go out to retrieve them and while she was out there, she had a good look around, discovering how the pirates set up their operations.'

In Queensland, Stevenson uses a very debonair ex-federal police detective-sergeant who is always immaculately dressed. In the Western states, a little old man, short, fat, sixtyish, grey hair and balding, strolls into video shops for the AFVSO wearing a cardigan and in a grandfatherly fashion selects suspect videos to send on to Stevenson. To add to the crew of undercover agents, one of Stevenson's men, covering Western Australia, has a beat over five and a half times the size of Texas. With places like Lake Disappointment, Mount Bruce and the Yeeda River as landmarks, the AFVSO man drives for weeks on end in a rented car from town to town, chasing pirates.

'You're printing money,' says Stevenson, of video piracy. 'It is very much like drug running. It's pretty easy to get the last fellow, the fellow who made the final sale, but for every stage up the ladder you go from there, it gets harder and harder. So, to get Mr Big is almost impossible.'

Stevenson is someone who does not favour ambiguities but the field he is in is riddled with them. 'If you are stealing someone's intellectual property, then it's a little bit different than if someone goes in with a sawn-off shotgun and holds up a bank. Here you've got someone who can steal something and you don't even know he's stolen it.'

Clug discusses the enormous problem the MPAA faces in a place like Japan where $170 million was lost in 1986. 'It is the largest pirate operation in the world. You can't get into the market,' he says. 'Jesus, they're swallowing it up. Theatrical managers have had to close doors. Piracy is such an easy business to get into. All you have to do is buy a couple of VCRs.'

Video piracy in Clug's opinion is 'the single most important issue the motion-picture industry is facing. It could destroy the industry. Just think of it,' he says. 'If everything could be pirated, it would no longer be worthwhile to invest in a picture. The motion-picture industry is a risky business to begin with. How can you justify being in business if 50 per cent of your business is gone?'

More to the point, if the financial opportunities required to transform ideas into film are further impaired by pirates, audiences may have little else to look forward to than uninspired forgeries.

Sea crimes

'If you're a woman, people allow you to put your feet in deeper. They're not so defensive. I've been playing this role for over ten years. I don't know how other people see me, but I'm confident enough that I don't give them a chance to look down on me because I'm a woman. I'm in a man's world . . . You just have to go and deal with them and forget who you are.'

SHIAO-LIN KUO, investigator,
International Maritime Bureau

They arrived in Bombay in knee-length kurtas and business suits, by third-class train and jet. Small-town merchants, petty and ignorant of the ways of life beyond their village limits, met with India's trading barons on a sultry morning in March 1985. The disparate gathering of 150 men was unified by the virtue of shared predicament. Together, they had pooled $4.5 million in precious foreign exchange for a cargo that had vanished.

The *Sea Falcon*, a 11,500-ton ship carrying their consignment of steel, clothing and chemicals, disappeared after leaving Antwerp back in October. The Indian merchants were counting on a December arrival date. When the goods failed to turn up after twelve weeks, the suppliers, scattered across Western Europe, received angry letters from the consignees. Anxious to restore their confidence, the Europeans turned to the International Maritime Bureau (IMB), a specialised division of the International Chamber of Commerce. Dedicated to the prevention of maritime fraud world-wide, the IMB has been operating since 1981 from its east London headquarters in Barking.

Captain Potengal Mukundan is a senior IMB investigator with a Cranfield Masters in Business Administration. Mukundan spent years tramping on merchant ships before he gained command while attending the Plymouth School of Maritime Studies. The son of a British Petroleum executive, Mukundan was born in Kuwait but grew up outside of Cochin, India. A thoughtful, modest man in his mid-thirties, Mukundan's quiet strength comes to the fore during volatile negotiations.

When he received the assignment to represent the Indian merchants, Mukundan immediately put a tracer on the *Sea Falcon*. He discovered the ship and its 36-member Greek and Indian crew had left Antwerp in October on schedule and sailed toward the Red Sea. The ship anchored at Port Said in Egypt because by then the charterer, Clipper Orient Lines, had gone into liquidation.

Chartering fraud is especially easy to commit during a depressed shipping market, when too many ships chase too few cargoes. Shipowners, anxious to avoid laying up vessels, are tempted to charter them to previously unknown and at times unscrupulous companies.

'All a person has to do is simply set up a chartering company, which can be done overnight, with no special qualifications required,' explains IMB director, Eric Ellen. 'He collects the full freight charges from the buyer or seller, pays one instalment to the shipowner to put the goods on the ship and quickly goes into liquidation. No law-enforcement agency considers this a criminal act, merely a civil infraction. Attempts to recoup losses are usually futile.'

After forty-five days, the crew scraped up enough money to pay passage fees through the Suez Canal. They sailed on, passing Bombay where the Indian crew wanted to land, but the shipowner forbade the vessel to dock in India. In order to offload some cargo, the ship pulled into Karachi, Pakistan.

When the *Sea Falcon* berthed, she was promptly arrested by six different creditors of the shipowners. They included the crew, who had not been paid for fifteen months, port authorities, three local ship's chandlers in Karachi, a ship's chandler in Antwerp and a bunker supplier. All together, the creditors sought $700,000. The crew alone demanded $380,000 in unpaid wages. The ship's arrest meant that its papers were confiscated and that it would be unable to get clearance to sail out of the harbour. The documents would not be returned until he debts were settled.

If the cargo was ever going to make it to Bombay, Mukundan needed to pay off the creditors. 'There was no way we were prepared to start negotiating with the creditors without enough money to meet the debts,' he recalls. 'It didn't make sense.' Unlike typical chartering frauds, the charterer did not take the money and run. 'The charterers, after collecting the freight monies, used them to pay off previous debts,' says Mukundan. They had a fleet of ships and a lot of problems.'

Clearly, the Indian consignees had title to the cargo. The problem was that the shipowner did not have the money to deliver it. Without the money, he was content to let the vessel remain in Karachi. Mukundan's only source of capital were the heated Indian merchants themselves. Asking them for more cash was not going to be easy.

Mukundan prepared for his meeting by placing an ad in the national press explaining that the IMB was aware of the problems affecting the cargo's voyage. He invited the consignees to a strategy meeting at the Nataraj Hotel in Bombay. When the ad appeared, some consignees saw hope, others found a target for their anger.

Many of the smaller consignees had staked their entire businesses on the imported raw materials. Without the goods, their factories were paralysed. For each day the merchants failed to receive their cargo, they drew ever nearer to financial ruin. Banks had begun to take liens against their property. Their wits and overdrafts were at breaking point. The chartering fraud had left thirty consignees too destitute to make it to the Bombay meeting. Those that could make it, came with the single expectation that Mukundan would deliver their cargo. Instead, he asked them for an additional $70 per ton, a requirement totalling $700,000. He explained that it was the only way their goods could be delivered.

The merchants were outraged. Rising to their feet, several leapt on to chairs and shouted abuse. 'There was a lot of antagonism,' recalls Mukundan. 'It was terrible. They were just ordinary businessmen. Some were small businessmen, the kind who have no clue about what is happening outside their own world. There were also big consignees who had shipping and chartering managers. The whole commercial range was present.'

In their eyes, Mukundan had a lot of nerve asking for money. 'The ship was already three months late. Some of them got really upset and aggressive, asking why we couldn't just get the ship to complete the voyage rather than coming to them asking for money. Meetings like that are very difficult,' says Mukundan. 'Initially they are all against you. You can feel the anger of the people directed at you because they perceive you as the only person who can speak to the owners on their behalf and they see you somehow as representing the owners. I addressed the group and explained in detail what had happened; what their options were and what might happen if they didn't take prompt action to protect their cargo.

'The choice was simple,' says Mukundan. 'If they didn't raise the money there was no doubt at all that the vessel would not leave Karachi. She would stay in Karachi and invariably, when the vessel was sold by public auction, for which we knew there were already legal proceedings in force at that time, they might be given two choices by the new owner of the vessel. Either they would have to pay an exorbitant ransom to get their cargo to

Bombay, or else they would have to go to collect the cargo in Karachi.'

In the second case, if they were to go to Karachi to get the cargo, it would be very difficult because of the political problems. Due to the political strife between India and Pakistan, Karachi port authorities do not allow trans-shipment of Indian cargo via Pakistan.

'I went by instinct,' he says. 'I told them what the problem was and slowly answered their questions, and the more I explained to them, as time went by, they realised I wasn't really their enemy. Even if I didn't have the information, they respected the fact that I could get the information from the owners or from other sources. They appreciated that it was a very difficult problem. It is not something that a commercial person locally could easily handle. It would have been very difficult for him to negotiate on his own. I said it was not my problem and I made it very clear to them that it was theirs. We would act on their instruction and if they didn't want us to investigate, we were going to leave. I told them they could solve the problem themselves.' Mukundan eventually convinced the consignees to pay the additional charges and started to collect funds for the creditors at the meeting.

His next rendezvous was across the border in Pakistan where for three months the *Sea Falcon* and her crew had waited it out in the Karachi port. Temperatures were creeping into the nineties. The hull's grey-and-white paint had started to peel under the blazing sun. Below deck, the cargo of steel, clothes and chemicals baked in sealed hatches. Normal maintenance had been suspended. The cargo crane was inoperable and the ship's engines had not been serviced. 'It floated,' recalls Mukundan.

Tensions were rising between the Greek officers and Indian seamen. The 36-member crew had divided itself into factions. None of them had been paid for over a year, as a result of the charterer's liquidation. To survive, they had broken the bond of their customs stores, selling the contraband liquor and cigarettes. By the time Mukundan arrived on board the ship, the whisky and tobacco had run out. The crew survived on lentils and water provided by a local trade union. The *Sea Falcon* was so low on diesel oil that at night her decks were completely blacked out. The local launch operators, taking pity on the despondent crew, ferried them gratis from ship to shore. The crew's morale had plummeted and they were, in effect, in a state of mutiny at anchor. The ship's captain had long since stopped giving orders and locked himself into his cabin at night for his own protection. 'I cannot do anything,' he told Mukundan. 'You must talk to them.'

Mukundan addressed the crew in the ship's saloon. Their mistrust of the man who wanted the cargo – their 10,000-ton bargaining chip – was palpable. They had retained a lawyer and filed a suit for $380,000 back wages in the high court. Mukundan wanted them to withdraw their claim, otherwise the vessel would not sail. 'It was a very big problem,' he recalls. 'Dealing with a crew under these circumstances is very difficult. They are on a ship and as they see it, there is nobody outside the vessel who is prepared to help them.

'They needed basic things: food, water, provisions, stores, and diesel oil to run the generator to keep the ship at a comfortable temperature. For the six months they were in Karachi, they received nothing,' says Mukundan. 'They were psychologically at the end of their endurance. It is very difficult to deal with people like that. You have to be very careful. There is always the possibility that what you're asking them to do may be the last straw. They might just do something desperate, like taking to the ports and sinking the vessel. All thirty-six just existed. You get the break down of discipline in situations like this. People didn't listen to what the captain told them.'

The more Mukundan learned of the crew's problems, his sympathy for them increased. 'It was terrible,' he says. The worst was that they couldn't send any money home and you can imagine what it's like when the main bread-winner is not able to deal with domestic problems. Family members were falling sick and, without money for education, some of the crew's children could no longer go to school. Their fathers were somewhere far away, stuck in a Karachi port. They had no money to send home to keep their families going. It was a very difficult situation. 'Crew members are basically very simple people,' says Mukundan. 'It's not fair to expect them to understand or to shoulder the burden for the problem of the shipowners.'

Following Mukundan's first meeting with the crew, one of the ship's officers came up to him to ask if he knew the vessel, the *State of Orisa*. Fifteen years before, Mukundan and the officer had been fellow cadets aboard the freighter on a journey from India to Japan. The unexpected reunion was a further boost to Mukundan's credibility with the crew. Yet another was his offer to deliver mail to their families.

But the crew was only one aspect of his problem. Mukundan was negotiating with a lot of creditors simultaneously. 'We had to reach a full and final settlement, or else the ship would never leave,' he says. 'We needed all the creditors to withdraw their cases and release the vessel from arrest, but before that could happen, we had to pay them.

'It was a catch-22 because we didn't want to pay them until the vessel had actually left Karachi,' says Mukundan. He did not want to risk paying off a handful of creditors only to have the last one engage in lengthy litigation. 'The real trick throughout,' he says, 'was to synchronise everything. The whole thing was like a house of cards. So long as you kept building and it kept going in one direction, you were OK. One false move and the game was over.'

The thing that worried Mukundan the most was the possibility that a bank with a $3.6-million claim against the ship would step in. If it did, Mukundan explained to the six other creditors, their claims would be brushed aside, since the bank's claim was far superior. In the end, the bank did not become involved, convinced legal fees in the complex case would cancel any financial reward.

'One key creditor probably knew he had a very strong card to play and he was trying to exploit it. Everyone was trying to do that. So you play one off against the other, don't tell anyone what you have just negotiated with the other person,' says Mukundan. 'Of course I was being difficult. But the creditors had a choice: they could either wait and take a gamble on getting their money after a very lengthy hearing in a Karachi courtroom or they could settle instantly.'

Two small ship's chandlers in Karachi refused to negotiate and to this day are still fighting for the 10 per cent of their claim – the amount Mukundan put up in the high court to release the arrest of the vessel. 'They felt that we would have to settle with them,' says Mukundan. 'First of all, because they are so small we would not risk the whole operation for them. We preferred, rather than pay them, to pay the court and let them fight it out. After all, we did give them the option to settle.'

In an effort to persuade the crew to withdraw their court action against the shipowner, enabling the vessel to leave Karachi, Mukundan promised that upon its arrival in Bombay, the IMB would pay the crew $130,000. The balance of their claim would be recovered from the proceeds from the sale of the ship. In the meantime, the IMB would provision the ship for the journey. Using the consignees' funds, Mukundan paid the crew pocket-money as a show of good faith.

Over a period of three months, Mukundan had become indispensable to both the consignees and the crew. 'It was really the only way to do it,' he says, 'otherwise you end up with people being totally unreasonable. At the end of the day, it is nearly impossible because you have two parties who are hurt here. If you look just at the crew and the consignees, it is not fair that the consignees pay to the crew everything, because it is not their debt. It's the shipowner's. So one has to be reasonable, although each person has his own reason for thinking he's completely right.'

As he negotiated with the creditors, Mukundan sometimes came close to despair: the case appeared insoluble. 'There was so much at stake,' he remembers. 'Sometimes, just before the sailing of the vessel, everything you've been working towards for the last three or four months hinges on the next few days. If something goes wrong at the last minute – the ship has an engine problem, which prevents her from sailing, or some creditor from out of the blue comes and slaps a notice on the ship – that's it. From what source are you going to find the extra $15,000 or $20,000 to satisfy them?'

After many long hours of negotiating, the crew finally withdrew its claim. The day before the ship was due to set sail, the chief engineer, a Greek, came up to Mukundan and stated that he would not withdraw his claim unless he was paid another $3,000. It was a simple case of blackmail.

'The ship cannot sail without me,' he told Mukundan. 'Unless you agree to pay me the money now, I will not agree to withdraw my claim. It doesn't matter what the rest of the crew does.'

Furious, Mukundan called his bluff.

'OK,' he said. 'Fine. I'm catching the next flight back and you can stay here and collect your money at the end of your court case in Karachi. Don't even think about looking to us for help. We won't give it to you.'

Mukundan met with the crew in the saloon and told them of his plan to leave. 'They were very upset,' he says. 'When this chap got back to the ship, they locked him up in his cabin. The cook refused to prepare any food for him until he agreed, like the rest of the crew, to withdraw his claim.' The next morning, the chief engineer withdrew his claim. 'I had a job to do,' recalls Mukundan. 'I wanted to get the ship to Bombay and I was prepared to do whatever was necessary to achieve that end.'

As heated negotiations with creditors dragged on, an explosive situation played in the back of Mukundan's mind. In the early days of the case, when he had just arrived in Bombay, Mukundan received a telex from one of the Western European traders, Intermaritime EP Fluvial, a chemical freight forwarder based in Paris. The telex informed Mukundan that the chemicals in the ship's cargo hold would become unstable if kept in a continuously hot or tropical climate for longer than four months.

There were over twenty tons of various chemicals on board the ship, including aviation fuel, acrylic acids, corrosives, flammable agents and a cocktail of two dozen other chemicals which could emit poisonous fumes. The temperature in Karachi was in the nineties throughout the ship's stay. Inside the vessel's hatches, the heat was oppressive. The *Sea Falcon* was to remain under arrest for six months. Clearly, Mukundan had a time bomb on his hands.

If that were not enough, because of her state of disrepair, and the dangerous cargo, no underwriter dared to insure the vessel for the two-day journey from Karachi to Bombay, not least because the ship would be sailing during the monsoon season. Delays caused by negotiations with creditors had pushed back the departure date. When she finally left Karachi, the wind registered force 7–8 on the Beaufort scale. It's rare that any ship heads out in such foul weather, let alone one carrying explosive chemicals. The Indian coastline from the Tropic of Cancer to Mangalore is littered with the flotsam and jetsam of top-deck cargoes that are washed overboard during the monsoon season. To Mukundan's relief, the *Sea Falcon* survived the journey.

Having been assured immediate access to a berth in Bombay, the crew were enraged to discover they would have to wait indefinitely at outer anchorage while huge freighters, made lifeless by the monsoons, discharged their cargoes. For ten days they waited on stormy seas, convinced they had been

154

duped. There were many trying conversations between the crew and Mukundan on ship-to-shore radio. 'At one stage, they threatened to go back to Karachi,' he says. 'It was an extremely difficult period.'

The crew, betrayed and angry, had become as unstable as their chemical cargo and when the *Sea Falcon* gained entrance to inner anchorage, the crew promptly deserted the ship. Stevedores were hired to unload the cargo, a process that lasted the whole of July. Amazingly, no consignee complained about the expired chemicals. The textile and steel buyers, so outraged in March at having to pay extra for their cargo, were delighted to be refunded $50 for every $70 they had contributed to retrieve the goods. Mukundan saw that the crew were paid. In the end, the *Sea Falcon* was sold for $600,000 to salvagers.

Mukundan had spent the better part of five months on the case. 'It was stressful,' he says. 'You just carry on doing it, and you don't think about the stress. It's very fascinating actually to see how different people respond to different situations. Playing the fly on the wall, making observations, it is interesting to predict outcomes. You stack all your bets on them and you proceed on that basis. It's very nice if you're right and if you're wrong, you start again. Intellectually, it's very satisfying. It's like psychological gambling and the chips are the success or failure of the whole project. That's what we're gambling on the whole time.'

Since it was formed nearly a decade ago, the IMB has gambled that it will succeed in all of the 150 cases it handles each year. The IMB's 1,000 members are drawn from over sixty countries and include traders, like the Indian merchants in the *Sea Falcon* case, insurance companies, shipowners, brokers, charterers, lawyers, commodity dealers and banks. Two-tiered annual membership fees vary from £660 to £2,500.

Through its extensive port contacts around the world, the IMB monitors ships and develops dossiers on vessels and people in the shipping industry. This can mean tracking a missing cargo of antique Buddhas worth $60 million lost in the Mediterranean or setting up a toxic waste hotline for information on illegal dumping. The non-profit-making IMB functions as a central intelligence agency of the high seas, providing bulletins and black lists to its members. Information geared to preserve trust among traders is crucial to an industry so vulnerable to criminal deception.

Shipping, despite the introduction of computers and high-tech communications, is beset with simply executed, major fraud. Often the culprits can rely on port and bank officials to accept without question forged documents or to neglect routine checks that are intended to save the innocent from financial loss. Because ships, unlike aircraft, take weeks rather than hours to reach destinations, the criminals have time to cover their tracks.[1]

Underwriters, too keen to make killings on premiums, can be hit by fraudulent cashing in on policies worth more than 500 per cent of the value of the insured ships and cargo. 'The sky's the limit,' says a Lloyd's claims adjuster. Filing fraudulent maritime-insurance claims is an easy and quick way to make a fortune. 'It's dead simple,' he says. 'There is very little communication in the international underwriting market. Big stings are rarely picked up.' The reason? 'We have very little commercial option. We have to survive.'

Survival comes in the form of premiums and shareholders' funds. At the end of the day, if an underwriter, who pays 20 per cent on a total-loss claim, should suspect fraud, they will either find it too embarrassing to admit, or unworthy of legal recourse. What they probably don't realise is that there are thirty other underwriters located in markets around the world paying the same percentage on the same claim. The conman behind the sham walks away from a group of silent victims, rich and free.

When he was head of the International Association of Airport and Seaport Police, IMB director Eric Ellen gave a presidential speech that shook the insurance industry. 'I accused the insurers of covering up for murder, conspiracy and fraud,' he recalls. 'They were just paying out on claims, not investigating, just looking at the bottom line.'

Ellen's speech made headline news the next day, but his candid approach did not win him many friends in the insurance industry. 'My comments raised a storm of protest from the audience,' says Ellen. 'But it didn't help me very much. I don't think insurers ever forgave me for what I did. They didn't share my passion. It's taken a long time for them to accept me. They'd like to quiet me, I know that. They haven't succeeded yet.'

'Insurance brokers are a very secret breed,' explains Peter Lowe, an IMB investigator. 'They've kept secret for years. Fraud is rather like sex, something to be swept under the carpet. They don't like Eric much because he's out in the open, trying to solve fraud cases.

'There is a lot of competition between different insurers. They tend to guard each of their patches very jealously. They also don't like other people to know they've been hit with very sizable claims. It has an effect on investors' confidence and the share price. For commercial reasons, they prefer to remain rather muted on the subject. Eric sort of brought it out of the closet. He was one of the first to talk about maritime fraud so openly throughout the world.'

Today the walls of Ellen's office are adorned with plaques and medals from governments including Nicosia, Taiwan and Bermuda as well as the American FBI. They attest to the level of international co-operation he has received in his case work. 'I've come to terms with the industry now,' says Ellen. 'They realise what I'm trying to accomplish.'

Before creating the IMB, Ellen spent thirty years policing the ports of London as Chief Constable, a job that brought him into contact with labour lords and the seamier side of the India, Royal and Surrey Docks. His career brought him the comforts of promotion and recognition, but one day, something happened that changed his life.

On the morning of 17 January 1980, a 213,928-ton Liberian-registered supertanker, the *Salem*, sank off the coast of Senegal. Originally bound for Italy and carrying a cargo of crude oil worth $56 million, the *Salem* had deviated to South Africa. There the crew illegally sold what was Shell Oil's fuel to the sanctioned government of South Africa. After discharging her cargo she replaced it with sea-water ballast. The sinking of the *Salem* had been part of an organised plot to defraud Lloyd's of London, whose syndicates had insured both the cargo and the hull for a total of $84.2 million. Eventually, culprits were arrested, tried and sent to prison. South Africa paid Shell a reported $30.5 million in settlement for claims arising from the case. Frederick Soudan was sentenced in 1985 to thirty-five years in jail for his part in the fraud, but escaped three years later from his cell in Houston, Texas. The *Salem* remains the largest, most celebrated maritime fraud case of all time.

'I could have soldiered on with the police force for another fifteen years, but the *Salem* came along. It was the case that had the biggest effect on my life,' says Ellen. 'It made the industry sit up. It made insurers turn white. It proved the need for an international maritime bureau. It was really as a result of the *Salem* that the IMB was set up.'

Shortly after the IMB gained finance from the International Chamber of Commerce in January 1981, it received recognition from the United Nations' shipping agency, the International Maritime Organisation. Many of the world's major shipowners and marine insurers became immediate members.

Sea crimes, to which the IMB is dedicated to thwarting, have many guises. The major frauds include criminal manipulation of documents, scuttlings, 'phantom' ships, deviations and piracy.

'Maritime fraud is big business,' says Ellen. When the IMB was formed, reported losses directly related to maritime fraud equalled some $130 million a year. Today, cases reported to the IMB equal £150 million a year, just 2 per cent of the overall shipping fraud losses. 'Until law enforcement gets involved on an international basis, it's going to get worse,' says Ellen. 'No one fears a civil writ for £200,000. It's the hands on the shoulder, the threat of ten years in prison that acts as deterrent. I do believe in hitting hard. You pacify the industry, you get nowhere. The most difficult part of my job,' he adds, 'is dealing with the establishment.'

The appeal of maritime fraud is simple: 'It's the easiest money in the world,' says Ellen. 'You stand a very high, 90-per-cent chance of getting away with maritime fraud as opposed to a fraud committed in your own country. The reason is that most maritime crimes are international and the police are very bad travellers. They don't cross national boundaries very well and they don't take their law-enforcement powers with them and they use co-ordinated centres like Interpol. As a result, maritime fraud does not get investigated very well . . . There are a lot of people who have never got caught.'

Finding the perpetrators of maritime fraud, shrouded in flags of convenience, hidden behind a chorus of nominee directors, is usually impossible. It takes talent and perseverance to track them down. At the heart of the IMB is an international team of twenty professional investigators. Master mariners, qualified lawyers, practising maritime solicitors, former British and colonial police officers, and transportation executives make up the highly motivated, hand-picked staff whose linguistic strength is equal to a minor United Nations.

Investigators from regions including Asia, India, Kenya, Canada and the UK all have practical sea-faring experience and commercial expertise in the fields of transportation and law. The casework calls for extensive analysis of shipping documents and report writing. But it is by no means a desk-bound job. Without power to prosecute independently, investigators work closely with law-enforcement agencies around the world.

For each investigator at the IMB, there is no such thing as a daily routine. Wrapped inside each assignment is an adventure.

When Shiao-Lin Kuo, a veteran IMB investigator, recently received a telex from a German company, a victim of cargo fraud, she knew her adventure would take her home.

Born in 1957 in Taipei, Kuo's parents gave her a name that means 'Little Bamboo' in Chinese. Kuo's father, a police chief in Taipei, died when she was 7. To this day he appears in her dreams at night, perhaps an indication of his impact on her and the loss she continues to bear. 'You wake up,' she says, 'struggling to believe he is alive.'

While it's tempting to think Kuo unconsciously followed in her father's footsteps when, at the age of 16, she became one of the first women to be accepted by Taiwan's central police college, it is more likely that she wanted to prove something to herself. 'I always wanted to be a soldier,' she once said. 'But my mother opposed.' At police college, Kuo quickly became the top student, a position she held consistently during her four-year course. She scored high marks with a .38 revolver in firing practice, garnered a black belt in judo and became adept at kung fu and conventional weaponry. To look at Kuo in a fashionable outfit and high heels, her black shiny hair in waves of curls, she does not appear dressed to kill in the literal sense. But beyond her looks is a woman that possesses consummate skills of self defence.

After her graduation, Kuo joined the Taipei Municipal Police where, as the only woman in her section, she frequently went undercover, posing as a prostitute to help break vice and gambling rings. In less than a year on the beat, she was selected to work in Taiwan's Interpol Division. On three separate occasions Kuo escorted extradited criminals who had fled to Taiwan back to Japan and Brunei.

Because Kuo had mastered English as an adolescent and

taught herself Japanese, she was in demand for liaison work with other police forces. In 1979, Eric Ellen, then president of the International Association of Airport and Seaport Police, visited Taiwan with his family. Kuo was assigned as Ellen's interpreter. One year later, Ellen returned to Taiwan in connection with a 'rust bucket' fraud, a case involving the scuttling of an over-insured, barely seaworthy vessel containing valuable cargo. Kuo assisted him by talking with the Taiwanese people involved in the case.

Ellen told Kuo of the latest development in his scheme to set up an international maritime bureau. The International Chamber of Commerce was prepared to finance the bureau with £20,000. The sinking of the *Salem* had sped up the process to establish a world-wide bureau to wipe our fraud and piracy. Ellen wanted Kuo on his team.

With permission from General Kung of Taiwan's National Police Administration, Kuo joined the fledgling IMB. Since she left her post at Interpol, her mobility has increased sharply. 'Police forces all over the world suffer from bureaucracy,' she says. 'Here, you make your own decisions and have your own responsibilities. We are able to go anywhere. . . . Unlike typical law-enforcement agencies, we have become the focal point for the shipping industry because we have a much more commercial approach to what the industry needs.'

Not surprisingly, most of the cases Kuo handles are based in Asia. 'I wouldn't investigate in the Far East without her,' says Ellen. 'She can give me that protection others are looking for. Lin is a vigorous and thorough investigator. She brings important Far Eastern experience to the international staff.'

Since joining the IMB, Kuo has worked on some thirty cases, usually three to five major investigations a year. 'If you've got common sense, you can do investigation work,' she says. 'It gets very difficult when it comes to problem solving. You should know who you're dealing with. You should never put yourself in a situation you can't get out of.'

Kuo speaks from experience. She has received a number of death threats since joining the IMB. In a case involving forged seamen's licences, she incurred the wrath of Taiwanese fishermen. 'You feel like you're doing something against the whole of society. Once they lose their licence, they lose their livelihood,' says Kuo. 'A lot of people are working solely because they have a licence. It's forged and they paid for it. I tried to find out who was behind this big operation.'

While she was in Hong Kong, the office received a death threat directed at Kuo from a Taiwanese businessman in Japan who wanted her off the case. The threat was genuine, but it did not shock Kuo. 'She has great determination and an aggression that makes grown men quake,' says Ellen.

Kuo's mother has described her as a jagged rock whose edges, over time, gradually become smooth. Not known for being especially tactful, Kuo asserts herself bluntly and directly to foreign taxi drivers and barristers alike. Her wilful manner betrays a quick temper. At the same time, she is kind hearted, possessing a delicate laugh worth every effort to elicit. Kuo has discovered that being a woman in her profession is an asset. 'If you're a woman,' she says, 'people allow you to put your feet in deeper. They're not so defensive.

'I've been playing this role for over ten years. I don't know how other people see me, but I'm confident enough that I don't give them a chance to look down on me because I'm a woman. I'm in a man's world,' says Kuo. 'I never deal with women. Only the criminal's wife or girl-friend. You just have to go and deal with them and forget who you are. They probably don't swear at me because I'm a woman. But they do accept me in my role and they talk to me. They might hide something from me because I'm a woman or they might be softer. You can never take 100 per cent advantage. I think before a case is settled, you're afraid really to relax with them. If you like the chap, you might turn soft when it comes to negotiating. To start with, you have to be calm.'

Before meeting her adversaries, Kuo researches every aspect of the case. 'I love going through documents. It's like putting together a puzzle in which every piece is strange and different. When you piece it all together, you see the beauty of it. It's exciting.'

When Dann Export, a German company, sent a telex to the IMB, their plight was a familiar story. They had paid $4.5 million for twenty-nine containers of high-quality teak rocking chairs to be made by a Taiwanese firm. Another container was meant to be a cargo of high-quality dolls. Dann Export had planned to distribute the goods to European department stores. When the goods arrived, fourteen containers held inferior bar stools. The dolls were substituted with cheap imitations and the remaining fifteen containers were filled with rubbish.

Dann Export sent the IMB a copy of the bill of lading. Frequently referred to by IMB investigators as a 'licence to steal', a bill of lading is an easily forged piece of documentary evidence that shows goods described therein have been loaded aboard a vessel. It acts as the shipmaster's acknowledgement that he has taken the goods aboard his ship, but, most importantly in this case, it is also the shipper's guarantee of accuracy in describing the nature and quantity of a cargo.

Once the bill of lading has been signed by the shipmaster, the supplier takes the document to a bank to receive cash through a letter of credit opened by the buyer. Dann Export paid the suppliers through a letter of credit, but when it received the inferior goods, it filed an insurance claim. In order to receive any payment from its underwriters, Dann Export needed to prove that far from bilking its insurers, it had been defrauded by its suppliers. In its telex, they asked the IMB if it would carry out an investigation on its behalf in Taiwan. 'I read the telex on the tube on the way to a meeting in London,' recalls Kuo. 'It's impossible to get the information you need in a case like this from just a telex. I knew I would have to go out there myself.'

Kuo's familiarity with Taiwan goes beyond the sort of feelings most people have about where they grew up. Taipei, the capital city, is where Kuo first learned the art of detection. Her undercover work for the police and investigations for Interpol provided Kuo with superb training for grappling with maritime fraud. She works fast, quickly gathering evidence to use during confrontations with criminals. Kuo's fearless approach during tense encounters catches them by surprise. More often than not, perhaps sensing they've run out of options, her quarry make outright confessions.

Soon after Kuo received the telex and further details from Dann Export, she flew to Taipei. Kuo did not register at a hotel, preferring the familiar surroundings of her mother's home. To reduce maternal anxiety or interference, Kuo does not discuss cases in her mother's presence. In any event, she does not see much of her mother during working visits. Kuo's hectic week-long stays are crammed with gathering evidence and appointments with suspects.

When she arrived in Taipei, Kuo took a taxi to her mother' home and had a quick bath. With a few hours left in the working day, she headed out in search of Growth Power Enterprise, the company that had inspected the cargo of chairs, dolls and rubbish before they were shipped to Germany.

'I asked a junior clerk who inspected the cargo,' remember Kuo. 'He told me Stephen Wong, the proprietor, dealt with all enquiries. He added that the inspector in this case had been John Knust. Both men were out of the office,' says Kuo. ' looked around and spotted a piece of paper on top of a desk Someone had written the names of the suppliers: Namson Industrial Company and Fugy Co. Ltd. At that point, I realised the inspector, who was supposed to be totally independent was connected to the suppliers.' Kuo discreetly took down the information.

'When I arrived at Namson, they were no longer there,' she says. 'Fugy's door was locked tight. I spoke to the neighbours

They said the company had moved out a long time ago.' Fugy's office was a flat located in a narrow alley. Kuo knocked on nearby residences, asking for Fugy's whereabouts. 'One neighbour told me something very interesting: Stephen Wong of Growth Power had been to his company, asking to buy some stock – cheap, left-over – goods for export to Germany.' The man said Wong had placed ads in papers seeking stock goods from scrap-merchants all over Taipei. Kuo traced Fugy through the shipping line they had used to forward the goods. When she spoke with the man in charge, he told Kuo that Wong requested only cheap bar stools, not rocking chairs.

When she met with Wong and Knust mid-week she was surprised to also see their lawyer, an elderly Chinese man. 'They said they had reported the case to the police. They were suing Fugy and Namson for supplying inferior goods,' says Kuo. 'They were trying to cover their own backs.'

Wong was a small, very energetic man in his thirties. Knust, the German, was tall and very thin. He was in his sixties, but with his wrinkles and grey hair, appeared a decade older. 'He looked quite ill to me,' says Kuo. Knust told Kuo that he was an inspector for a fashion company in Taiwan. He became ill recently and went back to Germany where he met the buyer from Dann Export. 'The buyer, he said, asked him to come back to Taiwan to see if he could do some business for him.'

Kuo had done some checking on Knust and learned that he did not have a proper working visa in Taiwan. 'Every two months he had to come back to gain a short tourist visa. He insisted that he had seen the cargo before it was loaded into containers. I asked him where he had inspected the cargo,' says Kuo. 'He couldn't tell me.' From that response alone, Kuo's suspicions were confirmed. 'I felt that there was something wrong, because if he inspected the cargo while it was being loaded, it's not very likely that you're going to swap the contents of thirty containers out at sea.' Turning to Wong, Kuo asked him for the precise address of where the cargo was loaded. Eventually, after much persuasion, he agreed to take her there.

'At the same time, I made other local enquiries to find out what Stephen Wong was actually doing. I visited the trading company who supplied the dolls. Wong had earlier shared an office with them and asked them if he could use their company name to send out goods. He was using other companies to send out inferior merchandise.' Wong defended himself by stating that the Germans (Dann Export) had come out to Taiwan, had seen the goods and knew what they were buying.

Kuo noticed on the way to the inspection site that the car Wong drove was brand new. She figured it was a recent acquisition that he could afford as a result of the shipment to Germany. 'We wound up near a field. Lots of small alley-ways, but no factory,' says Kuo. 'It was very unlikely that you could have a huge lorry going in and out to a main road, especially one capable of carrying a 20 foot container.' Wong parked the car and Kuo walked down the alley, asking residents if they had seen containers being loaded. No one had. On the way back into town, Kuo thought that although Wong might be charming and outgoing, he was not an especially mature or sophisticated conman.

Perhaps if he had been more experienced, Wong would have persuaded his suppliers to cover for him. Instead, Fugy told Kuo that Wong had showed the factory foreman a cheap stool and requested Fugy to make them. He never presented a model of a rocking chair. 'After I spoke to Fugy,' says Kuo, 'I knew the rocking chairs were never ordered, never shipped. But how could the inspector sign a certificate stating both that the goods were ordered and that he saw them actually loaded on to the containers?' To find out, Kuo returned to Growth Power. 'Stephen Wong could not explain. Gradually, I became very upset,' she recalls. 'I told him I was going to the police.'

Kuo stalked out of the office. Wong rushed out to follow her. 'He was very worried. He told me he had taken a 30 per cent commission on the deal. A letter of credit had been open to him from Dann Export. He transferred it to Fugy and Namson, but they received very little money. They couldn't afford to send out the chairs ordered in the first place because they didn't have a profit margin,' says Kuo. 'What Wong did was to charge $10 for the chair, but have Fugy make it for $7. The money from Dann Export would not arrive until they received an inspection report. What the Germans did not know was that Wong, besides taking a generous commission, employed his own inspector.

'Wong had basically told Namson, "I'm giving you an order. In return, you must give me 30 per cent, otherwise my inspector, John Knust, will not sign the inspection report. Without the inspection report, you can't get the money," ' says Kuo. 'He really controlled the situation by exploiting the inspection report, controlling the suppliers and making his commission with it.'

Leaving Growth Power, Kuo hailed a cab. Stephen Wong followed her. As the cab pulled up to the kerb, Wong blocked her from getting inside. 'He offered me some kind of repayment, but it was a very small percentage compared to what he made,' she says. 'It came to about £20,000. I told him I was not in the position to recover money from him and that it was nowhere near the full amount in the first place. He was quite worried. He chased me down the street.'

Kuo had told him she was going to the authorities. 'I was quite satisfied because I knew the legitimate cargo was never shipped. To make sure, I needed some information from the authorities to support my investigation.' Kuo made a trip to the courthouse and discovered that Namson had conducted a similar fraud in May. 'They had shipped rubbish instead of machinery goods to Norway. Nobody picked it up, which enabled them to do another fraud three months later.'

To solidify her case, Kuo made some last-minute checks. 'Before I left for the airport, I visited the factory which supplied the stools to Fugy. They confirmed that Stephen Wong and

John Knust had inspected the cargo in their factory when it was loaded into containers. Stools, not rocking chairs, had been loaded. I was able to prove that Stephen Wong and John Knust knew what they were doing.'

Kuo had spent six days cracking the case. She kept careful notes of every meeting, later incorporating them into a report for the client, Dann Export. Stephen Wong was arrested on fraud charges. John Knust is still at large. Dann Export, at the end of the day, ironically were unable to make an insurance claim. Since the rocking chairs were never shipped, no policy could be attached to what were technically, non-existent goods.

Kuo spends a considerable amount of time in the Far East. Chasing phantom ships and crews is a recurring adventure for her. Phantom ships – vessels that, once loaded with valuable cargo, disappear never to be seen again – were a popular form of maritime fraud in the 1970s. It was a cheap way of cashing in on an insurance policy. The present resurgence in phantoms is far more serious. With an average cargo valued at $7 million, the game has become more lucrative and organised with sophisticated criminal gangs forging crew and ship documents.

In December 1988, the ship *Cherry Navee* was detained when it left Java with a cargo of plywood. Investigators later learned that it had changed its name seven times. As phantom ships vanish and reappear, newly named under the stroke of a paintbrush, tracking them becomes nearly impossible. 'There have been cases of crews painting a new name on the ship's bow as its under way,' says Ellen. Thirteen ships in 1988–9 have disappeared in the Far East, their cargoes never to be seen by victimised cargo buyers.

'You can't trace a vessel,' says Kuo. 'It's not like a person. It does not have a birth certificate. You can't trace a ship or its owner because most of the time, they only set up a company a few weeks before the operation. They register locally, but the description of the vessel and the crew's passports are totally fictitious. The local authorities get paid highly for ignoring such details.' The crews are equally expendable. 'They use very cheap labour from the Philippines, Burma or Thailand,' she says. 'They are well organised and cover all of South East Asia. Flying under flags of convenience, they avoid banking regulations by bartering stolen cargoes.'

When cash is required, however, there is little delay. One organiser was able to raise $3 million in less than three hours in a recent deal. 'The same people involved in scuttlings in the 1970s are doing it again,' says Kuo. 'But today it's bigger money and they are better organised. It's also more dangerous. I've been warned,' she says. 'It's easy for them to get rid of someone who stands in their way. In Singapore, it's $300 to get rid of people. It's very cheap. In places like Thailand, there is no protection at all.'

Like criminal deception on land, maritime fraud is regionalised. The phenomena of phantom ships takes on a violent mien in the Middle East. Instead of disappearing, ships deviate to the Lebanon, where their hijacked cargoes intended for other ports are sold to the highest bidder.

With its currency almost worthless and its former trading economy in ruins, Lebanon has relied on piracy as a source of consumer goods and hard currency to maintain expensive private armies. The various militias have received at least 50 per cent of their revenues from the seizure of cargoes in the illegal ports. From November 1986 to November 1988, thirty-six ships diverted to the Lebanon where their cargoes worth $30 million were illegally sold. Sailing under Cypriot, Lebanese or Panamanian flags of convenience, the vessels have become statistics in the fastest-growing maritime fraud.

Since she was built in Bremerhaven, the *Sea Wind*, a 7,000-ton cargo ship, sailed under six different names before she deviated from her course in 1988. Originally loaded with $1 million worth of steel from Romania, she was due to berth in Port Sudan. The Lebanese Forces picked her up on radar, lying off the coast of Beirut and, suspecting she had deviated from her course, headed out for a closer look. When they came aboard the vessel, the Forces noticed the ship's course had been laid for the illegal port of Ras Sela'ata. The *Sea Wind*'s master had been awaiting instructions to enter the nearby port.

The *Sea Wind* was brought into Beirut under armed guard. Its valuable steel cargo was discharged and when the ship's captain failed to explain why he was waiting off the coast of Lebanon or the reason he was bound for Ras Sela'ata, he was promptly arrested. The cargo was kept under the safe custody of the Lebanese Forces who were in constant contact with the IMB. Mukundan informed the cargo underwriters of the situation. 'The London [insurance] market is fully aware of what is going on and they fully appreciate the circumstances. There have been only four cargoes that have been recovered from the Lebanon out of the thirty pirated. So they have lost a lot of money. They know once a cargo goes in, the chances are they will pay on a total loss claim. So anything which contributes towards getting some cargo back is a plus. It's not a magic show,' he adds. 'They are fully aware of the difficulties.'

Dealing with the Lebanese Forces has been an educational experience for the IMB. 'They are very pleasant to talk to; very soft spoken. But at the end of the day,' says Mukundan, 'they know they hold the power. If you tell them something that is not acceptable to them, they just say, "Well, you can't do it." And you know there is no way you can do it. They are very hard to negotiate with, but once they give their word, there's no problem. They like to portray themselves as a government body, above all these kinds of commercial matters, so it is done between a number of people who are go-betweens.

'We have negotiations in Cyprus,' says Mukundan. 'Going in, you're wary of everyone. You're very insignificant in the overall power game and once you get caught in it, you are totally at the mercy of forces over which you have no control, as I'm sure the hostages have found out. The events that determine whether they will be released or not are totally remote from them.

'The underwriters gave us their approval,' recalls Mukundan. 'They agreed that we should go ahead and pay the Lebanese Forces $300,000 and we would arrange for the safe shipment of the cargo outside the Lebanon and pay them only after the cargo had been shipped.' The Lebanese Forces having intercepted the *Sea Wind*, and taken the ship into port, discharged the cargo, reloaded it on to another ship. The cargo sailed safely to its destination. 'For that we paid them a fair reward for their endeavours,' says Ellen. 'They in fact said it cost them a lot more.'

Ellen admits that the Lebanese Forces were pirates themselves up until 1985, when there was a leadership change. He is quick to justify the IMB's involvement with them. 'The industry has to do something. You can't leave everything to governments and law enforcement. Our decision to deal with the people of Lebanon was a commercial decision. In any case, I'd deal with the devil if need be,' says Ellen. 'These are dangerous cases. On a couple of occasions I had to go over to Beirut and although I had the protection of the Lebanese Forces, they've been ousted from power anyway.

'At the talks they are surrounded by armed guards at all times and that always causes tenseness. These are large, international frauds with lots and lots of money involved. Every situation is dangerous because the cost of having me or any one of my staff done away with is considerably less than the size of the frauds we're talking about. There is a continual element of risk. My mandate is to make sure that they have what we're after and to get it back as cheaply as possible.'

− 6 −

The enforcers

'Anybody in my business is very sceptical of the honesty
of corporate executives. We handle the worst. Companies get desperate and do desperate things.'

THOMSON VON STEIN, senior counsel,
Division of Enforcement,
Securities and Exchange Commission

On an afternoon in May 1988, Bruce Baird, head of the
securities and fraud unit in the New York US Attorney's office,
looked into the future and saw a bit of history in the making.
During his eight years in the federal prosecutor's office, he had
tackled big investigations, including the case against Carmine
'the Snake' Persico, head of the Colombo crime family. The
resulting eight-month trial crushed the top leadership of one
of the most powerful syndicates in New York, sending away
thirteen members for over 200 years on charges of conspiracy,
racketeering and extortion.

Baird's boss, US Attorney Rudolph Guiliani, had launched an
impressive attack on organised crime, but even the mob could
not compete with the action down on Wall Street. Financial
frauds, linked to takeover wars, competed with the mob for
front-page ink. In the wake of the Wall Street insider-trading
scandals, Guiliani appointed Baird to the fraud unit. Nabbing
stock-market tycoons provided him with comparative insights.
'For the most part, you can understand why members of the
Mafia get involved in criminal activity. A lot of them dropped
out of school at a very young age. These Wall Street guys don't

have that excuse. To catch them, you have to use every tool you can.'

Traditionally, Baird's most potent weapon has been the Racketeering-Influenced and Corrupt Organisations (RICO) Act. Named after the gangster portrayed by Edward G. Robinson in the film, *Little Caesar*, RICO was passed by Congress in 1969 to help federal prosecutors crack down on organised crime. With RICO, the government can seize assets before a trial and demand repayment of any proceeds of illegal activities. The statute also opens the door to civil-law suits that make defendants liable for triple damages if found guilty.

In the spring of 1988, Baird was giving RICO wider consideration. 'I have,' he said, scanning Wall Street's distant skyscrapers, 'enough practical confidence to try it.' Ten months later, on 29 March 1989, Baird's office brought the full force of RICO down on Michael Milken, junk-bond king and West Coast vice-president of investment bank Drexel Burnham Lambert. Milken, his brother Lowell and another Drexel trader, Bruce Newburg, were charged with ninety-eight counts of racketeering and fraud. They faced 700 years in prison and were asked to forfeit a staggering $1.8 billion. 'Our job is to bring the most serious charge that is justified,' Baird would later say. 'The more serious, the more likely the defendant is to co-operate.' Drexel, itself threatened with RICO and resultant bankruptcy, pleaded guilty to six felony charges and paid $650 million in fines in December. This co-operative move from Milken's former employer effectively left him out in the cold.

These events marked the first time in American legal history that RICO, a potent weapon against the Mafia, had been trained on Wall Street insiders. Baird's vision of the future had been nothing short of reality.

The case against Michael Milken began with an investigation launched by the Securities and Exchange Commission (SEC), following admissions made by Wall Street arbitrageur-turned-felon, Ivan Boesky. In September 1988, the SEC filed a 184-page civil suit against Milken. The litany of allegations included insider trading, stock manipulation, reporting violations and falsifying records. On the heels of the SEC's civil probe, the US Attorney's office drafted its criminal charges.

When he was the director of the SEC's division of enforcement between 1985 and 1989, Gary Lynch was at the fulcrum of the insider-trading investigations that led to a succession of milestone cases: Dennis Levine, Ivan Boesky (and with him, Ernest Saunders), Drexel Burnham Lambert and Michael Milken. The division of enforcement during Lynch's four-year leadership was responsible for over forty successful cases against illegal traders, roughly equal to the same number filed during the first half-century of the SEC's existence.

For Lynch, the attack on criminal insiders was long overdue. In January 1984, the SEC had accused Paul Thayer, former director of LTV Corporation and a former Assistant Secretary of Defense, of passing inside information on to eight people while he was a director of two major corporations involved in mergers. Thayer received a sentence of four years in federal prison, the longest ever meted out at the time for insider trading violations. But, 'By 1985,' says Lynch, 'the cases that we had brought were having absolutely no effect, were having no impact on conduct because we had yet to bring a case against someone who was a major figure on Wall Street. The impression that we created through the bringing of all these cases against people who were, for the most part, small fry, with the exception of Thayer, was that if you were a smart sophisticated trader, you got away with it.'

Cracking down on insider traders, those profiting from non-public material information made available in advance of an announced deal, had been a priority set by former SEC chairman John Shad since his appointment in 1981. At the time, he vowed that the Commission would come down on violators 'with hobnail boots'. Lynch had made manifest Shad's commitment. As it began to move effectively from one celebrated case to the next, the division of enforcement became known as the 'Lynch Mob'.

The RICO statute may have been drafted for the prosecution of organised crime figures of the latter half of the twentieth century, but it conjured up confrontations between the feds and gangsters of the 1920s and 1930s. The fact that it had now been used against a $550-million-a-year bond dealer in Beverly Hills revived the image of men in pin-striped suits. Instead of violin cases, the new criminals carried portable computers.

Eliot Ness and the 'Untouchables' who cracked down on Al Capone and his Chicago gang have much in common with Lynch and his division's war on Wall Street. Ness worked for the US Department of Justice, prohibition detail. He had grown up, the son of a wholesale baker, heavily influenced by Conan Doyle's Sherlock Holmes, and he was a potential tennis star. Lynch, the youngest by many years of five children, grew up in Middletown, New York, a homespun agricultural community. Lynch picked onions and dreamt about being a professional basketball player a natural ambition for any 6' 1", 14-year-old.

Both men had unpopular laws to work with. The hate mail the division receives, that derides the SEC for prosecuting insider-trading cases, equals the bitter sentiments Americans expressed about Prohibition. Drinking alcohol, like insider trading, was something that had always been taken for granted. The saloon had been an integral part of the American west; champagne the fuel that made the 1920s roar. Instantly, with the passage of Prohibition, drink was done for.

To keep the illicit bootlegging industry alive, Capone's lieutenants rigged elections. With their leverage and inside information, Wall Street's equivalents rigged corporate take-overs. Capone paid off people on the take. His Wall Street counterparts paid off informants with suitcases filled with banknotes in Manhattan's back alleys. Ness's brief was to loosen the stranglehold Al Capone had on Chicago. He caught him in a way Capone least expected: a tax return. Lynch was to snare big insider traders with the same kind of unexpected reach: gaining access to their secret off-shore accounts. Capone's pin-striped Chicago gang were hitmen for the mob. Wall Street's pin-striped warriors use an arsenal of 'dawn raids', 'shark repellent', 'poison pills' and 'scorched earth' strategies.

Insider information, leaked in advance of public announcements concerning takeovers, rights issues, and so on, was power in the hands of those in a position to trade on it. No law specifically forbade insider dealing. For decades, if the SEC was lucky enough to detect it, the Commission relied upon anti-fraud provisions of other federal securities laws to prosecute violators. It wasn't until Foster Winans, the *Wall Street Journal*'s 'Heard on the Street' columnist, was arrested for giving 'market-affecting information' to Peter Brant, a stockbroker with Kidder, Peabody and Co., and his case taken to the Supreme Court that the SEC was forced to come up with a definition of the crime.

The Insider Trading Sanctions Act, signed into law on 10 August 1984, allows for imposing fines up to three times the profit gained or the loss avoided by use of material non-public information. Designed to curb the misuse of confidential information unavailable to the general public, the new law was geared to make the markets fairer for all investors.

Four years later, in the waning hours of the 100th Congress, the Insider Trading and Securities Enforcement Act was passed. The statute increased criminal sanctions and fines and added a controversial bounty provision which allows the SEC to reward persons who provide information which leads to a successful prosecution. Additionally, employers or 'controlling persons' of the violator are now liable for penalties if they disregard new obligations to curb insider trading. Finally, the new law enables the SEC to conduct investigations on behalf of foreign authorities.

With the passage of these acts, Wall Street theoretically became 'dry'. The new 'Untouchable' was Lynch, a plain-speaking, poker-faced man who had left the family farm business in upstate New York to attend law school. Soon after he joined the SEC as a staff attorney, the 27-year-old Lynch completed an investigation into a Los Angeles brokerage house accused of manipulating stock prices. It proved to be an important case for Lynch. 'I would wake up at night thinking about questions, and where it was going next. I really loved the whole investigative process. I also enjoyed being given something and told to run fast with it.' After several months of digging and compiling evidence to back up allegations, Lynch called a meeting with the defence counsel, Frank Wheat. An imposing man with decades of experience in securities law, Wheat also happened to be a former SEC commissioner.

Lynch was two years out of law school. He had spent the first with a Washington firm, the second, driving a truck across the United States. 'I had gone straight from undergrad into law and I wasn't certain that I really wanted to be a lawyer. I thought it was time for a radical change.' The firm granted him a year's leave of absence and Lynch packed his bags, threw them in the back seat of his car and hit the road. He headed south to Florida and got a job as a truck driver. The year was 1976. When he reached California, Lynch, his long hair in a pony tail, decided to return to Washington. He applied for a job with the SEC and was hired by the then chief of enforcement, Stanley Sporkin. Like his colleagues in their late twenties and early thirties, Lynch received immediate, hands-on experience, comparable to that which senior partners would experience in established firms.

With the stock-manipulation case, Lynch was offered the chance to prove himself against one of the best the American Bar had to offer. Lynch had done his homework but was still apprehensive. Sporkin, now a federal judge, recalls the meeting Lynch had with Frank Wheat: 'For every question, Gary had an answer. Instead of saying he was going to contest the case, as defence lawyers almost always do, Wheat sat back and said, "Well, you got us." '[1]

Sporkin, heavyset and dishevelled with dark circles under his eyes, has the pasty look of someone who has spent his career inside climate-controlled buildings.

'You know what we are?' he once demanded. 'We're just a schnookie little government agency, nibbling at the toes of giants – and they're screaming.'[2] Sporkin, during the Watergate era, forced powerful companies including Exxon, ITT, Firestone, Occidental Petroleum, Northrop and Gulf Oil 'voluntarily' to disclose the fact that they had paid bribes to domestic and foreign officials. Known by his adversaries as 'Attila the Hun', Sporkin's seat of power was surrounded by a hectic shuffle of headline-making cases, and an ever expanding division of enforcement. It was a chaotic time. One Wall Street lawyer said that visiting Sporkin in his office was like being at 'a whorehouse during a fire-drill'.

The tone of Gary Lynch's division of enforcement compared to the free-wheeling style of Sporkin, is less mêlée, more teamwork. When he was appointed director of enforcement in 1985, Lynch inherited a department that was woefully overstretched, and in the eyes of an American Bar Association task force, too meagre 'for the Commission effectively to discharge its statutory responsibilities'. The New York Stock Exchange in the 1980s referred an average of a hundred documented cases a year of insider trading to the SEC; the National Association of Securities Dealers, the self-regulatory body of the over-the-counter markets, sent another hundred. An average of only 75 per cent a year was investigated. In the last decade, to complement the staggering 700-per-cent rise in stock transactions in the US, the number of people employed in the securities industry rose 400 per cent.[3]

As the market boomed, investor complaints doubled to 25,000. The SEC staff, meanwhile, actually shrank. 'It's like a city tripling its size, while its police force declines by 4 per cent,' said Richard Phillips, a former SEC staffer and prominent Washington attorney. Today the Commission, one-third of which is devoted to enforcements, is made up of some 2,200 people. Roughly 260 enforcement personnel are based in Washington, another 450 in nine regional offices around the US. The Commission is composed of lawyers, accountants, financial analysts and other professionals who handle a regular case-load of 700 to 800 investigations. The SEC's divisions of enforcement, corporate finance, market regulations and investment management are served by the office of general counsel.

Like Phillips and a legion of lawyers before him, most SEC staff attorneys come to the SEC to gain experience in securities law and then gain wealth and prominence in private practice. At the SEC, located near the Justice Department buildings and Washington's Chinatown, young lawyers walk the halls in striped shirts and braces, the uniform of ambition. Most are committed to the SEC, its bureaucracy, low pay and learning curve, for a maximum of three to five years.

The continuous migration presents problems, namely, a chronic lack of institutional memory. In such a high turnover environment, every departure signals the loss of case-work expertise. The SEC faces other problems. The agency can only enforce civil laws, usually through injunctions, fines and penalties, 90 per cent of which are settled out of court. The SEC does not have the authority to prosecute or to file criminal charges and so, in big cases, frequently it must convince federal prosecutors to become involved. 'There's a lot of securities violators for whom an injunction doesn't mean very much,' says Joseph Goldstein, associate director of enforcement. 'We try to involve the US Attorney's offices,' adds Lynch, 'the biggest deterrent is jail. There is nothing a person in the securities business fears more.... They lose control of their lives.'

For US attorneys who are capable of sending white-collar criminals to prison, there is a general unwillingness to take securities cases unless there are headlines and political capital to be made. For instance, shortly after New York US Attorney Rudolph Guiliani retired in January 1989, he announced he would be running for mayor of New York. Landmark insider-trading convictions did nothing to hurt his popularity.

With the exception of a few US Attorneys in California, New York and New Jersey, most federal prosecutors are not very keen on stock-market fraud. The reason is simply that securities cases are complex and much harder to present in court, versus the quick rewards of a typical bank robbery. Securities fraud is a quiet crime. Nobody dies from it. There are no smoking guns or dead bodies, just stacks of telephone records, cancelled cheques and stock transactions. Therefore, it is harder to convince an unacquainted judge and jury of the criminality involved.

'Some of these things really are technical,' says Phillip Parker, the SEC's associate general counsel. 'When you go in before a judge who's got murders and kidnappings and bank robberies and a million and one drug cases, he doesn't want to be bothered with something he knows is going to take two weeks and, in the scheme of things, he has to be convinced it's a big deal.'

SEC attorneys who stay at the Commission despite the low pay and judicial reluctance to handle their cases remain, for the most part, for what Parker calls 'psychic income'. 'You're dealing with people that you've read about,' says Gary Sundick, an assistant director of enforcement. 'People here get to take testimony from prominent and interesting people and they're not sitting in the back room of a law firm, or camped in a library, doing research for their partner to use. They aren't preparing questions for someone else to ask.'

The added challenge of battling with some of the best-paid legal minds in the US offers high stakes, on-the-job training.

'People here get a lot of responsibility at a relatively young age,' says John Sturc, associate director of enforcement. 'Their decision-making is based upon what they think is the right thing to do, as opposed to what narrowly would serve a client's interest. There is a lot of pick and choose. If we don't think the case is good, or we don't think that it's worth pursuing, we don't pursue it.

'I don't think you're going to find people that are raving moralists here,' he adds. 'But no doubt people at the SEC have a strong feeling about what's right and wrong, what's ethical and what's not.'

The legislation, that created the SEC in the wake of the 1929 Crash and the Depression that followed, was the product of public anger and anguish over the uncontrolled financial collapse of the market. The mission of the SEC whether crash, 'correction' or corruption is to administer federal securities laws aimed at providing protection for investors.

The government investigative lawyers who work at the SEC aren't the sort of heroic crime-fighting figures we're used to. Thomson von Stein, senior counsel for enforcement, pale and pudgy, is a man who usually eats lunch at his desk. Surrounding him are stacks of documents, residue of a 350-page chronology distilled from 4,000 pieces of subpoenaed paper.

Von Stein's features are pleasant: an even-toothed smile above a cleft chin, a face framed by receding black wispy hair and large aviator spectacles. While he speaks, he fiddles idly with a surgical stapler, a keepsake from a case involving American Surgical. Von Stein's easy manner hides the fact that he is being sued for $50 million by a firm under SEC investigation. 'It comes with the territory,' he says. 'Anybody in my business is very sceptical of the honesty of corporate executives. We handle the worst. Companies get desperate and do desperate things.'

Uncovering corporate *angst* in a blizzard of paperwork, can be overwhelmingly tedious. 'The most creative part of our usiness,' says von Stein, 'is trying to figure out why the dog idn't bark.' The whodunit in this case becomes a game of everse chess: the match is over by the time it lands on von tein's desk. His task is to retrace the players' moves following confusing maze of documentary evidence. 'By function we re reactive when it comes to financial fraud,' says von Stein's olleague, William McLucas, associate enforcement director who would later replace Lynch upon retirement). 'We follow he parade and pick up the manure.'

'When I played baseball in high school,' says von Stein, 'our oach said, "We got two speeds: standing still and going like ell." It's the same at the SEC, only in our case, it's standing till and going. It can be argued that in the big scheme of hings, the SEC may not be effective; that we're a day late, a ollar short with our enforcements. Our sanctions aren't really exible. We can sue for an injunction, that is to say, you go o a federal court and say "these people have broken the law nd they will probably break the law in the future, therefore, ve want a court order, that is, an injunction saying don't do again." It's the traditional slap on the wrist,' he says. 'We lon't have the authority to make people pay penalties except n insider-trading cases. . . . We are always out-lawyered. The eople we deal with are as bright as we are but because securities s a big-money business, their clients have unlimited resources. or every one lawyer there's an army behind them. They can eally outgun you.'

Perhaps part of the problem is the fact that the SEC, unlike streamlined law firm, must contend with the bureaucracy nherent in any government agency. 'There are times when ve need to get urgent documents posted, so we'll try to DHL package,' says Lynch. 'Someone in the mailroom will say, What's the justification for this?" You say, "Wait a minute, 2.50 is our contract rate and you're asking me to justify to ou why I want to send something overnight?" Occasionally,' e says, 'bureaucracy will raise its ugly head.'

When he retired in July 1989, Lynch, despite his thirteen years tackling some of the biggest securities fraud cases ever recorded, made about $78,000 a year, a salary figure most first-year law graduates make in established New York firms. The SEC budget in 1987 was $111 million. Michael Milken's take-home pay the same year was over five times that amount. 'I think the SEC is going to have big problems down the line if the disparity between salaries here and private sector salaries continue to widen,' says Lynch.

Faced with low pay and bureaucracy, the continual draw for many SEC lawyers is the undoubted power they wield. This also presents a catch-22 situation, since the mere mention of the SEC investigating a company can have a devastating impact on its stock price. 'A subpoena from the SEC with a telephone call doesn't make anyone's day,' explains Joseph Goldstein. 'We try to make sure everyone is accountable and we make sure we exercise that. We don't let people run off. There are no Lone Rangers here.'

'It's a very close knit operation,' says Phillip Parker. 'There are no independent fiefdoms warring with each other. With Gary [Lynch] there is a kind of presumption of rationality about everything he does. He's the kind of person who inspires confidence in people both above and below him. He does not make rash decisions.' Parker, who used to car pool with Lynch to work, adds that, while he may not be predictable, Lynch is consistent.

Among the SEC's collective of associate directors (known at the SEC as the 'Front Office') Lynch is regarded as the master of the forty-second meeting. 'I don't sit around with eight people at a table wringing hands for three hours trying to make a decision,' he says. The key reason is that the division of enforcement is pushed to come up with rapid results. Funded by tax payers, the SEC must demonstrate regularly to Congress that it is worthy of federal funding. Its mandate is maximum deterrence. 'You can't go for every case,' says Edward Herlihy a former SEC enforcement attorney now in private practice. 'You *have* to get as much bang for the buck as possible.'[5]

During his years in the enforcement division, Gary Lynch looked forward to cases that involved a lot of digging. 'I've always liked the process of doing investigations and solving puzzles and learning the facts. Every time you learn a new important fact in an investigation it's like a victory. It's important to do things quickly, to bring cases while the facts are still relatively fresh and while you can still have an impact.

'If you get into an investigation three years after the fact, it's going to be very difficult to put it together,' says Lynch. 'And if you bring the case in three years later, who cares? It's dealing with conduct that's so old that not only is it not going to have much of an impact on other people, but a defendant can go in and say look, this is ancient history. What are they doing dredging up something from so long ago?

'Part of the defence strategy in any investigation is to delay the process,' says Lynch. 'These things always take longer than first expected. It takes time to put them together. It's very rare that a six-month investigation is finished in three months. The more usual situation is when a six-month case takes from a year to 18 months. It's by making quick decisions on our side that we don't prolong a case.'

Before he became director of enforcement, Lynch had earned the unofficial title, 'Mr Tender Offer'. The fast-action skills Lynch learned on the basketball court helped him during these pivotal meetings that brought together a group of sworn enemies: raiders and their targets.

During a hostile takeover bid, in which a corporation or individual seeks to control another company through the purchase of its shares on the open market, the targeted company can protect itself in a couple of ways. To repel an unwelcome bid, a company will usually employ the first line of defence. In this case, it will raise as many legal issues as it possibly can to fight off the predator, filing suits in federal and state courts and through regulatory agencies. Under the Williams Act, the SEC has adopted a number of disclosure rules that describe potential takeover violations. The defending company, through its lawyers, has the right to challenge any disclosures as materially incomplete or incorrect.

Lynch became an expert at assessing the strengths and weaknesses of corporations under pressure by observing the grounds on which disclosure violations could be charged. These were: the purpose of the offer, the financing of the offer, prior contacts with management or directors of the target company, the impact of regulatory requirements and unreported misconduct or violation of law. If there were grounds for violations, the defending company could buy time until they were corrected; their ultimate aim being to unveil a grievous violation, a 'show stopper' that would end the deal.

'Tender offers are extremely fast moving,' explains Phillip Parker. 'You have to spin on a dime. Both sides come in screaming. These people who were banging down your door one minute no longer answer your phone calls. They're up all night, going over the fine print of a deal to meet an 8 a.m. deadline. They use defensive tactics like poison pills, lock-ups and shark repellent. They are remarkably creative. Disclosures have to be made. Boardrooms divide into troops. It's like mobilising an army within twelve hours. It's a military procedure.'

During his tender-offer work, Lynch became aware of the impact the news of a takeover had on the target company's stock. The announcements were the stuff members of Wall Street's 'Golden Triangle', the corporate raiders, arbitrageurs and investment bankers, lived and died for. As Lynch participated in the disclosure violation hearings, arbitrageur's lieutenants lurked in the backs of courtrooms ready to place urgent calls to buy or sell huge blocks of the target's stock, based on the latest twist in the case.

Lynch understood the power of the information they relayed. An arbitrageur who speculated on stocks could have millions riding on a raider's bid. With so much risk, especially considering so much of their capital could be borrowed to the hilt, the veracity of direct sources was crucial. Leaked information in advance of a deal ultimately took the risk out of risk arbitrage. Lynch and his colleagues at the SEC understood the capital elitism that grew out of trading on insider information: it removed any chance of an average investor making the same risk-free, high return investment.

Their unenviable job was to put an end to it.

For the deal junkies on Wall Street – the men and women who make corporations merge, divide and disappear – the 1980s became the ultimate fix. The market and its celebrity players transformed the language of high finance, creating a vocabulary for strategic corporate warfare. Predators were portrayed as villainous asset strippers, while arbitrageurs like Ivan Boesky risked millions speculating on takeovers and became legends.

Invited to the UC Berkeley campus to deliver a commencement address to its business school in 1985, Boesky announced, 'Greed is all right by the way. I want you to know that. I think greed is healthy. You can be greedy and still feel good about yourself.'

By the time he met Dennis Levine, Ivan Boesky was a living legend. Levine, a managing director at Drexel Burnham Lambert, had seen Boesky's hallmark smile light up newspaper and magazine profiles. He had read how Boesky worked eighteen-hour days, living off caffeine and the adrenalin of a deal.

Boesky operated out of his white-carpeted office on Fifth Avenue, a high-tech throne room replete with video monitors, computers and a telephone with 160 direct lines that kept him in constant touch with bankers, targets and raiders. Boesky's life revolved around the telephone. Even the one he had installed in the limo that he took to work each day had three lines.

He would chase every scrap of Wall Street information he could get his hands on, spending millions of dollars a year for researchers, consultants and lawyers. He even paid a clerk at a private airport to monitor the destinations of corporate jets carrying corporate Chief Executive Officers. Boesky didn't make it a point to keep well informed; he made it an obsession. Whether it was during his six a.m. commute from his $10 million Georgian mansion in Westchester County or over dinner with a raider, Boesky dominated the risk-arbitrage business. He had become a principal player in virtually every takeover deal of significance on Wall Street. His presence in a target stock was seismic.

By 1985, with the help of investment bankers Drexel Burnham Lambert, Boesky formed a staggering $900 million war chest of junk-bond collateral to increase his leverage in the market. The interest of arbitrageur (arbs) in a stock was often enough to excite takeovers, rather than the other way around. Boesky had enough borrowed money at his fingertips to take over companies himself. In fact, CBS, afraid he was prepared to do just that when he bought $250 million of its stock, filed a law suit against him. Boesky retorted, 'I didn't think that was a very nice thing to do to their largest shareholder.'[6]

Because Boesky's fees were triple the competition, he had to take more risks to make his investments pay off. To do this, Boesky purchased a seat on the New York Stock Exchange. This allowed him to leverage up to four times his fund's capital compared to the average investor's ability to leverage only twice as much. The leveraging, which is the power to invest through borrowed money as a means of increasing returns, heightened profitability on deals that were successful, but exposed creditors to terrific risks.

When Boesky took big stakes in deals, the market rumbled with expectations of shares on the rise. Fuelled by the presence of other speculators shadowing him, the price of the target's share would erupt. As the Street's most high-profile arb, Boesky was unabashedly cutthroat, they say, developing a love affair with stocks that sometimes only lasted minutes. The takeover fever on Wall Street fortified his position as the king of the arbitrageurs and he wrote *Merger Mania*, a largely self-financed book, to explain how.

Boesky, silver haired, poised and diplomatic, won kudos from the establishment through donations to Republican political campaigns and by teaching business classes at New York University where he was on the board of trustees. His generous contributions to Jewish charities and his involvement with the Harvard Club gave Boesky the patina of an elder statesman, the silver fox of arbitrage.

The volatile nature of Boesky's business was obvious by the swings in his annual figures. In 1982, his investors received a buoyant 57 per cent return on their investment. The market, meanwhile, dropped almost 11 per cent the same year. Boesky suffered a $15 million loss when Gulf Oil decided to withdraw its offer to buy Cities Services. In 1984, his losses were replaced with the staggering rate of return of 142 per cent. Helped by oil-company takeovers, Boesky was back as king of the arbs. But, petroleum stocks were hardly risk-proof investments. When raider T. Boone Pickens surprised everyone by selling back his shares in Phillips Petroleum, Boesky took a beating, this time sinking $40 million into a deal that didn't materialise. When the Hunt brothers of Texas nearly cornered and then annihilated the silver market, Boesky lost $10 million in a day.

Boesky's company, Ivan F. Boesky Corporation, represented wealthy individuals and a handful of institutional investors. By the time of the Phillips débâcle, they witnessed Boesky's magic edge in the market evaporate. While Wall Street was caught up in the biggest takeover boom in history, Boesky's firm was delivering a bland 7.7 per cent return to its investors.

He was struggling to recapture the magic that had made him famous. Boesky needed a player who knew how to make a killing on corporate hostility, someone who guided corporate raiders through the Wall Street war zone. Boesky wanted an insider willing to disclose their plans of attack.

He found his ally in Dennis Levine at Drexel, the investment bank of choice for Wall Street raiders. Levine was valued at Drexel for bringing in clients and priming them with an arsenal of borrowed down-graded equity (junk bonds) with which to wage takeover battles. Boesky was in the market for reliable, inside information on up-coming deals. Levine, who had been trading on such information since 1981, had done well enough, but Levine knew if more stock had been snapped up by other players, namely arbitrageurs, the share prices and his profits would have soared even higher. The arbs and their copycats had billions of dollars of buying clout. Knowing in advance that a powerful arb was shadowing your purchases was a guarantee that the share price would escalate.

While no one is sure who made the first move, Boesky and Levine crossed paths at the beginning of 1985. Levine had moved up through the ranks on Wall Street in a way Boesky could appreciate: a network of informants. In a way, they were *nouveau riche* doyens of high finance who had begun their lives as sons of small businessmen and rose unspectacularly through the ranks until they landed lucrative jobs on Wall Street. Levine, who grew up in Queens, NY, was the son of an aluminium-siding salesman. After he graduated from high school, he lived at home with his family for a couple of years, helping his father with his business.

Levine attended Bernard Baruch College, a branch of the City University of New York, and enrolled in its MBA program with aspirations of a career in investment banking. Levine's goal was to become a millionaire by his thirtieth birthday.

For nine months following his graduation, Levine sent out a blizzard of résumés to investment houses. Citibank Corp in Manhattan eventually hired Levine in March 1977 as a management trainee at a starting salary of $365 a week. A year later he landed a job at Smith Barney, Harris Upham & Co. When he did not receive a promotion, Levine left for a job at Lehman Bros. Kuhn Loeb Inc. Denied promotion to a managing director's post, Levine, devastated, contacted an executive recruiter who landed him a $1 million a year job as managing director in the mergers and acquisitions department at Drexel.

By that time Levine had more to celebrate than a seven-figure salary. He had amassed a fortune through some fifty insider trades. On one transaction alone, in June 1984, Levine made a net profit of $1.2 million after Jewel Cos Inc. received a takeover bid from American Stores Co., a deal in which Lehman was involved. Levine covered his tracks by making his trades through the Bahamian subsidiary of a Swiss bank, Bank Leu International Ltd.

Boesky, the son of a Detroit restaurant owner, attended three separate colleges in Michigan, but dropped out before completing his studies. A college degree was not a prerequisite at the Detroit College of Law, where Boesky enrolled, only to withdraw twice before graduating in 1964. While he was studying law, Boesky married Seema Silberstein in 1962. The connection to the Silberstein family became vital for Boesky who could not find a job after graduating.

Boesky, having been turned down by prestigious Detroit firms, landed a position as a clerk for a federal judge, who was a Silberstein friend. Within a year he left the judge's chambers, eager to prove himself with the big law firms, but they again rejected him. Boesky worked as an accountant, only to give it up a year later. Ben Silberstein, infuriated that his daughter, who had just become a young mother, had married a man who could not keep down a job, derisively nicknamed Boesky 'Ivan the Bum'.

Silberstein, none the less, put Seema and Ivan up in a Park Avenue apartment while Boesky looked for work. After several stints with banks, Boesky's first serious job was as an arbitrageur, a profession introduced to him by an old school chum. He joined the firm, Kalb Voorhis. On his first day, Boesky was fired for losing $20,000 on a deal.

In 1972 Edwards and Hanly, a small brokerage house, took a chance and hired Boesky as head of their arbitrage department. He began by breaking all the rules. Instead of honouring co-operation agreements among arbitrageurs, Boesky would buy all of the available stock in a company, driving up the price without any regard for the livelihoods of his fellow arbs. Boesky's aggressiveness earned him the new title, 'Ivan the Terrible'.

For Ivan Boesky, a man keen to make up for lost time, there was only one thing that mattered. 'It may seem callous,' he said, 'but I am indifferent to who succeeds or fails as long as I make a profit.' Carl Icahn, Wall Street raider and head of TWA in the heady days of the takeover wars, joshed, 'I've told my wife, if I need surgery, get me the heart of an arb. It's never been used.'[7]

His habit of overextending capital got him into trouble when the New York Stock Exchange censured and fined Boesky $10,000 for selling securities in excess of Edwards and Hanly's ability to deliver. The firm went bankrupt in 1975 and, with his wife's $700,000 inheritance, Boesky decided to make it on his own and created Ivan F. Boesky & Company. By operating out of the former trading rooms of Edwards and Hanly, Boesky and his team of a dozen employees solicited investors for limited risk-arbitrage partnerships. Grooming well-placed sources was vital to the operation's success.

Boesky and his fellow risk arbitrageurs had information networks second only to MI5. These men, who moved millions of dollars in a blink of an eye, gambled on gossip. Every tip contained a potential clue to the outcome of a deal and directives to buy or sell. The news was as precious as profit and it came from all over the world; from lawyers poised in congressional hearings on a takeover, people in printing offices handling the proxy statements, cleaners, clerks, secretaries, decision makers. . . It all counted.

With his sophisticated information network, Boesky worked the market to his distinct advantage over other arbitrageurs. Among the stocks that Boesky invested in, based on solid tips, were Nabisco Brands which earned him a cool $4 million, the same amount he earned on Houston Natural Gas. Boesky profited by nearly $1 million on FMC Corporation and made millions by trading on tips about mergers or tender offers involving American Natural Resources, General Foods and Union Carbide. Deals involving SCM Corporation, AVCO Corp., and ARA Services Inc. helped Boesky amass a fortune estimated at $200 million by *Forbes* Magazine.

No one matched Boesky's capacity to move mountains of cash. He took the biggest stakes in prime-target stocks before other players realised their potential and his educated gambles paid off magnificently. By the end of the fiscal year 1984, with the help of important oil-company takeovers, Boesky's rate of return for investors in his partnership fund was a staggering 142 per cent.

Boesky's reputation as the king of the arbs, grew from an uncanny ability to know what stocks to buy, usually in advance of takeover or merger announcements. Part of this could be explained by the fact that Boesky was a workhorse who slept, on average, two hours a night and that he was exceptionally well connected. His influence was transatlantic: Boesky controlled London-based Cambrian & General Securities Plc in which he had holdings of $50 million. His critics, however, said that he was too smart, too well-informed, that his research was too good. His timing, they said, defied the laws of chance.

On one takeover alone, Boesky and his investors made $65 million. As his influence grew, the investment bankers, raiders and traders gravitated towards Boesky. His power to control vast amounts of stock drew the interest of T. Boone Pickens Jr., chairman of the Mesa Petroleum Company, and Carl Icahn. He also began to draw the interest of the SEC.

What concerned the commission was the fact that someone like Boesky, with his close ties to the raiders and investment banks, might be influencing takeover deals and profiting from them in a way that no ordinary investor could. The SEC's concern became more acute whenever it was determined that Boesky had invested heavily in a target prior to the announcement of a deal. Boesky's trading records were devastating, one source close to the SEC said, 'You didn't need to be a Dick Tracy to figure this one out, but you needed one last piece to make the case.'[8]

Dennis Levine was the missing ingredient.

'High rollers like Boesky and Levine are among the most intelligent and sophisticated crooks America has to offer,' wrote Craig Copetas in *Regardies*, July 1986. 'Their edge is an acute understanding of the velocity of money; they can keep ill-gotten capital moving so fast that no one (except the people involved in the scheme) knows where it came from or where it's going. That the SEC can nab insider dealers is evidence of remarkable detective work.

'But the eerie spectacle of the mega-merger has created a new breed of conman who generates money through his intimacy with the powerful. As a takeover gets closer to consummation, so many people catch wind of the deal that the news invariably seeps out. The people who platoon the SEC's front line try to keep tabs on the lawyers, the merger advisers, the paralegals and the janitors who clean up the offices, but it's nearly impossible for them to plug all the leaks.'

'Our focus on insider trading is a function of the explosion in the market,' explains William McLucas, 'and the apparently irresistible temptation, given a risk/reward analysis, for people to go ahead and take a chance.' As the profile of the division of enforcement grew with each case, insider-trading investigations generated 'a lot of sex appeal', says commissioner Aulana Peters. 'Especially as they involved highly placed, very wealthy and powerful individuals.'

But the attraction of insider-trading investigations can quickly wear off, as Phillip Parker quickly discovered. 'I was able to establish that fourteen members of the same Palm Springs country club bought the same stock within a ten-day period. We couldn't find any link between these individuals and the companies in question. In addition, most of these people were extraordinarily wealthy and if you ask somebody like that why they bought the stock, they just say, "What did you say – was it 5,000 shares? . . . I had pocket change, I can't remember." The easy case,' says Parker, 'is where somebody goes out and invests his net worth in a very speculative investment. Looked at objectively, it makes no sense unless he had insider information.

'Often in insider-trading cases, you know statistically that X hundred thousand shares are going to trade that day. I think what's difficult is that you have to assume that most of the people that you talk to are innocent: they were lucky, they bought the stock at the right time, or whatever.

'To prove someone is guilty of insider trading, you have to conduct a very thorough investigation and they tend to be the most intrusive investigations into personal privacy. The key evidence in our cases is very often telephone records, credit-card bills. . . . We want to be able to establish that this individual was in this hotel room at this time, that he made an eight-minute phone call and all that kind of stuff. And sometimes that involves taking testimony from their spouse, their secretary and personal friends. Nobody wants to do that unless they have good cause.'

Parker majored in English at Kenyon College, located in his home state of Ohio, and attended law school at the University of Virginia. He worked in the division of enforcement for thirteen years before moving over to the general counsel's office. Parker has the look of a university dean: tall, academic, purposeful. 'Insider-trading cases are frustrating because very often, you don't know whether somebody was guilty, or whether you'll be able to prove it,' he says. 'He can play dumb or very, very smart. If you get a market professional or an investment banker or someone who bought stock at the right time, and you bring that person in and say, "Why did you buy?" They'll give you forty-three reasons and it will be very complicated and convoluted. They'll say they're chartists, for example, and that they follow a technical method of stock analysis.

'I've had these people come in and unfold a big graph with arrows everywhere. They come up with all these theories about how, for example, women's hemlines and superbowl victories determine stock-market behaviour,' says Parker. 'It's a lot of mumbo-jumbo. Before my staff attorneys took testimony, I used to make them read a book depicting all of these charts because, invariably, they would meet one of these people.'

Frequently, insider traders will perjure themselves in an attempt to salvage their case. In doing so, their fate is sealed. 'There have been a lot more perjury prosecutions in the last couple of years and it's had an effect,' says Parker. 'Lawyers tell their clients, "Whatever you did, perjuring yourself is worse."' To Gary Lynch it didn't make any difference what caused insider traders to be convicted. 'Do people really care?' Lynch has asked. 'It's going to be the same jail and they will spend the same amount of time there.'

The deal that brought Boesky and Levine together was Coastal Corporation's hostile takeover bid for American Natural Resources (ANR). It was the first deal Levine handled in his new position at Drexel. The beauty about Boesky's inside trades was that they could easily be masked by his regular performance as a speculator. Levine's trades could also be overlooked in the tidal wave of copycat investors. Operating on Levine's tip, Boesky bought blocks of ANR stock prior to the public announcement of the Coastal bid. He accumulated nearly 10 per cent of the stock and liquidated at a profit of $4 million soon after the deal was consummated. On the heels of the takeover, Boesky, using advance information from Levine, invested $16 million in Houston Natural Gas. When it merged with InterNorth, Boesky walked away with a profit of $4.1 million. The mere announcement of merger talks between Nabisco and RJ Reynolds sent stock soaring. Levine, as with the other two deals, invested a modest amount compared to Boesky, who, running with his leaked information, invested $25 million in Nabisco. After the official announcement was made, Levine and Boesky together made $4 million on the transaction.

Boesky was trying to recoup his astounding success in 1984 and he was beginning to realise how Levine was helping him do just that. He struck up an agreement with Levine whereby if Boesky did not already own stock that Levine tipped, Levine received 5 per cent of Boesky's profit. If Boesky already had the particular stock in his portfolio, Levine's 'buy more' or 'sell' tip would deliver 1 per cent of Boesky's profit or losses saved, to Levine. Any losses were to come out of Levine's payments.

For 14 months, beginning in 1985, Levine fed Boesky information on mergers, takeovers and acquisitions. Boesky, the man Levine liked to call 'the Russian', made over $50 million on at least seven trades. Levine's share was $2.4 million. The only problem was to explain to the IRS how he made the money. Boesky came up with a solution that underscored Levine's value to him. On 24 April 1986, he offered him a job as head of Ivan F. Boesky Corp.'s merchant-banking operation. Levine's $5 million signing bonus, the biggest in Wall Street history, would cleverly conceal the illegal trading proceeds.

Levine was elated by the offer, a career peak. The kid from Queens had made it big. Already he flaunted his wealth: a summer cottage on the Hamptons, an expensive apartment on Park Avenue, a Ferrari Testarossa. Life for Levine was nearing perfection. There was only one slight bother: Bank Leu, his Bahamian trading facility, refused to engage in any more investments on his behalf. Levine knew the SEC had expressed concern about the bank's prescient trades capitalising on hot takeover stocks. Levine had prepared phoney documentation to back up the suspect manoeuvres, giving it to bank officials for any questions the SEC might have. That he had not heard further about the SEC's interest, led Levine to believe all was well.

'At a certain point we ceased all contact with anyone on the Street,' recalls John Sturc. 'We did not seek any information from brokerage firms in order to give Levine the impression we'd gone away.'

The SEC had come incredibly far in its investigation of Dennis Levine. They were in no position to blow it. In May 1985, an anonymous letter accusing two Merrill Lynch investment brokers in Caracas of insider trades arrived at the central headquarters of Merrill Lynch in the heart of New York's financial district. The brokers were linked by shadow trades to Brian Campbell, a former broker at Merrill Lynch. Campbell's largest client had been Bank Leu International Ltd in Nassau. It was obvious from the records that Campbell had been shadowing the bank's trades. The compliance men at Merrill may have seen the tip of the iceberg when the letter from Caracas arrived. With the Bank Leu connection, they had reached the waterline.

Bob Romano, head of compliance at Merrill Lynch, contacted his former colleague at the SEC, Gary Lynch. Over the next several months, the Commission had assigned fourteen people to a formal investigation. The size of the trades were big enough to warrant the attention, but more importantly, the SEC wanted to learn who was behind them.

'We began to collect transaction records, noticing a strong

success pattern in the selection of merger and acquisition securities,' says John Sturc, as the attorney who led the investigation. 'In July of 1985 we made the initial request for Bank Leu's co-operation and asked them to submit trading records.' Bahamian and Swiss bank secrecy laws prevented the release of the name of the account holder who dictated the trades. The bank's lawyer, and former SEC counsel, was Harvey Pitt. His proposal to the SEC was simple. If the Commission would drop its case against the bank, the bank would release the name of the person behind the trades. To sweeten the deal, he promised that the unnamed individual was a major player on Wall Street.

The Commission had spent as long as five years on previous insider-trading cases persuading foreign banks to release the names of clients. It did not want to risk losing access to the violator in the course of a lengthy legal battle with Bank Leu. 'It would have been conceivable to have Bank Leu consent to be a defendant in a subpoena enforcement case,' says Sturc. 'But it would have taken years of litigation with a possible adverse result for the Commission. Our real concern was that Levine would move his money before we concluded the case.'

It took almost a year for the name of Dennis Levine to be released to the Commission. 'There had been forty-two trades by Bank Leu in takeover securities so that was enough to begin looking at these securities and looking at who and when, talking to Bank Leu and trying to work out a deal,' recalls Michael Mann, chief of the Office of International Legal Assistance at the SEC. 'By the time we went to the Attorney General of the Bahamas, we had a very good circumstantial case that whoever it was knew an awful lot,' says Mann. 'The Levine case was important. It showed that we could work in a creative way to develop a solution which allowed us to get the information. It was the largest insider-trading case involving a foreign connection brought to date.'

Mann's message is simple: 'Look, if you trade from abroad, you're going to be treated like anyone else. If you violate the law we're going to bring a case against you. We're going to pursue you and we're going to get the foreign government involved, be it France or England or Egypt, to help us. And they will help us because they don't like fraud any more than we do.' On Wednesday, 7 May 1986, Gary Lynch, Michael Mann, Lev Dobriansky, the American ambassador to the Bahamas, and a justice department attorney met with Paul Adderly, the attorney general of the Bahamas. The point of the meeting was whether Adderly would allow Bank Leu to release the name of its customer without fear of prosecution.

Back in Washington, John Sturc had a hunch the meeting would go well. 'We had a discussion with the attorney general in an earlier case, Louisville Cement, in which there was trading in the Bahamas and he had discussed with us then that transactions in securities were not banking transactions covered by the Bahamian bank secrecy law,' says Sturc. 'We knew that going in. Michael [Mann] and I participated in those discussions.'

Two days after the meeting in Atterly's office at 5:30 p.m., a messenger delivered the attorney general's letter to the bank. In four paragraphs he gave the bank permission to disclose the identity of its customer because, as Sturc predicted, the securities activities did not involve a 'banking relationship', thus the bank secrecy laws of the Bahamas did not apply. Immediately, Harvey Pitt, Bank Leu's lawyer and the architect of the deal, phoned Gary Lynch to tell him that the name of the customer was Dennis Levine.

That evening, Levine, oblivious to the chase, was feeling the ego boost of Boesky's job offer. He was eager to begin trading again and was prepared to break his ties with Bank Leu to do so. At 6:00 p.m., he sent written instructions to Bank Leu to transfer $10 million to an account at Morgan Grenfell in the Cayman Islands. It was too late in the day for the transaction to take place.

Once the SEC received Levine's name on Friday, a team led by John Sturc worked throughout the weekend preparing a complaint with supportive papers to request a temporary restraining order on Levine's assets. On Monday morning, in an emergency session held without Levine's knowledge, the SEC was granted its request and froze the $10.5 million remaining in Levine's account.

The SEC obtained its temporary restraining order without evidence for a hearing only for ten days. After that, the SEC had to present solid evidence to justify continuing restraint pending the outcome of the case. The Commission had won the right to freeze Levine's assets on the basis of its civil complaint that said Levine had made $12.6 million in profits through advance inside information on fifty-four stocks from 1980 until the end of 1985. The complaint described Levine's means of obstructing justice by persuading a bank official to lie to the Commission and to destroy important evidence.

Theresa Pritchard, an assistant director of enforcement, whose staff were directly involved with the Dennis Levine and Boesky investigations, explains that insider-trading cases have the illusion of glamour, but apart from the personalities and the money involved, they are incredibly tedious cases to solve. 'We look for patterns,' she says. 'If you look at phone records, you could easily tell if A talked to B; hung up his phone and then called his broker. On one side, you're learning as much about the deal as you can. On the other side, you're learning as much about the traders as you can. With insider trading generally, there are certain types of documents we would routinely ask for. They would include a person's roladex, their business and home telephone records, their trading records. From that you would put together who knew about the deal.'

On the night of 12 May, Levine was scheduled to go to a black-tie charity dinner at the Waldorf Astoria. Instead, summoned to the US Attorney's office in lower Manhattan, Levine arrived to pick up a subpoena and a copy of the SEC complaint against him. In the office of Charles Carberry, the assistant US Attorney who had compiled evidence for the criminal case against him, Levine was handcuffed and arrested on criminal charges of obstruction of justice, securities violations and tax evasion.

The next day, after spending the night in the Metropolitan Correctional Centre, Levine was freed on a bail of $5 million, secured by $100,000 in cash, his Park Avenue apartment and shares in Drexel. On 5 June Levine pleaded guilty to four felony charges brought by the US Attorney's Office. The charges were one count of securities fraud, for trading the stock of Jewel Companies on the basis of inside information; two counts of income-tax evasion for failing to report his profits; and one count of perjury based on testimony earlier given to the SEC. Levine settled additional SEC charges and agreed to pay $11.6 million, which included the $10.5 million frozen in his account with Bank Leu in the Bahamas. Levine also accepted a permanent injunction barring him from the securities business for life. The Commission could have levied a $35-million fine against him, instead the government took his Ferrari which had less than 4,000 miles on the clock. Levine kept his apartment, valued at nearly $1 million, his BMW and about $100,000 in cash. The criminal counts against Levine carried maximum penalties of twenty years in prison and $610,000 in fines. Levine was sentenced to two years in federal prison and fined $362,000.

When Levine told Judge Gerard Goettel that he had obtained inside information about a bid for Textron Inc., the admission confirmed fears on Wall Street that Levine was implicating others. Between the time of his arrest and his guilty plea, Levine made calls to participants in his insider-trading ring. The sounds of an operator and coins dropping assured them that Levine was using a public telephone. What they had no way of knowing was that the public ambience of the calls came from a recorded tape made by the US Attorney's office that played while Levine, wired, pumped his old friends for information.

Judge Goettel would later say at Levine's sentencing, 'Through the information he has provided, an entire nest of vipers on Wall Street has been exposed.' Among the six insiders Levine implicated, none carried the weight of Ivan Boesky, the richest stock speculator on Wall Street.

'Generally when you have a co-operating witness,' says Pritchard, 'the first place you start is to get the story of their culpability down and to understand it. With an insider-trading case you look at their trading and go through it deal by deal, stock by stock. You try to find out where they got their information from and how they came to take their position and how they followed the progress of the deal.' Pritchard inherited the Levine case from departing branch chief Paul Fischer. It was during her staff's interviews with Levine that his involvement with Ivan Boesky and others was revealed. The case was all consuming and Pritchard, a wife of a university professor and mother of a young daughter, frequently took it home with her, spreading documents over the kitchen table and working into the small hours.

'I used to say, plenty of times, that I would love to walk away and spend more time with my kid, but this was probably the closest to making history that I would probably get,' says Pritchard. 'You can't just turn around and walk away. My anniversary was ten days before we actually filed suit against Boesky and I was putting in a lot of hours. My daughter was about two at the time so I used to be fairly rigid about going home and spending the evening with her and then going back to work (at the kitchen table) after she went to bed.' Fifteen minutes into the morning of her anniversary, Pritchard's husband presented her with a dozen roses and a card that read, simply, 'Attention: I love you. Happy Anniversary. Now you can go back to work.'

The case continued. Like all insider-trading investigations, it wasn't easy. 'There are days and probably weeks when it's just frustrating because you know that something had to happen to that stock before the announcement was made because the volume of the price sky-rocketed and you just can't put the puzzle together,' says Pritchard. 'Or you know there's something wrong with the financial statements you're looking at but you've been through three years of accounting records and you can't figure it out.

'These things get put together by nothing but drudgery and hard work, where people sit down and go through months and months of trading and telephone records. It's really great when the headline hits, but somebody spends hours going through single pieces of paper – rooms of them, sometimes.'

On 14 November the SEC shocked the financial establishment with the announcement that Boesky, the king of the arbs, had been caught in the Levine investigation. He agreed to pay $100 million in penalties and returned profits. In addition, Boesky was expelled from the securities industry for the rest of his life. He pleaded guilty to one, unspecified criminal charge that would carry a maximum of five years imprisonment. Boesky was sentenced to three years and allowed to sell off $440 million worth of holdings, mostly in takeover stocks, before it was announced he had co-operated.

Roundly criticised for the 'sell-off clause', the SEC justified its actions by delivering a fleet of insider traders fingered by Boesky. The forthcoming case against Drexel Burnham Lambert and its west coast vice-president, Michael Milken, was viewed as a primary justification for Boesky's extraordinary plea bargain with the prosecution.

In the fall of 1986, Boesky allowed the government to monitor his telephone calls with a wide number of major financial figures around the world. Boesky snitched on everybody. 'He led the government through an otherwise impenetrable thicket,' said Boesky's lawyer, Leon Silverman, 'and permitted them to obtain admissible evidence which would otherwise have been unavailable.' His co-operation sent the scandal across the Atlantic.

On 23 September 1986, the SEC and the Commodity Futures

Trading Commission entered into a Memorandum of Understanding (MOU) with the Department of Trade and Industry (DTI) in the United Kingdom. The Memorandum, like the handful of other agreements the SEC has with other governments, establishes a working agreement with securities regulators in the US and the UK. It makes assistance available in cases involving insider trading, market manipulation and misrepresentations relating to market transactions, as well as in the oversight of investment businesses and brokerage firms.[9]

The transatlantic co-operation signalled by the signing of the MOU was implemented almost immediately. On 24 November 1986, the DTI received a thick file from the SEC containing sworn testimony from Ivan Boesky that linked Guinness to his stock-market manipulations. Boesky's admissions implicated Guinness chairman Ernest Saunders, who would later face thirty-seven charges relating to the Guinness takeover of Distillers including allegations of theft, false accounting and stock-market manipulation.

The Guinness affair triggered a renewed awareness of fraud in the City of London and a flock of self-regulating organisations (SROs) formed in the wake of de-regulation, began to test the limits of their powers. Their creation, while good in theory, was unco-ordinated. Regulatory bureaucracy was spread between small and ineffectual organisations that moved in complicated layers of protocol.

The problems of splintered bureaucracy inherent in numerous SROs was compounded by the fact that at their head was an organisation whose *raison d'être* is the promotion of British business – the DTI, known in City circles as 'Great Britain Inc'. As time passed, complaints rose concerning the meagre number of insider-dealing cases the department pursued. It seemed that the DTI's endorsement of British industry had taken priority over the enforcement of securities laws.

Since 1986, only 15 insider-trading cases have been prosecuted by the DTI, the most notable being that of Geoffrey

Collier in July 1987. At the time, Collier, a former stock trader for Morgan Grenfell, was fined £25,000. The lack of official action was highlighted in the spring 1989 *Sunday Times*/Mori City Opinion Survey. Asked how effective arrangements were for monitoring insider dealing, more than half the 147 institutional fund managers polled said they believed the monitoring efforts were completely ineffectual.

Michael Feltham, head of the insider-dealing group at the International Stock Exchange, thinks he knows why. 'Insider trading is one of the purest forms of fraud. Ninety-nine per cent of it is you telling me something,' he says. 'We've got to prove it happened.' The fact that Feltham, who has been at the Exchange surveillance division since its inception in 1984, and his fifteen-member crew can nab any of the inside traders is rather incredible. C. W. Dickson, assistant director of the Serious Fraud Office, stated in a December 1988 letter to University of Cambridge researcher John Naylor, 'On its own [insider trading] is essentially a regulatory offence and as such, is unlikely to qualify as a serious or complex fraud.'

Without question, the most vital circumstantial evidence in any insider-trading case are telephone records. In this regard, Feltham says his hands are tied. 'We cannot subpoena the records because each night British Telecom destroys them,' he says. 'The only hope of gathering that evidence is knowing about the inside trade as it is happening.' Even in the most successful Wall Street insider-trading cases, months passed before the SEC was aware of the first illegal transactions. None the less, the Commission was able to retrieve important telephonic evidence with subpoenas. Feltham says he cannot do that because what he's after simply won't exist anymore by the time he needs it.

The ability to deal with insider trading tends to be seen as the yardstick against which the effectiveness of security regulation is measured. The absence of an independent, publicly funded regulatory body, the diversity of unco-ordinated organisations and lack of available resources for enforcement not only has inhibited policing of insider trading but characterises the British approach to security regulation generally. That the Stock Exchange may soon be granted power of prosecution is a move in the right direction. 'What we need,' says Feltham, 'is an SEC right here.'

– 7 –

California scheming

'I need to pray about it.'
'If God didn't want you to buy what I'm selling, you
wouldn't be here.'

'I need to talk it over with my wife.'
'I don't know about your wife, but mine doesn't know
a thing about business affairs.'

'I need to talk to my accountant first.'
'Let's face it. All accountants are conservative. If they
knew how to invest, they wouldn't be accountants.'

Sample from boiler-room
'pitch' book, 'Objections'

Stephen Bederson, deeply tanned and talkative, sported a bright-
yellow Hawaiian shirt, green corduroy shorts and white leather
trainers. His Ray-Ban sun-glasses were the finishing touch of an
outfit designed to make the most of the day's warm, southern
Californian sunshine. Each time Bederson took a sip of the
Cherry Coke in front of him or puffed on his Benson & Hedges,
he raised both hands. He had to. Apart from the gold bracelets
on his wrist, Bederson sported a pair of handcuffs.

In the dim, smoke-filled room he occupied, Bederson's outfit
was at odds with the sombre atmosphere created by the presence
of two investigators from the Orange County District Attorney's
office. Perhaps due to the fact that he made a living as a
high-pressure salesman, Bederson attempted to talk his way
out of his handcuff dilemma. He didn't have much to lose.
Bederson faced three felony charges that would have easily

sent him on a one-way, ten-year ticket to 'Club Fed' – cop slang for federal prison.

Bederson's lawyer, a few years before, had bailed him out of a similar scrape in New York. This time he was on his own as he listened to Larry Lambert, a cross-sworn DA investigator and US marshal, read him his rights for the second time. 'You have the absolute right to remain silent,' said Lambert. 'Anything you say can and will be used against you in a court of law. You have the right to consult with an attorney, to be represented by an attorney and to have an attorney present both before and during questioning. If you cannot afford to hire an attorney, one will be appointed by the court free of charge to represent you before any questioning if you wish. You can decide at any time to exercise these rights and not answer any questions or make any statements. . . . With these rights in mind are you willing to talk to me now?' asked Lambert.

'Yes I am,' said Bederson.

Whether it was naïvety or salesman's bravado that prompted him to deliver his spiel, Bederson could never have counted on a customer like Larry Lambert. Bederson's pitches up until then had always been conducted over the telephone. Lambert's negotiations, including the defusing of twenty-five armed-hostage situations, have always been face to face. Bederson's reward for verbal dexterity has been easy money. For Lambert, it has been the rescue of human life. His experience includes naval intelligence operations and a stint in Northern Ireland. Presently, he is an investigator in the organised crime unit in the Orange County DA's office. Lambert, a stocky six-foot man in his early thirties with brown eyes and salt-and-pepper hair, is also founding member of the Southern California Fraud Task Force.

Before Bederson began talking, Lambert and his colleague, Doug Miller, another investigator from the DA's office, had a distinct advantage. When he was arrested, during a morning raid on his Costa Mesa office, Bederson was on parole. Breaking the law while making amends for previous criminal activity is no way to impress cops, prosecutors or judges. 'The guy's looking at ten years of his life, if he's good,' Lambert would say later. 'We owned him.'

As he addressed Bederson, Lambert sat in a chair normally occupied by the director of Bederson's company – a firm that changed names three times in eighteen months to avoid civil charges, and, with the immediate arrest of its entire workforce, had just gone out of business. As Bederson answered questions, a small tape recorder, the size of a microphone, captured his rambling confession. He was generous with accusations and admissions of his own guilt. Bederson blamed his boss, Jerry Nabridge, for blackmailing him into staying with the company. Nabridge, a paunchy bejewelled man in his fifties, had created a classic boiler-room operation.

Boiler rooms have been popular for more than half a century, growing in strength hand in hand with the popular, wide acceptance of the telephone. Operating in basements filled with boilers and steam pipes, telephone salesmen dialled and persuaded unsuspecting investors to sink money usually into mineral rights, property, worthless stock, precious metals or commodities. The high returns they pitched over the telephone were irresistible. The products they sold were non-existent.

Operators took deposits from clients, but their order forms were frequently tossed into buckets instead of being forwarded on to relevant trading markets. Boiler rooms, particularly in Northern Europe, thus earned the name, 'bucket shops'. In terms of technique, not a lot has changed over time. Salesmen continue to peddle too-good-to-be-true deals to gullible investors.

In recent years, stiff laws have been implemented to crack down on boiler rooms in New York and New Jersey and after the fly-by-night outfits migrated to Florida, the same laws ushered them out of the state and towards the Pacific coast. Today, Orange County accounts for the lion's share of

America's staggering $1-billion-a-year fraudulent boiler-room industry.

Nabridge, like many before him, left Florida to set up his operations in California. He devised a scheme to acquire property rights in Illinois, Oklahoma and Nebraska. He and his salesmen, Bederson, 37, and Timothy Guth, 29, convinced investors that various properties, for which Midwest Minerals was a broker, contained valuable mineral rights. In fact, Midwest Minerals' clients were led to believe oil had been discovered on the land and that oil-drilling wells were in full production. In fact, no oil wells existed. By Orange County standards, Nabridge achieved moderate success. In eighteen months, Midwest Mineral Properties Inc. made $2.5 million.

All Nabridge had to do was keep one step ahead of the authorities. In so doing, the company changed names each time it moved to a new address. Midwest Mineral Properties became Nebco Inc. which, in turn, became Kelim Inc. One of Nabridge's biggest clients, Robert McDowell in Beaver, Pennsylvania, invested nearly $250,000 in Midwest Minerals. Another victim, an Arizona man, lost $403,000.

From September 1985 through to January 1988, McDowell continually received calls from eight different salespersons from Midwest Minerals. On one occasion a salesman told him that two wells he had invested in were producing so much oil that the tanks could not hold all of it. He asked McDowell to send $28,500 so that additional oil-storage tanks could be installed. Eager to secure the funds, Midwest sent a Federal Express courier to pick up McDowell's cheque.

Despite the considerable outgoings on his land and oil-drilling projects, McDowell never received money back on his investment, despite continual promises that he would. He became disillusioned and eventually sought legal advice. When McDowell called the authorities, he learned that the mineral rights he had invested in did not even belong to Midwest Minerals. The real owner of the property was an elderly woman named Elva King. As it turned out, Midwest had paid Mrs King $489 for a two-year gas-and-oil lease in August 1986 for 40 acres of her property. But King, who lives on the property, told authorities that there were never any gas or oil explorations conducted on her land. No one from Midwest, she said, had even bothered to visit the property.

From that point on, Midwest Minerals was closely monitored by Pennsylvania law-enforcement authorities who ultimately charged Nabridge and his associates Bederson and Guth with theft by deception, criminal conspiracy, and theft by failure to make required disposition of funds received. The trio was also charged in California for operating without registering its telemarketing business with the California Attorney General's office.

During his confession, Stephen Bederson pinned a fair portion of blame on Jerry Nabridge, who had recently used investors' funds to purchase a new $120,000 Rolls Royce. Larry Lambert wanted to know if Nabridge realised he was making his fortune by engaging in fraud by (telephone) wire and theft and whether Bederson would admit that he was breaking the law. Bederson said they both knew what they were doing but that he tried to convince himself everything was above board. Perhaps aiming to receive some of Lambert's sympathy, Bederson said, 'I was stupid . . . totally stupid. I was desperate. I had no money.'

Bederson's approach backfired.

Lambert pressed Bederson about his earnings during the last year and a half that he worked the phones for Nabridge. When Bederson said, 'A substantial amount . . . well over a hundred thousand', he added that he blew most of it in Vegas and that he doubted if Lambert would find more than $500 in his bank account.

Because Mr McDowell in Pennsylvania had lost a substantial amount of his life-savings to Midwest Minerals, Lambert aimed to fortify the evidence the task force had about the McDowell deals. He asked Bederson what pitch he used. Bederson said he told McDowell that he needed to buy more acreage to complete a property deal that Midwest had arranged on his behalf. The buyer, Bederson said, was only interested in large parcels of land. McDowell, believing there was a standing buyer for his property, wired thousands of dollars to Midwest. Bederson admitted in his confession that the land McDowell was purchasing never existed. Bederson later secured more funds by telling McDowell that there was a surplus of oil on his land, so much, in fact, that Midwest was incapable of storing all of it and thus needed capital to invest in storage tanks. 'There were a lot of stories,' said Bederson. On every deal he closed Bederson said he made a 15 per cent commission while Nabridge took the rest. He described his boss's 'lavish' lifestyle: trips to Italy, France, expensive cars, a luxury home in Florida and an apartment in California. The two residences were convenient for Nabridge who escaped to Florida for the weekends.

An important revelation during Bederson's confession occurred when he admitted that he and other salesmen at Midwest Minerals adopted different identities when talking with clients over the telephone. Bederson, for instance, became 'Ron Holt' when he dealt with McDowell. When Lambert asked why he and his colleagues preferred using aliases, Bederson said, 'Because we knew that what we were doing was wrong.' Bederson also mentioned that he lived in constant fear of being caught which prompted Lambert's partner, Doug Miller, to ask, 'Did you think that any day when you were doing this that the authorities would come knocking on your door?'

'Always,' said Bederson. 'That's the thought that never left my mind. It always bothered me, always worried me.'

On the morning of 19 April 1988, a five-car convoy of eleven task-force agents from the Orange County District Attorney's office, Newport Beach Police Department and Postal Inspection Service, parked outside the Bristol Street offices of Midwest

Mineral Properties Inc. in Costa Mesa. Apart from Mark Fisher, a police detective who wore a khaki uniform, complete with badge and bullet-proof vest, agents donned everything from jeans and sweat-shirts to suits and ties. Everybody carried a gun. In single file, a group of seven agents climbed the stairs and took positions outside the door of Midwest Minerals. The rest of the task force surrounded the building, waiting below windows in the event of an escape or, more likely, the disposal of incriminating evidence.

Stephen Bederson had just put some client files into a cabinet when he heard Fisher knock at the door. He looked out the window and noticed a man wearing a dark-blue windbreaker with POLICE, emblazoned in yellow letters on the back. Outside, the officer-in-charge, Randy Sorley, began conducting the dramatic half of his first boiler-room raid. As he pounded on the door, he shouted, 'Open up. This is the police.' Silence greeted him. Fisher tried again, but there was no response. The task force was certain the men for whom they had arrest-warrants were inside. Cars belonging to company employees were parked close to the entrance, including Timothy Guth's racer with the telling licence plate, UV BNHAD. Minutes passed, but no response was issued from the office. Outside, agents' hands tightened on gun grips while Fisher applied his custom, steel-enforced boots to the door. The following silence was lengthy and strained. Eventually, the handle slowly turned as Jerry Nabridge opened the door.

'What took you so long?' asked Sorley.

Nabridge, dressed in a bright yellow sweat-shirt, slacks and lots of gold jewellery, refused to speak without legal counsel. Stephen Bederson, who felt differently, accompanied Larry Lambert and Doug Miller into a small office. Timothy Guth appeared shaken. A few months earlier, Guth had left a more sophisticated boiler room the day before it had been raided. This time, his luck had run out. His licence plate had become for Guth a little too ironic. Following a brief meeting with Fisher, Guth sat, handcuffed, in the middle of the largest room in the five-office suite.

During Bederson's confession, Lambert and Miller fed pertinent information to other agents. Referring to an arrest-warrant the police took with them to the raid for one salesman who conned $245,750 out of Robert McDowell, an agent remarked, 'If Bederson's Ron Holt, he's dead meat.' At about the same moment, Stephen Bederson told Lambert that 'Ronald Holt' was among the many aliases he invented for himself. Bederson also divulged that Nabridge kept all of the company records in the trunk of his Audi 5000. Fisher moved quickly to have it impounded.

In police-raid choreography, agents methodically posted identifying labels on office doors and furniture and began to gather evidence: everything from sales records, ledgers and customer-lead cards to invoices, brochures and telephone bills (one monthly telephone bill totalled $1,482). An agent with a clipboard drew a floor plan of the office, while Jan Anderson, a reserve police officer with the Newport Beach Police Department and former network cameraman, filmed the proceedings with a portable video camera.

Kacy McClelland, an Orange-County-based postal inspector, who heads a team of mail-fraud investigators, took over desk '4D'. While he sat in Nabridge's former seat, McClelland combed through correspondence. Dressed in a red tie, button-down shirt and blue blazer, McClelland was the most formally attired member of the task force. He is a veteran of more than a dozen boiler-room raids. While he organised paperwork, behind McClelland on a wall poster a man holding a flute of champagne sat on the bonnet of a Rolls Royce. Beneath him, the message: 'Poverty Sucks'. 'That's standard decor,' said McClelland. 'Every boiler room we've hit has that one.'

As Lambert emerged from an office down the hall, a telephone connected to an answering machine rang. A man by the name of

Max Morottz in Ashton, Idaho, began to leave a message. He wanted to know how his $80,000 investment in Nebco was doing. Lambert picked up the phone. 'Hi,' he said. 'This is Larry.' In a matter of minutes Morottz became the first outsider to learn of the demise of Nebco Inc., the successor of Midwest Minerals and the firm that had liquidated his savings account. 'We've got arrests,' Lambert told him. 'Security fraud . . . local violation of state statutes. . . . I don't know if there is or isn't . . . there might be. . . .'

Lambert jotted down Morottz's details. More calls came in. A Virginia Morris wanted to know when she'd receive a K-1 tax form so she might file a deduction for her investment in Midwest's oil-and-gas drilling projects. An agent explained that Morris, apart from losing her entire investment, will, like other victims, most likely be penalised for not paying taxes on it. Contrary to what she was told by Midwest, oil and gas investments are no longer tax deductible. Investigators gradually learned about other people who fell for the Midwest sales pitch. Two cheques totalling $23,000 from Albert Ruehlmann in Cincinnati, Ohio, and E. C. Fortunato in Oakridge, California, were tucked inside Nabridge's brief-case, awaiting deposit into one of his US or Swiss bank accounts. 'We saved a couple,' said Fisher.

Roger Wright, who works with Kacy McClelland on the mail-fraud postal-inspection team, quietly paged through stacks of records and slips. Nicknamed 'the Terminator' for his sheer size, Wright attempted to organise the surprising volume of paperwork that had amassed during the last eighteen months of Midwest's operations.

Timothy Guth sat next to office amenities: a microwave oven, refrigerator and miniature television set. A visitor asked him how he and his colleagues were introduced to victims such as Robert McDowell. 'The federal government has a list of everyone who has purchased mineral rights in the US,' he said. For $120, said Guth, Midwest purchased a list of Alaskan mineral-right holders from the Department of the Interior's Bureau of Land Management.

The government list became an invaluable source of qualified leads – people who had previous investment experience with mineral rights. Midwest's most current sales pitch, found in Bederson's desk, appeared tailor-made for the unsuspecting investors:

'Hello ____, this is ____ with Kelim Inc [Midwest's latest name]. How have you been? Great. ____, six months ago I spoke to you about some oil-lease property which we had acquired under speculation in Oklahoma. You told me then that you were still holding on to some leases in Alaska, and that you weren't too happy with the results so far. So, I didn't want to get back with [you] until I had something that was definite. . . .'

What was 'definite', said Bederson in his confession, was that Midwest's land and mineral rights were guaranteed to be snapped up by waiting oil consortiums. Because the oil companies would only buy large lots of land, Midwest, as a broker, needed to line up initial buyers for these discounted land parcels. Why discounted? Because the sellers needed to liquidate holdings to shore up their losses following the October 1987 stock-market crash. The ruse worked.

In the vernacular of the boiler room, Midwest's salesmen were 'yaks', their customers 'suckers' or 'mooches'. Enticing a new client into sending money meant 'dancing' with them. Naturally, the longer the potential client danced or stayed on the line, the better chance the salesman had of closing the deal. Once Midwest's customers sent money, the salesmen's goal was to 're-load' them or sell them more of whatever they bought. Jerry Nabridge decided instead of selling more land, he'd sell his 'mooches' oil-drilling production equipment such as platforms, pumps and storage tanks.

As the raid progressed, agents slowly put together evidence. During his confession, Bederson admitted that Midwest had told clients that there were thirty full-production oil wells on various acreage sites.

'Did any exist?' asked Lambert.

'No,' said Bederson.

The task force worked through the lunch-hour and by three o'clock, when all the evidence was neatly packed into cardboard boxes, the group moved *en masse* to a restaurant in Newport Beach. Randy Sorley, the officer in charge of the raid, drove a shiny red pick-up that looked like it normally hauled surf boards instead of court documents. Dressed in a blue sweat-shirt and charcoal acid-washed jeans, Sorley carried a black portable phone with him to the table. He needed to secure the level of bail to be set for Nabridge, Bederson and Guth. He did not want to risk missing the return call from a local judge who would make the ultimate decision. Because of Nabridge's considerable net worth, Sorley had mentally aimed for a minimum $1-million bail.

In the restaurant, the team of investigators washed down hefty sandwiches with beer and loosened up to tell stories about some of the characters they had met on the boiler-room beat. One day Kacy McClelland got a phone call from a landlady who said her former tenant had left behind some suspicious documents. When McClelland and his team arrived, it became clear that the man, James Eglitis, had worked for one of the most notorious boiler-room operations in Orange County. As agents carefully assembled his incriminating paperwork back at headquarters, one by one, they began to feel itchy. As they scratched their arms and legs, they realised that the papers from Eglitis's flat were infested with fleas. Task Force agents dubbed the operator Jimmy 'the Flea' Eglitis.

During one raid an irritated boiler-room operator shouted, 'If you don't get out of here, I'm going to call the police.' Greatly amused, McClelland replied, 'We *are* the police!'

Raids on Hollywood boiler rooms have produced unusual twists, continued McClelland, like the time a group of agents, busy hauling out boxes of documents from a boiler room on Sunset Boulevard, were solicited by a prostitute.

The jovial atmosphere around the table was suddenly punctuated by the ringing of Sorley's portable phone. He grabbed the receiver. 'Hello sir,' said Sorley. Judge Russell Bostrom had returned his call. Carrying his beer in one hand and the portable phone in the other, Sorley disappeared to a quieter room. When he returned ten minutes later, Sorley was wearing a smile. He had secured the $1-million bail for Nabridge. Voters in conservative Orange County traditionally endorse tough, anti-crime measures and the people who implement them. Judge Bostrom's name, as it happened, would soon appear on the local ballot. 'I love election years!' shouted McClelland.

Before being extradited to Pennsylvania to face further sentencing, Nabridge was sentenced to six years in federal prison in California and was required to pay $650,000 restitution. The state of Pennsylvania, where victim Robert McDowell had lodged complaints with the authorities, sentenced Nabridge to a concurrent two- to six-year prison term and fined him $25,000. Timothy Guth was sentenced to six months to five years in Pennsylvania prison. Despite Bederson's two confessions (he made another in Pennsylvania), he was sentenced by the state of Pennsylvania to a jail term of six months to five years. Because his federal probation was revoked, Bederson is likely to face another five years behind bars.

The Midwest Minerals case illustrates a phenomena that has swept Orange County, catching locals and authorities by surprise. Despite the crack-down efforts of the Task Force, today an estimated 150 boiler rooms are in full operation. In the two years since the Task Force was created in January 1986 leading up to the Midwest Minerals raid, 110 people were convicted in Los Angeles federal court for related fraud charges.

Boiler rooms in Orange County have mushroomed not only in volume but turnover. 'When I first started,' remembers

Lambert, '$5,000 was a lot to lose. Then there were $100,000 victims in million-dollar cases and I thought that was a lot. Today,' he says, referring to Midwest Minerals, 'it's $1,500,000. I'm doing this for a drill. Fifty, 60 million – that pricks up my ears. That's what we're seeing today.'

The raids conducted by Lambert and the rest of the Task Force take place in one of the most beautiful and chic locations in America. In the rarefied atmosphere of Newport Beach, $1,000,000 yachts bob at anchor in front of isle properties costing $42,000 per linear foot. There are 9,000 yachts moored around seven man-made islands in Newport Harbour, more per capita than anywhere else in the world. Most of the boats are luxurious business write-offs and never set sail. Those that venture out into the fast afternoon winds of the Pacific coast, tack and jibe in jagged competition. The scissoring triangles of taut canvas appearing like shark's teeth.

Touted as the 'American Riviera' and the 'Côte d'Orange', this slice of Southern California, forty miles south of Los Angeles, lives up to the fantasies most people have about the Golden State. The warm weather, palm trees, beaches, and attraction of Disneyland promote a holiday atmosphere. And yet, were it a nation by itself, Orange County would displace South Korea by its annual production of valued services and products. The region's wealth is laced with decadence, and Bank of America's local ad reads, 'We finance anything that's fun'.

What is ironic is the fact that Bank of America, the largest bank in California and the third largest in the US, reported losses totalling $1,810 million between 1985 and 1987. These losses ($955 million in 1987 alone) prompted shareholders to file a massive civil suit, charging the bank's officers and directors with violating federal securities law by concealing the bank's financial condition and lending problems. Accused of 'reckless and wholly imprudent loan and investment decisions', the bank settled out of court in January 1988 and awarded shareholders $39.25 million.

'A floating financial crapshoot' is how one investigator describes Orange County. The local chapter of the Better Business Bureau, a consumer-protection agency aimed at promoting high standards of business conduct, is no longer in business. Boiler rooms thrive in this sun-drenched county. Their presence has bestowed upon the region a new name: Conman's Coast.

A con artist couldn't select a better place to make a killing. Orange County's household income registers 80 per cent above the national average. It is situated in the middle of the richest half of the richest state in America. The area's growth in financial stature is mirrored by the exponential leap in population the area has experienced in the last thirty years. In 1960 704,000 people lived in the citrus county. Today it is home to 2.1 million residents, most of whom are strangers to one another.

Such anonymity and conspicuous affluence make it difficult to tell the good money from the bad. Predators blend in with their prey on palm-fringed boulevards where the lustre of Lamborghinis, Ferraris and Excaliburs outshines the common appearance of BMWs and Mercedes. In the superficial small talk of strangers, Orange County drivers communicate through personalised licence plates: REZULTZ on a Porsche 944, PREMACO (short for Precious Metal Accumulation Corp) on a ragtop Cadillac Biarritz. A red Ferrari is tagged CONARTIS while a white Rolls Royce has licence plates that brag N 1 WEEK, the time, presumably, it took its owner to earn the cash for the car.

There are other reasons Orange County has become so popular with boiler-room operators. 'It's called a soft real-estate market,' explains Kacy McClelland. 'They can't get enough people to fill the space. Landowners are willing to rent to people without much background information on them.' Boiler rooms, usually offices outfitted with rows of desks with telephones, have sprung up in the gleaming harbour-view offices of Newport Center, in sprawling industrial-park suites and newly constructed buildings in the centre of town.

The concept of telephone sales is nothing new to most

outhern Californians. 'The Los Angeles metropolitan area s tuned in to telemarketing,' says McClelland. 'Everybody is ccustomed to it. You have essentially a ready-made employee ool to draw from. The first ten you get, you can weed out ight of 'em, keep the two good ones, get replacements and eep going like that. Recruiting is no problem at all.'

'You get an out-of-work actor,' says Lambert, 'slap five grand n the table and they'll say anything. A good slammer,' he adds, an make $4–10,000 in a week; his manager, $40,000. The eam has come across boiler rooms pulling in $600,000 a week.' Naturally, the lifestyles of the operators and slammers reflect heir new-found wealth.

'They want the best,' says Mark Fisher. 'Fast cars, $100 unches and they pay for it with the best credit in the world: ther people's money.'

Where better to spend it than Orange County? 'It's a glorious lace to work,' says McClelland. 'There is a lot of wealth ere to attack.' If the money, weather and easy targets fail o provide enough incentive, McClelland adds one more reason vhy Orange County is now America's boiler-room capital: 'We re,' he says, 'outnumbered.'

At any given time McClelland is investigating thirty different oiler-room operations. There are five times that many known raudulent telemarketing firms in the county. One indication of he size of the problem is underscored by the fact that boiler-oom operators in the greater Los Angeles/Orange County rea have bilked an estimated $500 million from telephone ompanies by using stolen phone-access codes to call their ictims. And while the Task Force is officially comprised of nembers from eleven different law-enforcement bodies, in prac-ice, McClelland, Fisher and Lambert spearhead an overworked d hoc boiler-room detail that is perpetually stretched for lack f manpower.

McClelland and his colleagues in the Santa-Ana-based postal-nspection fraud unit, enforce federal mail and wire statutes as well as those prohibiting the interstate transportation of stolen or fraudulently obtained property. Consistently, 98 per cent of the criminal cases postal inspectors bring to trial result in convictions. The sheer growth of boiler-room operators presents a far more serious challenge. McClelland draws an analogy between the odds against the Task Force and a scene from the movie, *Jaws*.

'Remember when Roy Scheider is standing on the deck and the shark suddenly leaps out of the water and Scheider tells the guy, "We need a bigger boat"? Well,' he says, 'we need a bigger boat.'

McClelland first became acquainted with boiler rooms during his days as a postal consumer-protection specialist in Pittsburgh, Pennsylvania. One case he recalls involved a group of telephone salesmen who swindled $2 million from investors by peddling worthless coal-mine contracts, or 'selling dirt', as it's known in the trade. Victims believed the coal they had bought would be later dug from the ground and sold at substantial profit. What they weren't told, however, was that they were expected to pick up the coal themselves, remove it from the mine and sell it on the open market.

In Orange County, McClelland had come across a handful of similar boiler rooms. He decided to test the waters by mailing out questionnaires to victims. 'The phone didn't stop ringing for months,' he recalls. At the same time, other victims who had lost their savings to fraudulent telemarketeers sought help from local enforcement agencies.

Detective Mark Fisher, in his office at the Newport Beach police station, had received several complaints about an operation called Capital Trust. As more duped investors began to tie up the phone lines at the station, Fisher contacted McClelland for some advice on bringing a case against Capital.

'I'll be happy to sit down and talk to you about the case,' McClelland told Fisher, 'but I'm not going to have the time to do it.' Within a day or two of that conversation, Mark

Fisher and Larry Lambert arrived in McClelland's office, a cramped room adorned with maps of Kentucky mineral mines. 'We talked about Capital,' recalls McClelland, 'and they were willing to bite off a chunk of it.' Fisher's and Lambert's support meant a lot to him. Enough to break his original resolve not to get wrapped up in the case. 'I was willing to join them because, all of a sudden, we were going to get some stuff done.'

It was a turning-point meeting from which sprang the beginnings of a task force. McClelland shared his boiler-room experiences – from the operators he came across in Pittsburgh to the boiler rooms of Orange County. He described how he went about proving fraud by wire and how that often meant going to unheard-of locations to gather evidence. McClelland told Fisher and Lambert how he learned, on the job, that with purported oil and gas finds, it was up to an investigator to prove with physical evidence that the deal was fraudulent. For McClelland, this meant, in one case, travelling to Kentucky in the middle of winter to examine non-functioning oil and gas-drilling equipment.

Adventures aside, convicting boiler-room operators usually began with gathering as much information about the company as possible, explained McClelland. Through victims of boiler-room scams, investigators could piece together enough evidence to mount charges against a firm. Fisher and Lambert listened closely to McClelland. They had just begun hearing from Capital victims and wanted to know more about turning these complaints into an indictment. 'I told them what proof I intended to use to make another case work and I drew an analogy between that case and Capital Trust, because they were similar.'

Over the next couple of months, McClelland, Fisher and Lambert would co-ordinate information on Capital victims in preparation for a raid. They learned that Capital Trust, Inc. was formed in 1984 by Richard O. Kelly, Sr. a man in his early fifties who cultivated a charming 'Southern Gentleman' demeanour.

Kelly's son, Richard, was the sales manager at Capital and James Harvey, the president. The investigators discovered that Capital was an amalgamation of eight boiler rooms throughout Orange County with central offices in El Toro, Irvine and Newport Beach. Capital made money by purportedly buying and selling commodities, including silver and gold bullion and coins, platinum, palladium, and copper.

In a matter of weeks, McClelland, Fisher and Lambert figured out that five of Capital's 'account executives' had 'churned and burned' victims by recommending their clients sell one commodity and purchase another. The point of which was the creation of huge commissions for themselves without regard for their clients' investments. The churning amounted to a double-win situation for Capital. It guaranteed that any investors' profits would be converted into income for Capital while at the same time reducing any equity clients had wrapped up in the company, therefore reducing Capital's liabilities to its clients.

As the mastermind behind Capital, Kelly Sr. used part of the proceeds to finance Shangri-La Farms Inc., essentially a private residence in Talladega County, Alabama. 'Unlike his son who treated client funds as his private chequing account, making house and car payments with it and paying off the kids' school fees with the money, Kelly Sr. wouldn't take out bits and pieces for this and that,' says Fisher. 'He would take out a $3-million loan to buy a piece of land and then another $2 million to build a house on it.' The homestead consisted of 505 acres, more or less, with a 55-acre lake, 45 acres of waterfront property, 280 acres of pasture and preserve and 125 acres of woodland. 'Structural improvements' included a 7,000 square-foot main house, two guest houses, a barn, a boathouse and a tennis court.

Kelly Sr. hired Dorothea 'Dee' Tomczyk and Alex McCord as senior account executives. According to the draft indictment brought against them, both were responsible for inducing various clients into investing with Capital and with lulling those

ame clients into a false sense of security regarding Capital's
nancial stability. Dee Tomczyk's seductive voice 'made you
eel warm and tingly all over', reported the investigators. 'She
nade you feel good about sending her money.' The fact that
he spoke with her victims over the telephone and not face to
ace, gave Tomczyk, in particular, an added edge to make a
illing. Investigators say Tomczyk's flirtatious manner earned
er a cool $70,000 from one male victim. 'Women do well
onvincing men to invest,' says Larry Lambert. 'It's kind of
ke phone sex.'

But if Tomczyk's clients could have seen who they were
ending money to, perhaps they might have been more prudent.
Jnlike the sex kitten she portrayed herself to be, Tomczyk is
n fact closing in on her fiftieth birthday and weighs some
wenty stone. As the investigators closed in on Capital in
reparation for an eventual raid, McClelland jokingly warned
isher and Lambert, 'For God's sake, don't shoot Dee Tomczyk
- Green Peace will sue your ass!'

Tomczyk, despite her physical appearance, was an incredible
lammer. One day she convinced an investor to sink $100,000
nto silver. When the market went up Tomczyk called him with
he good news: he had just made $20,000. She asked him if
e wanted to liquidate or roll the money over into platinum,
ecause, she explained, the precious metal was about to go
hrough the roof. The man liked the idea so much, he not only
ollowed Tomczyk's advice but he convinced his 22-year-old
laughter to invest in the same thing. Both father and daughter
ad 'purchased' platinum on a margin. In other words, they
ad placed money or collateral as a deposit in order to serve
s a performance guarantee. If the market were to fall, or slip
elow a performance guarantee level, both would be required
o deposit more collateral to maintain the equity level of their
nvestment.

Most boiler rooms naturally operate best during a bear
narket. Once investors are hooked on a commodity that may

have been oversold to them, as in the case of boiler-room investments, market forces take their course. The legitimate downward spiral in price helps to conceal the outright theft of their original investment.

Despite Dee Tomczyk's continual assurances to the father and daughter that their investment was safe in Capital's hands, they eventually lost everything. In an interview with Fisher and McClelland he explained that he personally wasn't devastated. He knew that although it would take time, he would postpone his retirement and make it back somehow. What brought tears to his eyes was his daughter. She had invested her life-savings with Capital and was left penniless. He volunteered during the interview that his daughter had just been diagnosed as having terminal cancer.

Tomczyk's colleague, Alex McCord, played a different game. One of his victims, Irene Zelma Osmond, a widow in her eighties, recalls him as 'a gentleman from the word go'. When they first met, McCord drove down from Irvine to San Diego and treated Osmond to lunch at a French restaurant. Following their meeting, he sent her a three-pound box of chocolates. 'You can't help but like Alex,' says Osmond. 'He told me he was an adopted child. I felt sorry for him.'

McCord lavished considerable attention on Osmond and called her several times daily beginning usually at 5 a.m. Amidst the flurry of phone calls, McCord would apprise Osmond of the performance of her various precious-metals contracts that he had secured under the auspices of Capital Trust. McCord assured her, 'You'll be receiving cheques left and right on this thing.' After sinking $110,000 into Capital over a three-year period, Osmond says, 'I haven't received a god-damn one.'

Osmond's husband, who died in 1981, took care of all the couple's financial decisions, to the extent that she never had a checking account or credit card. 'When it comes to bookwork,' she says, 'I'm just lost.' Clutching a sheaf of Capital margin-call announcements that she fulfilled, Osmond says, 'When I look at hese sheets, I want to kill him.' The margin calls would often be sent, as in the case of the following, the day before action had to be taken:

> Due to a recent price movement in the precious-metals market, your account requires additional funds in the amount of $19,487.95. If the funds are not received by 12:00 p.m. on 28 February 1986, your position will be liquidated at the market closing price.

Less than 2 per cent of the Capital Trust assets recovered by investigators actually went into precious metals. The remaining 98 per cent of Capital's investors' funds, according to Mark Fisher, has either been spent, hidden or tied up in other schemes.

Irene Osmond, who, following her losses, now lives in a modest mobile home in Escondido, California, describes herself as an easy mark. 'I've been a damn fool,' she says. 'Every time I wanted to sell, Alex said, "Not now". I had faith in him. . . . There's not another son of a bitch that's going to get the tail off a Buffalo nickel from me. Maybe I'll get some back some day. Do you think there's a chance?'

Four east-coast Capital investors are asking the same question. Each lost more than $150,000 through their affiliation with Capital. In preparing an indictment against the firm, 'We will bring in the high dollars to show the jury Capital stole a lot of money,' explains Fisher. But to prove just how ruthless the Capital operation was, Fisher is planning to introduce the jury to Joseph Chaperlo.

When Chaperlo, 74, a retired Pomona, California, labourer realised he lost $23,114 – nearly 70 per cent of his life-savings – he was devastated. 'I just feel I want to do away with myself,' he wrote in a letter to the police. Persistent slammers at Capital began calling Chaperlo in 1984. Over a three-year period he was 'churned and burned' by greedy silver, palladium and copper 'brokers' who switched him from one investment to another as often as twice a day, extracting high commissions at every turn.

Chaperlo now lives in a shack he shares with a small mongrel dog. His haggard face is a picture of despair. 'I used to always think that victims of violent crime suffered more than targets of fraud. Now I'm not sure,' says Fisher. 'At least they have someone else to blame. But in fraud, these people are so mad at themselves that they have no outward anger. It's the anguish that comes from knowing you've helped someone, a person you've trusted, rip you off.

'I think victims of this type of thing suffer more. You get mugged on the street, or say your home gets broken into or you get beaten up. It's a bad deal – you lost money or you got hurt, but it's like being hit by lightning. You're just in the wrong place at the wrong time. Things happen. If you get robbed at gun point, the guy wasn't smiling at you, pretending to be your friend, using your name thirty times in the first three minutes of conversation. You didn't help him both by believing him and handing him your money.

'These folks can be angry at the criminal, but they're also very angry at themselves. They helped. So it's like you not only take their money, you leave them totally demoralised. Who then wants to come to the authorities or the police and admit they're not only a victim but a stupid victim?'

On a four-day, 1,400-mile journey through central California and Nevada, Fisher and McClelland came across other Capital victims. A woman horse trainer in Reno sent 57 lbs of silver dollars to Capital's chief rival, Intech. The Newport Beach firm was meant to sell it on the precious-metals market. The woman was counting on the proceeds of the sale to finance an indoor arena. With the total loss of her investment, her plans have been permanently shelved. Ron, a Vietnam veteran, has a wife and three children. He gave Capital $15,000 – all of his spare cash. The market went down so they told him he would have to start making margin calls to maintain his equity or he would lose his investment. He took out a second mortgage on his house and paid in an additional $13,000, and then he lost it all. He now works in an orange-juice bar factory, double shifts three times a week to make ends meet. 'In this case, we're not talking getting back to where you were,' says Fisher. 'We're talking about treading water.'

The Capital 'victim trip' made an impression on McClelland and Fisher and they were anxious to pull together enough evidence against Capital to secure search-warrants for the company's premises. By late January 1987, 2,000 small investors had lost a total of $14 million to the boiler room. Fisher, McClelland, Lambert and colleagues from the IRS, Postal Inspection Unit and District Attorney's office raided Capital on 31 January 1987. Besides gathering all relevant paperwork, the Task Force wanted to take pictures of key figures. Dee Tomczyk and Alex McCord were nervous but obliging. Richard Kelly's southern gentlemanly demeanour evaporated when he flatly refused to be photographed. It was only the beginning of greater problems the Task Force was to experience with Capital Trust.

Several weeks after the raid (there were no arrests), the company claimed bankruptcy in Texas, a move that stymied any court proceedings in California where civil charges are pending against eleven Capital Trust employees. Police have evidence that indicates thirty-three separate boiler-room operations or related schemes have sprung from Capital Trust, including a consultancy firm that offers instruction on how to set up a boiler room and takes beginners through the legal minefields.

Fisher, none the less, has interviewed more Capital victims and has worked closely with the IRS in pursuing tax-evasion charges against the main operators. In the winter of 1989, heavy rains caused flooding in the old Orange County postal-inspector's office where evidence against Capital Trust was stored. The water damage to cheques and documents prevented any proposed indictments from being drafted until the spring. By mid-September 1989, Richard Kelly Sr. and four Capital Trust employees including McCord and Tomczyk were arrested. The final indictment charged them with defrauding $12.3 million from investors. In the months following the arrests, the Task Force compiled over 17,000 pieces of documentary evidence against the five.

Victims of Capital Trust as well as other boiler rooms, if not churned and burned, have fallen prey to 'bucketing', a scheme in which boiler-room operators accept orders to buy or sell from clients without any intention of executing them. The broker gambles that the market will move against the customer enabling him to pocket any loss the customer may incur in closing out the transaction. Bucketing also refers to the illegal use of margin deposits without disclosure to the customer, as in the case of Osmond. 'The amazing thing,' says Fisher, 'is that people send money to a faceless voice over the telephone.'

Reckless disregard for truth is the hallmark of account executives or 'slammers'. Some have attempted to sell platinum by saying it cures AIDS. One slammer in San Diego pitched iron oxide, describing how demand was rising for the commodity. Naïve investors failed to note the product was also known as rust. Strategic metals (like cobalt), walnut oil, gems, artichoke farms, jojoba beans, coins and mineral rights are just some of the bogus investment vehicles developed to abscond with investors' money.

Names of potential investors are supplied to boiler rooms on lead cards, unwittingly filled out by the investors themselves responding to certain junk-mail offers. World Equity Mint, raided in April 1987 after allegedly stealing $20 million from 4,000 investors, had a network of 22 affiliates fuelled by many thousands of lead cards.

Boiler rooms in Orange County vary in size from two or three desk operations to outfits with 100 or more 'account executives' working the phones. 'All you need is a few thousand bucks,' says Lambert. 'You rent the space, get your phones on credit, lease the furniture, get some crooks to deliver the pitch material and you roll.'

In 1986, California passed a telemarketing registration law that required firms to register with the attorney general. Aside from information on the identity of the company, firms are now required to submit pitch sheets. But it has done little to stem the tide of boiler rooms. Fisher compares it to the man in the early 1900s who thought if everyone got a driver's licence, it would cut down on the car-theft problem. But the law prohibiting fraudulent telemarketing is hardly toothless. 'When the Department of Corporations hits you for selling an unregistered security with a cause and desist order (a civil restraining order), it is a felony,' says Fisher. 'If you sell it or even offer it to ten people after that, it's ten separate chargeable felonies.'

In addition, when pinning a fraud rap on a slammer is made impossible through a plea of no knowledge, that is, the 'I'm just a salesman' defence, tax laws come in handy. 'Eighty per cent of them are going to go down for tax evasion,' says Fisher who has come across cases of salesmen reporting salaries of $52,000 but omitting to file returns for their $110,000 annual commission. 'The IRS gets respect from these people,' he says, adding that whenever his colleague from the criminal investigation division walks through the door during a bust, he never fails to make an impact, dressed in a black raid jacket with 'IRS' in big letters on the back.

Large operations gain credibility with investors by placing ads in the *Wall Street Journal*, *Barrons*, and by appearing on the nationally cable-broadcasted program, *Financial News Network*. While the outward appearance of most boiler rooms is convincingly rich (even the fashion-model receptionists look expensive), the firms are strictly fly-by-night. On occasion, operators, feeling the heat of the law, have literally vanished, bagging everything except the carpet. One investigator related how one day a bustling boiler room with well-appointed furniture, boardroom, potted plants, telephones, office equipment – all of which belonged to a leasing company – disappeared the day after a routine inspection.

There are other means of escaping the law. Account executives often use a 'good faith' defence, basically meaning that, like their victims, they believed what they were selling actually existed. But slammers can get hit for other reasons. Narcotic abuse is rampant in boiler rooms, say police, with cocaine being the drug of choice. Marijuana joints circulate, they say, as a way of spotting potential informers.

Slammers are very persuasive, and come equipped with handy references, or 'pitch' books to counter any rejection:

'I need to pray about it.'
'If God didn't want you to buy what I'm selling, you wouldn't be here.'

'I need to talk it over with my wife.'
'I don't know about your wife, but mine doesn't know a thing about business affairs.'

'I need to talk to my accountant first.'
'Let's face it, all accountants are conservative. If they knew how to invest, they wouldn't be accountants.'

Larry Lambert attributes the audacity of slammers to the fact that they conduct business over the telephone. 'If they met face to face with their victims, they'd feel more responsible,' he says. 'The telephone reduces the guilt created when a victim says all they worked for in life is now gone, that the legacy they planned to leave their sons and daughters no longer exists.'

The fraud slammers commit counts as one of the most difficult on the books to prove. 'Homicide is fairly simple,' says Fisher. 'Dead body – who did it? How many drug cases would be prosecuted if it took the lab a year and a half to analyse some white powder and say it was cocaine? I need eighteen months and two IRS auditors to tell me, "Yeah, they stole the money."'

The Newport Beach Police Department on Santa Barbara Drive looks like a well-heeled firm of solicitors, with framed lithographs hanging on colour-co-ordinated walls and comfortable furniture in the lobby. Between well-appointed offices and a library is a door leading to a large, fluorescent-lit room with rows of desks. It looks like a news room, a sales room, perhaps, but everybody's wearing guns. Mark Fisher's desk is dominated by a metal spike festooned with telephone messages.

Before his assignment to the department's fraud section, Fisher was a traffic investigator handling hit-and-run and fatal accident cases. He has the black-leather motorcycle boots to prove it. During his first month in the fraud division, Fisher became aware of a different kind of hit-and-run victim. His first case involved fifteen investors who had lost $40 apiece on a bogus property-listing scheme. By the end of the month, the loss to victims incurred in a separate case amounted to $2 million. The fraud assignments, dominated by boiler-room cases, have continued to escalate in financial importance. Capital: $14 million; World Equity Mint: $20 million; Intercomex: $40 million. An operation, in its infancy, pulls in $250,000 a week.

One of the benefits of working on the boiler-room beat is the chance to perfect investigative techniques. 'We are dealing with the best crooks in the country,' says Lambert. The latest twist involves bank-financed boiler-room investments in which banks purportedly maintain the collateral on an investment. Lambert has seen cases where Mafia funds have been laundered through bank-financed accounts. Organised crime is involved in boiler rooms throughout the US. One recent case linked the Chicago Jewish Mafia to a narcotics smuggling ring that had laundered $60 million through one of the Orange County bank-financed boiler-room operations. At present there are some 97 bank-financed telemarketing operations in the Los Angeles-Orange County area. 'It is the perfect instrument for organised crime,' says Lambert.

Perhaps as a result of the tremendous odds they face, McClelland, Fisher and Lambert have grown close as a team. 'There are no inter-departmental rivalries,' says Fisher. 'We don't fight to get our names in the press releases.' While most of the smart set of Newport meet up at watering holes like the Rusty Pelican and Bobby McGee's, the three investigators have impromptu board meetings at the local Taco Bell. Terree Bowers, who heads the LA-based Major Frauds Unit of the US Attorney's office for California's Central District, says of the Task Force, 'It's evolved into one of the most positive expressions of inter-agency co-operation.'

Says McClelland, 'I'd just as soon go out and get drunk with these guys as work on a case with them.' The three of them speak about the 'luxury of doing the right thing', and of each bust making other telemarketers 'sweat a little bit more'. Both Lambert and Fisher tease McClelland about an especially guileless remark he made on *60 Minutes*. McClelland said, 'In many cases, these people are like lambs and the telemarketers are like wolves. Someone has got to do something about them.' Soon after the programme was aired, McClelland answered his phone with, 'The people's shepherd. At the sound of the baa just leave a message.'

The man who fleeced 400 investors out of $2 million was a wolf in rock-star clothing. Matthew 'Matt' Valentine, according to Mark Fisher, was a cross betwen Rod Stewart and the Pillsbury Doughboy: 'A chubby little blond-headed thug'. Valentine was the president, director, incorporator, majority shareholder, chief executive officer, chief financial officer, secretary and owner of Intech, a company that purportedly purchased and sold commodities, including silver and gold bullion and coins, platinum, copper, gems, equity investments, metals and other minerals for its clients.

Kacy McClelland describes Valentine as 'a big game hunter in the modern world'. Valentine took over five other boiler-room operations and combined their assets with Intech's. With the proceeds of investors' money, he bought a house on Lido Island, and with the spare change, a $50,000 diamond ring and a full-length fox coat for his girl-friend.

Matt Valentine was not an especially pleasant man to do business with. He allegedly ran up over $10,000 worth of credit on his sister Debbie's American Express Card. When Amex reached her, she referred them to Valentine, explaining that he had run up the charges. American Express contacted him but Valentine denied on three separate occasions that he had a sister named Debbie Valentine.

Valentine had a legion of slammers who worked the phones in an office on Old Newport Boulevard. In the course of two years, investors sent Intech $2 million, often in the form of tangibles such as those mentioned in the indictment against the firm: $85,000 in hard silver, two diamond rings valued at $13,000, and gold krugerrands from a woman in Texas valued at $25,000.

Fisher, McClelland and Lambert were fielding calls regularly from Intech victims who feared that their valuables were lost for ever. Intech account executives had told investors they stood a chance of gaining 625 per cent returns on their investments, but Intech did not trade in the market on behalf of clients. Instead, the $2 million from the 400 investors went to finance the life-styles of the operators. Valentine's weekly salary, for instance, amounted to $2,500.

Like other boiler-room operators, Valentine had the facility to eavesdrop on his salesmen's telephone conversations. Valentine caused one of his account executives, Randy Elvidge, to be severely beaten when Elvidge began advising his own clients that their investments were in jeopardy and that they should attempt to recover their money. Elvidge was jumped from behind by two large men who pummelled him until, says the former Intech employee, 'There wasn't a part of my body that was not bruised.'

Before Valentine was charged with twenty counts of mail fraud and ten counts of interstate transportation of stolen property taken by fraud, Valentine decided to take the law into his own hands. Perhaps this wasn't a bad decision for someone who was looking at 215 years behind bars. Valentine decided to take contracts out on McClelland, Fisher and Lambert. He allegedly planned to have hit men do away with the three investigators.

Part of Valentine's paranoia may have stemmed from his alleged cocaine addiction. Police had prepared narcotics-dealing charges on Valentine, a conspicuous newcomer to the quiet island neighbourhood of Lido Island, a chic residential isle divided by avenues with European names such as Via Ithaca, Via Waziers and Via Palermo. Here, expensive homes are wedged close together on well-maintained, identical streets. From a private jet, Lido Island looks like a row of piano keys. The sharps and flats of its black-top alleys offer the only contrast to an otherwise bland housing development. Valentine had moved on to Lido Island where legend has it there is a Mercedes for each of the island's 700 dwellings. His was black.

Fisher, McClelland and Lambert had located Valentine's house and by talking with neighbours their suspicions about Valentine's involvement with drugs was confirmed. 'It's a nice quiet neighbourhood of affluent people,' says Fisher. 'And then this thing out of *Miami Vice* appears one day driving a black Mercedes 500 SL convertible with the hair and the sun-glasses and a new girl every night and drives down the alley like a bat out of hell. He hits the garage-door opener and he's inside and the door is half-way down before you can see anything. There are lots of late-night parties and foot traffic. . . . We knew that we were going to get him on the [boiler-room] fraud but we thought if we could throw in a heavy-duty drug case, we could go for racketeering and show that his whole life was one continual criminal enterprise.'

Because of the layout of the island, surveillance on Valentine's home presented a problem for the investigators. The conventional method was to conduct a stake-out from their unmarked car 'the silver bomb', an American make that stood out among the German saloons. 'We might as well have had "FBI" and "postal inspector" painted in fluorescent orange on the car,' recalls Fisher. 'We might have looked less conspicuous!'

A neighbour, relieved that the police were finally taking notice of the activity surrounding Valentine's house, described the parade of limousines and quick visits paid by unsavoury characters. 'It sounded like Colombian-style stuff where the pedestrian walks up to the garage door, knocks, the door opens and shuts. Ten minutes later, the door opens and he walks out,' says Fisher. The investigators, dressed in jeans and warm jackets, spent the night on the roof of the neighbour's house, monitoring the activity in Valentine's place. 'We could hear what was going on inside the house, but most importantly, we got foot traffic,' says Fisher. 'We used all the things we heard on the street about him from his associates and put that into a search-warrant.'

Apparently, if police cannot tell a judge that recent foot traffic has been observed, a search-warrant based on suspicions of narcotics dealing is usually impossible to obtain. 'It's the foot traffic that tells you it's there now, so we waited until we saw some. We got a warrant and then we shut down one night because nothing happened the next night and we were all so tired from working these eighteen-hour shifts. We said, "Wednesday night, what the hell, there's nothing going to happen tonight. . . ."'

'We got there the next morning and the neighbour said, "Till four in the morning! I mean, it was like a drive-in *movie lot*!"

So we used what she saw, put it in an affidavit and the judge says, "Fine". We figure he's either sold out and we're not going to find anything or we're going to have to wait until he gets his next shipment and that might not be for three weeks. It gets in and out so fast, we decided to hit that night.

'We stopped him in the alley. He doesn't have a thing on him, except in the left front-door pocket of the car, there's a prescription vial of antibiotics, in his girl-friend's name. California law states that prescription medication has to be in the possession of the person it's made out to. We essentially arrested Valentine for the possession of penicillin and read him his rights.

'He said, "This is harassment!" I go, "No, this is an arrest." He says, "This is harassment!" I go, "No, this is an arrest." We book him for possession of prescription drugs without a prescription. We search the house and we find the safe and we find 15 ounces of cutting agent and then a series of sifters where you take the rock and break it down into smaller rocks and sift until you finally have powder. The holding containers, the measures, the triple-beam scales, everything. You know, the gun in the living room under the seat cushion by the front door. The .45 auto on the night stand. The shotgun in the rafters of the garage where you just pull it down and . . . no cocaine.

'Everything we found in the safe was the cutting stuff, but no coke. We found a bindle. It was made out of a whole newspaper sheet and the narcs that were helping us said that there had been a half-pound in it.'

Valentine's victims were among the most sophisticated hit by a boiler-room operation and included lawyers and business executives. After one investor told Intech to sell his stake in the precious-metals market, 'Nobody answered the phone,' he says. 'They had gone to lunch for ever. When the market escalated, I had $40,000 equity in my account and suddenly, it was vapour.' He says that if he had the money today, he could retire. To make matters worse, he had borrowed it.

'It's really hard to tell people they aren't going to get their money back,' says McClelland. 'The older they are, the harder it is. There's a chance that most will recover one to five per cent of their original investment, if they're lucky. They might as well kiss it goodbye.' In the case of Intech, says Fisher, 'One could say the money went up in smoke, but it would probably be more appropriate to say that it went up various noses. It was a nice party while it lasted.'

Matthew Valentine made the mistake of publishing in one of his brochures the line, 'Today's decisions affect tomorrow's life-style.' 'We're going to make him choke on that one,' said McClelland. Upon his arrest in November 1987, Valentine was arrested and charged with twenty counts of mail fraud and ten counts of interstate transportation of stolen property. In April 1988 he was sentenced to six years at the Lompoc Federal Penitentiary, in central California. Valentine managed to score big in the cell-mate department. His dormitory companion was none other than Ivan Boesky. Says Fisher, 'What those two could have taught each other is frightening.'

'Compared to a narcotics case, it's a very attractive way to steal money,' says Lambert. 'A good way to finance your life. You can steal a couple mill, put contracts out on the cops and get a light sentence.'

Kacy McClelland is behind the wheel of the silver bomb, looking out over the sun-drenched sands of Newport Beach. The sailboats are kicking up a lot of spray this afternoon. In front of him, a Zimmer Excalibur moves into the fast lane. 'I'd love to live here,' says McClelland, 'but not if some guy in Pomona has to eat dog food.'

It's a Saturday morning in March 1989 and Mark Fisher is taking advantage of the uncommon silence of his open-plan office at the Newport Beach Police Station to do a little catching up. It has been a hellish week. On Tuesday, the day before proposed indictments against Capital Trust and Premaco (Precious

Metals Accumulation Company) were due to be reviewed by the US Attorney, a gangland assassin gunned down William King, the president of Premaco. The assailant entered the Newport Coin Exchange, a precious-metals dealership owned by King's wife. He opened fire, killing King's wife with a shot to the back of her head. A courier who happened to be in the Exchange at the time was also murdered. William King received gunshots to the head, leaving him blind in one eye and with little chance of meaningful survival.

Fisher arrived on the scene approximately ten minutes after the gunman had left. He had only just finished the draft indictment against King that alleged the Premaco president had participated in mail fraud, wire fraud, tax evasion and interstate transportation of stolen property.

Premaco had been raided in June 1988 and, at that time, ten individuals, including King, were arrested for felony and misdemeanour violations. McClelland and Lambert interviewed King who said that he was being pursued by the Las Vegas mob for embezzling some $150,000 of Mafia funds. King also had other enemies. 'His ex-employees despised him for cheating them out of their commissions,' says Fisher. 'The investors were being ripped off and were angry and his competitors didn't like him for taking over bits of their territory.'

Fisher, McClelland and Lambert cancelled their appointment with the US Attorney and began working with homicide. For the moment, cases against Premaco and Capital Trust have been temporarily shelved until the murder case has been cracked. 'It's the kind of work that keeps me lying awake at night,' says Fisher.

It's six a.m. and the sun is beginning to rise over Orange County. Doughnuts and coffee, the perks of the trade, are consumed by boiler-room salesmen. Lead cards are shuffled, phone books and government registries paged through. The lines are open. The day begins with a dial tone. A call is answered on the east coast. A deal is done. The process is repeated and pitches are made in every time zone. Scores of slammers cold call and cajole, pressure and close. The boiler room reaches a fever pitch. The sun is at its zenith above Southern California. Sailboats tack and jibe on the horizon. There are sharks in the water.

Collapse of an empire

'No one could begin to conceive of the impact of Carrian.'

RICHARD PARRY, detective inspector,
Royal Hong Kong Police,
Commercial Crime Bureau

Despite his delicate features that made him appear far younger than his 35 years, Jalil Ibrahim had a daunting responsibility. He was charged with solving 'a heinous crime', in the words of the Prime Minister of Malaysia. Jalil's mission was vital. Selected from an internal audit team to the post of assistant general manager of a Hong Kong deposit-taking company, the subsidiary of the largest bank in Malaysia, Jalil had been given direct orders by the bank's chairman to investigate and recover £600 million in unsecured loans.

The money, like the rest of the funds in the bank's vaults, had been earmarked for the economic ascent of Malaysia's 'sons of the soil' or Bumiputras. Bank Bumiputra Malaysia Berhad (BBMB) embodied the dreams of economic stability and financial growth for the race of indigenous Malaysians in a business sector dominated by ethnic Chinese.

Five months after his new appointment, Jalil was in over his head. 'Honestly,' he told his wife and children in an unfinished letter dated 9 June 1983, 'I've reached the limit of my patience here. . . . The problems in Hong Kong are not my making and from today onwards I am going to think of myself and my family first and put the interest of the Bank, the race and the country behind me. If those directors had thought of the interests of the Bank, the race and the country first, they wouldn't have made all those blunders in the first place.'[1] Two weeks later, Jalil's body was discovered in a remote banana grove in the New Territories.

An exhaustive man-hunt for Jalil's murderer was launched by detectives of the Organised and Serious Crime Bureau (OSCB). Because Jalil worked for a bank, Norrie Mackillok of the OSCB contacted Michael Farnham, head of the police Commercial Crimes Bureau (CCB). It was clear how Jalil had been murdered. He was found with a four-foot judo belt twisted around his neck. What police wanted to know was who killed Jalil and why.

The opulence of the Carrian Group's Hong Kong headquarters, with its Persian-rugged marble floor, potted plants and statues of curly-haired lions, was a mere shadow of the grandeur upstairs. George Tan, as group chairman, commanded his empire from a throne room. 'The moment I walked into Tan's office, with the marble statues, a fountain and Louis XIV furniture,' recalls one US banker, 'it was too surreal to be believed. He just impressed me as a used-car salesman.'[2]

The American banker was one of the distinct few who did not loan money to Carrian. Plenty of his peers sank into Tan's elegant furniture and raised toasts to the man who adorned his office in 'Hong Kong baroque': a tiger-skin rug, Venetian chandeliers and the accoutrements of an instant museum – rare clocks, expensive lamps and wall-to-wall oils and water-colours. Tan acquired art 'as one would buy meat from a butcher', according to a former aide, measuring his purchases in bulk. With the sweep of his arm, Tan would describe how a wall of art cost him £40,000, a table of trinkets, £30,000. He never referred to singular pictures. Quantity mattered rather than quality. Despite Tan's lapse in subtlety, some fifty lenders were reassured by the presence of the Hong Kong and Shanghai Bank which led Carrian's list of 'principal bankers' in a glossy annual report audited by Price Waterhouse.

Carrian, one of the largest conglomerates in Asia, appeared out of nowhere in 1979 and within two years was being compared to the colony's oldest and most prosperous trading concerns, the great 'hongs': Jardine Matheson, Hutchison, Wheelock Marden and Swire Pacific. Each had shared in the history of Hong Kong and so, too, would Carrian. Founded by Tan, a Malaysian engineer, Carrian's meteoric growth was a phenomenon that captured people's imaginations. In less than two years, the value of Carrian stock soared nearly 2,000 per cent from HK 40 cents to HK$7.80 by 1981. With its war chest, Carrian rapidly grew into a multibillion-dollar conglomerate, involved in insurance, banking and shipping, with real estate at its core. When Tan failed to capture imaginations with blockbuster deals, the Carrian logo, a puffed C and P (chosen for the firm's first company, Carrian Pest Specialist Ltd), promoted the conglomerate around the clock.

At the Group's peak, a person could live in a Carrian property debugged by Carrian Pest Control, insured with a China Underwriters policy, or they could take a Carrian holiday and stay in a Carrian hotel. They could also dine on Carrian meals, marketed under the 'Carrianna' brand name, featuring high-quality Chinese fast food and when they were finished, they could hop into a Carrian taxi. The Carrian Group was a complex hinterland of over 600 companies whose ultimate owners, Carrian Nominees, were unknown and undetectable. The way Carrian always paid over the odds for acquisitions made people think the mysterious nominees were happy to pay extra for a haven for flight capital. Rumours abounded that Carrian was secretly backed by money from Imelda Marcos, or wealthy oil sheikhs.

Tan easily won friendship and attention in high places. He

referred to Michael Sandberg, chairman of the Hong Kong and Shanghai Banking Corp., as 'Uncle Mike'. Tan doted on Sandberg, with anticipated returns. The Hong Kong Bank group was Carrian's merchant banker and largest lender after Bumiputra Finance. Despite the fact that the Hong Kong office was sceptical of Carrian, the Tan companies were able to secure millions of dollars worth of loan capital from the bank. In Sandberg, Tan found a sympathetic friend.[3] With over 600, there were plenty to choose from, including 'Outwit', 'Knife and Dagger' and 'Grand Zodiac'.

The icing on the cake was Tan's appearance next to Sandberg in the Royal Box at the Royal Hong Kong Jockey Club. The reassuring involvement of the Hong Kong and Shanghai Bank Corporation, who ultimately loaned Carrian HK$1.5 billion, encouraged other bankers to loan to the conglomerate. Many had no clue of either Tan's identity, or his source of wealth or the fact that he was in the country illegally.

The man's image made up for a lot of the unanswered questions. His charm and generosity were legendary. 'Tan was a man who knew who he could buy, when he could buy and how to buy,' said one observer. For he was, 'practised in the art of corruption'.[5] Tan's enthusiasm came out in sweeping gestures. His bespectacled face was divided by a thick, luxuriant moustache. He had the exuberance of a politician ahead in the polls. In a place where there are more Rolls Royces per capita than anywhere else, Tan had five. He was seen in all the right places by the people that mattered.

The Hong Kong Bank, the colony's largest and most august financial institution and banker to the Hong Kong government, may have been the biggest local lender to Carrian, but it certainly wasn't alone. Among the fifty-odd banks who gave Tan US$1.2 billion were Bankers Trust in New York, Barclays Asia Limited and Westdeutsche Landesbank of Germany.

Tan acquired credibility by surrounding himself with prestigious, highly respected professionals. His accountants worked for Price Waterhouse. Wardleys was his financial adviser. Tan's legal team came from one of the largest and most prestigious law firms in the colony, Deacons Solicitors and Notaries. Tan's right-hand man was recruited from Chase Manhattan.

Tan had everything: luck, timing, contacts and credit lines. The fact that he fled bankruptcy proceedings in Singapore, leaving behind a wrecked construction company, would not surface until years following his arrival at Kai Tak airport in 1972. Hong Kong, caught in the midst of a huge property-speculation wave, complete with a banking system swimming in liquidity and anxious to extend credit, would provide Tan the means to start over and to wage his remarkable conquest.

While his origins and date of birth have been the subject of much debate, it is widely believed that George Tan Soon Gin (his Chinese name) was born on 22 December 1938 in Sibu, Sarawak, a Malaysian region located south of Brunei. The son of a dentist, Tan studied engineering in Britain, but returned home without a degree. Unhindered by lack of qualifications, Tan engineered on construction sites in Malaysia, Singapore and Brunei.

Shortly after he arrived in Hong Kong, Tan purchased cheap land in the New Territories during the 1974-5 property slump. Tan was a Chiu Chow, owing to his family origins in the north-eastern corner of Guangdong Province. It's an area known for producing entrepreneurial heroes.

Being a Chiu Chow meant that Tan had something in common with Chung Ching-man, an experienced developer and hotel owner. Chung was a generation older than Tan and approached his work in a traditional and conservative way. He typified Hong Kong's old money. Tan's boldness, flash and unsophisticated manner was at polar opposites with Chung's steady-as-she-goes techniques. Chung's father and Tan's father-in-law had several joint ventures in Singapore. It was through his early association with Chung that Tan gained a lot of his property knowledge. In an interview with the *Asian Wall Street Journal* in 1982, Tan acknowledged, 'He's 56, I'm 43. He's been a developer for the past quarter of a century; I was new. Of course, I looked to his experience.' Together, they would set the Hong Kong property market ablaze.

Tan stayed with the Chung family business until he struck out on his own in 1978. A year later, Tan engineered the takeover of Mai Hon Enterprises Ltd, the publicly traded property arm of Stelux Manufacturing. Mai Hon's name changed to Carrian Investments Ltd (CIL), the publicly traded company of the Carrian group, between late 1979 and early 1980.

The takeover of Mai Hon was perfectly timed to profit from the Hong Kong stock-market's strongest boom in almost a decade. At the beginning of 1979, the Hang Seng index stood around the 500 mark; at year end, it was up to 879 and rising. The boom reflected the fantastic growth in the property sector where values and rents were skyrocketing.[6] Tan, now armed with a quoted property company, was ready for a piece of the action. What was significant about the birth of CIL was the fact that by paying more than HK$700 million[7] for Mai Hon, roughly four times its market price, Tan let it be known, right from the start, that he was a major player in the market. His staid mentor, Eda Investment's Chung, described Tan as 'an intelligent young man who was able to prove himself resourceful in a very short period of time.'[8]

Tan's first major deal dazzled the colony. In January 1980, a company, owned 75 per cent by the Carrian Group and 25 per cent by Chung, purchased Gammon House, a major Hong Kong office building, for HK$1 billion ($163.6 million).[9] The amount was HK$280 million more than Hong Kong Land had paid two years earlier. The record-breaking price and the fact that Tan hadn't borrowed a penny to buy it shocked the market.

Carrian Investments quickly became Hong Kong's most talked about firm. Rumours abounded about Tan's invisible backers and his bottomless bank account. The mystery only whetted investors' appetite for CIL scrip. By August, the company's share price had increased some 50 per cent from the previous December.

With a flair for the theatrical, Carrian announced in September that it would sell Gammon House for HK$1.68 billion. Tan began to demonstrate in his deals the dexterity of a magician. The rabbit he pulled out of his hat in the Gammon House transaction were buyers Rogerio and Stephen Lam, heirs to the Hang Seng Bank and directors of Bylamson & Associates Limited. The deal changed the face of Hong Kong, creating a boom in the property market and sending Carrian's share price skyward.

With the Gammon House deal, Tan had emerged from the shadows as a property mogul with a Midas touch. Carrian's early success with Gammon House convinced critics that Tan was a genius who understood the importance of timing in a booming market. Overnight, Carrian became a corporate force to be reckoned with.

The Lams paid a deposit of HK$108 million and signed an agreement to pay HK$150 million every three months. If they failed to do so, the HK$108 million would go into forfeit. After the 'deal', the Lams could not meet the first payment and told Tan that they would have to forfeit. Rather than risk the embarrassment of publicising the news, Tan asked his lawyers to put together a proposal that would allow the deal to go through, if only on paper.

In the end, Tan returned the HK$108 million to the Lams and sold Gammon House to various concerns including Bank of America, whose name is now on the building. Through implementing his lawyers' scheme, Tan was able to save his reputation and prevent any loss of face for the Lams. Their indebtedness to Tan would prove useful to him in a future deal.

Tan had carefully created the company's parents, Carrian Holdings Ltd (CHL) and Carrian Nominee Ltd, in 1977–8.

The private drama in which Carrian's secret financing was played out among these three companies was intentionally kept far removed from the investigating public.

CIL, the publicly quoted flagship of the group, had more than 100 poetically named subsidiaries, including Deciding Deed, Perfect Combination and Beat the Bush. CHL had many more. 'It got pretty crazy,' recounts a former employee who adds that company names were chosen on the basis of 'the most sex appeal'.[10]

Any loan officer intent on understanding the structure of the borrowing firm, even if he got past the maze of peculiar-sounding companies, would still not know the identity of the mysterious owners of Carrian Nominee who ultimately backed Tan's empire. Frequently, the registered offices were apartments of Carrian secretaries or employees. Directors included janitors and tea ladies. One employee, Chan Kwok Ho, a construction-site foreman, was made a director of Gold Come Limited despite the fact that he did not understand English. He attended 'board meetings' that never took place and signed loan applications, unaware of the consequences. Like other employees assigned to directorships, he was required to sign a declaration of trust pledging proceeds of shares to a company known as Thousand Good Ltd, a George Tan company.[11] This did not remove any directors' legal responsibilities.

Tan sufficiently removed himself from the sharp end of his business, never signing important documents until they were already signed by associates. He bestowed directorships and their attendant responsibilities to underlings and kept above the spectre of criminality by declaring that he only acted on the advice of professionals.

From the beginning, Tan's primary backer was Bumiputra Finance Ltd (BMFL). In its first recorded deal with Tan, the bank allegedly loaned his company at least HK$60 million, more than twice the value of the property purchased. Between late 1979 and early 1980, George Tan received an alleged

US$292 million, the largest unsyndicated advance made to any borrower in the history of Bank Bumiputra. A portion of this loan had allegedly been set aside for Gammon House. Tan had an exceptionally close relationship with BMFL. He referred to BMFL deputy chairman Lorrain Osman as 'Uncle Lorrain'. Tan's generosity towards the bank's directors, Osman, Rais Saniman, Hashim Shamsuddin and Ibrahim Jaafar, was legendary.

On 1 December 1979, Tan allegedly gave Jaafar a new Rolls Royce. On 19 December, Bumiputra Finance made the first in a series of alleged large loans which would transform its relationship with Carrian. Between that date and 12 October 1982, BMFL allegedly gave twenty-six money-market loans to the Carrian Group of companies totalling more than US$841 million.[12] The alleged size of the loans increased from HK$437.5 to HK$7 billion by 1983.

Shamsuddin, who was not only executive director of the parent, BBMB, but also director of BMFL, pleaded guilty to receiving airline tickets, shares and cash amounting to HK$15 million from Tan. His wife received a £40,000 Daimler. Such was his clout Tan even set up an alleged retirement fund for local staff at Bumiputra Finance.[13] The gifts coincided with his receipt of unsecured loans such as one of US$97 million in early 1982. If there was security, it was usually a post-dated cheque for the amount of the loan which would be rolled over with a new post-dated cheque.

The arrangement with the BMFL directors was well concealed. Conveniently, Rais Saniman, as general manager of BBMB's international banking division, determined what, if any, information about George Tan and Carrian would be submitted to the management committee of the parent bank in Kuala Lumpur.

With Tan, Bumiputra Finance had found a charming dynamo, a generous man who was quick with favours. He appeared to be an excellent vehicle for investment. Above all, he oozed charisma. Tan's 'mystique' was aided by the hundreds of millions of dollars he absorbed from BMFL. It gave him more than cash flow. It gave him confidence.

A person could not help but feel special, being granted an audience with George Tan. To gain access to his inner sanctum, a person had to have a special badge. He would refuse to be photographed, only saying, in a Fukian accent, close to Mandarin, 'I don't want to give assistance to potential kidnappers.' By shunning the press, Tan naturally drew media interest and fascination. Whereas lack of information usually generates suspicion, with Carrian, it created an aura of wonder, and myths of endless wealth.

Gradually it became known that Tan was the eldest in his family with three of his brothers residing in Hong Kong. Tan's wife and two daughters spent a great deal of time in Singapore. Though there was never any doubt Tan was the brain behind Carrian, predictably, he left the most exalted ranks of chairman and managing director to Carrie Woo, his then secretary, a situation he did not revise until July 1981.

Part of the mystique surrounding Tan had much to do with his belief in *fung-shui* or Chinese spirits. Bad *fung shui* amounted to a kind of curse that needed to be rectified, usually by a *fung-shui* man, gifted with an understanding of the basic requirements for good *fung shui*, i.e. the proper juxtapositioning of a site in consideration of the earth's elements. Like an astrologer, a *fung-shui* man is paid for his reading. All properties held by the Carrian Group had to be vetted by a *fung-shui* expert. In the case of Gammon House, a *fung-shui* man was consulted and paid, on a per-square-foot basis, HK$180,000.[14]

Tan refused to travel outside of Hong Kong, claiming that his *fung-shui* man instructed him never to cross over water or risk being chased by evil spirits. This arcane omen had some merit. Tan's Singaporean passport had expired in 1974. If he elected to leave Hong Kong it would be discovered he was staying in the colony illegally. Concomitantly, Tan's citizenship would be revoked when it was discovered he possessed Paraguayan and Tongan passports, as holding more than one passport in Singapore is an illegal offence.

In his *fung-shui* beliefs, Tan appealed to a wide Chinese population who shared the same superstitions. Before hiring anyone, Tan studied a person's ear-lobes to determine if they would bring good fortune to the company. Mindful of his lucky numbers, Tan only signed contracts at special times, on auspicious days. These practices made the firm distinctly Chinese. Bumiputra Finance would pull the strings, keeping Tan in tow. He would make a good front; a clever puppet for the powers that be at 'Bumi'. Their mistake was in miscalculating Tan's ambition. 'George learned the tricks of the trade as we went along,' says a former associate. 'He was very shrewd and very quick.'[15]

In no time at all, the puppet would become the puppet-master.

With the help of Hong Kong's banking establishment, Carrian's magnificent expansion took off. Each deal seemed bigger than the next. From the beginning, and especially after the Gammon House transaction, Carrian had to run hard to keep up with itself. In a joint venture with Hong Kong Land, the company made plans to pay a world-record price for the old wing of a hotel in Kowloon. Overnight, the Miramar hotel, in the heart of the Tsimshatsui tourist belt, was deemed to have more value per square foot than the Pan Am Building on Park Avenue, New York. It was sold for HK$2.8 billion.

Most notable of Tan's American business coups was his successful bid for a 49 per cent share of an Oakland Plaza development by the property branch of the Peninsular and Oriental Steam Navigation Company. But Tan, a novice in the maritime trade, was also moving into ground transport, with the largest fleet of cabs in Hong Kong, replete with 27 rental Mercedes and 200 tourist coaches.

Carrian's capital value had accumulated in two years to a staggering HK$5.5 billion. Tan and his company had become a stellar phenomena. Vickers da Costa, the highly respected London brokerage house with expertise in Asian markets, published a detailed review of Carrian that would boost the company even higher. The report amounted to a glowing tribute to Carrian's dynamic management style, solid financial base and gilt-edged future.

As the first published look inside Carrian by a professional financial analyst, the review attracted international attention. At the time of the report, Carrian shares were selling at a discount of a third to Vickers da Costa's estimate of their net asset value of HK$9.15 billion. The hype of the Vickers' review accelerated Carrian's succession of five scrip issues. Providing he retained them, the holder of ten Carrian shares in July 1980 would have thirty-three shares in less than two years. Share values fluctuated between HK$5 to HK$7.80.

Using its shares as collateral, Carrian plunged into an assortment of industries in which the firm had no previous experience. With his travel business, Tan started with tours, then built up interests in hotels and transportation. Carrian's travel network soon stretched from Hong Kong to most South East Asian nations as well as California.

The beauty of Carrian's complex corporate structure – its flowchart resembled an intricate computer circuit board – was that Tan could sell his properties, on a floor-by-floor basis, to the various Tan-related companies. In this way, Tan could control the buying-and-selling price of his assets and thus wield tremendous influence over the Hong Kong property market. With the inevitable 'profits', Tan could then justify more bank borrowing for more acquisitions. As the excitement spread and the prices rose, the Tan property portfolio could be mortgaged for more than its real value. The spiral continued ever skyward.

The false profits, generated by the incestuous trading of Carrian property, allowed the company to float more equity on the Hong Kong stock-markets, generating even more capital for Carrian to invest. For fiscal year 1981, fully 40 per cent of Carrian's profits turned out to be fictitious, based on reported sales for which no payment was ever received.[16]

In 1981, Carrian moved into shipping and transportation, purchasing controlling shares of Grand Marine Holdings. The company, with sixty ships and ten more under construction, was Hong Kong's fourth largest shipping company and one of the colony's largest transport companies. For this acquisition, the board of Bumiputra Finance approved loans totalling US$138 million to seven of Tan's nominee companies. There was no evaluation of the seven companies, four of which were incorporated after the loans were approved and released.[17]

While the charade lasted, Tan exercised phenomenal control of Carrian, rigging both property and stock-markets to distinct advantage. Like the role played by the Price Waterhouse accountants whose audits helped secure funding, bankers like Sandberg played a significant part in the creation of the Carrian empire. The fact that some needed encouragement was no matter. 'What was good enough for the Hong Kong Bank,' said one banker, 'was good enough for us.'[18]

Even when the property market began to fall in 1982, banks continued to lend Tan's conglomerate cash. One foreign banker who approved a loan to Carrian days before the company declared bankruptcy told the *Asian Wall Street Journal* in January 1983, 'Banks were so eager to fulfil their budgets that they forgot other prudent banking policies. Demand for loans [in Hong Kong] wasn't very strong last year and banks just went overboard on Carrian.'

Gerald Dobby, assistant general manager of the Hong Kong Bank, remembers, 'At the time George Tan was a rising star; one of the many who'd arrived in Hong Kong with an idea that started small and got bigger. Not every one of them ended up in disaster. . . . Was George Tan a victim of the times? Or was he, as alleged by the prosecution, from the very outset hell bent on defrauding the banks of HK$10 billion dollars? I don't know.'

By the end of 1981, Carrian was so highly geared, that any significant dip in CIL's share price would be disastrous. Many of CIL's shares had been used as security for hefty bank loans. To maintain their buoyancy, the company engaged in 'two-sided trading', whereby shares were sold through one stockbroker and bought through another. While often this had no effect on the price, it would increase the turnover and enhance the marketability of the shares and improve the shares' image to the public.[19]

Fearful that investors were selling Carrian short in a market that dropped some 500 points in a three-month period in 1981, Carrian effectively propped up its own share price while the market lost 22 per cent of its value. During this period, while all stocks nosedived, CIL actually rose. Tan, exasperated that his assistant Amos Tse was not buying shares quickly enough, would snatch the phone and talk to the brokers himself, complaining that Tse was too slow.[20]

At the time, almost nothing was known about CHL's balance sheet or the identity of its true owners, Carrian Nominees. By early 1982, several big institutions were becoming wary of the public company, CIL. Their doubts were not so much centred on its mysterious origins but more so on whether the company, in a fluctuating property market, could continue to sustain its momentum and profit margin. While Tan made brilliant deals, the company was seen to lack proven and rigorous management standards. To counteract the criticism, Tan hired John Marshall, a partner for twenty-four years with the auditing firm of Price Waterhouse. Marshall, appointed by Tan to be Carrian's managing director and group chairman designate upon Tan's retirement, was a highly respected Hong Kong figure.

When Carrian Investments in its 1981 interim report announced a 40 per cent drop in net attributable profits from HK$440.7

million to HK$262.6 million, it hastened to add that much of the previous year's profits were due to the Gammon House sale. But investors learned that the Gammon House deal had never been completed. Tan bailed out the Lams and secured US$124 million from Bank of America who bought fifteen of the thirty-nine floors. The remaining space was divided between Tan's silent partner, Chung, the Lams and Carrian.

With the sobering news, Carrian made an optimistic forecast. A number of 'significant transactions' would be completed in the second half of 1981 and these would deliver profits in excess of HK$615 million. Tan badly needed to fuel investor confidence, for it was against the value of CIL's shares that he borrowed millions to build his empire. Carrian, in a bid for more time, pushed its financial year forward to 31 December.

To make good on the projection, CHL planned to transfer a large package of assets into CIL. These included the China Underwriters' stake bought earlier in 1981, and the office block, which would later become the Carrian Centre, on Gloucester Road in Wanchai. Carrian would also acquire a substantial stake in Union Bank, owned by CHL. To pay for the new assets, CIL issued 143 million shares to CHL.

Market conditions towards the end of 1981 and the first half of 1982 were not particularly favourable for unloading any more shares on to the public. CIL faced a dilemma: to get more funding it would need to sell shares, but to do so at this stage would depress the market. A share buy-back scheme was the answer.

In April 1982, merchant bankers Jardine Fleming placed 95 million CIL shares. Carrian Holdings Limited guaranteed the purchasers the right to sell the shares back to CHL the following year at a big premium over the purchase price. Unfortunately for the London institutions and Jardine associates who took most of the shares, there was no one to guarantee the guarantors.[21]

It was nearing the end of the year and Tan had yet to make

good on his promise to CIL shareholders. He decided it was time to sell his minority stake in Union Bank in the hopes that it would boost CIL's earnings. On New Year's Eve, the Lam brothers came to Carrian's rescue, purchasing 17 million Union Bank shares for nearly twice their value, netting Carrian a profit of HK$313 million.[22] The deal, agreed on deferred terms, was secured by an 'unconditional bank guarantee'.

Perceived as a confidence boost for Carrian, the deal was, in fact, an elaborate window-dressing exercise. Statements made in the 1981 CIL annual report about the Union Bank transaction later became the grounds for criminal charges brought against Tan in October 1983. A banker who met with Rogerio Lam of Bylamson described in court how Lam admitted never paying 'one single penny' to Carrian for 17.2 million Union Bank shares.[23]

By mid-1982, the situation had worsened. In an interim report, Carrian announced profits of HK$269 million. Seventy-five per cent of it was from the late-June sale, on deferred terms, of four residential buildings in Hong Kong to undisclosed 'overseas investors'. As with other pivotal Carrian transactions, this deal was never completed. By the late summer of 1982, Carrian, dangerously geared and financially extended beyond logical means of survival, was in serious need of cash. Its huge property stake was rapidly becoming a liability.

In 1980 1.3 million square feet of office space had been built in Central district, more than the combined total of the previous four years. As Central and Tsimshatsui vibrated to the sounds of pile drivers, the face of Hong Kong changed beyond recognition. The old Hong Kong and Shanghai Banking Corporation headquarters came down, replaced by an extravagant new headquarters. The venerable Hong Kong Club vanished as mirror-skinned skyscrapers rose up, jostling up-market neighbours for square feet and tenants.

During 1982, vacant office space increased by 80 per cent, signalling the beginning of the end of the property boom. Rents and capital values plummetted. The gold-shrouded Far East Finance Centre was especially hard hit. In February 1982, a floor in the building was bought for HK$4,300 a square foot. Seven months later, the price was slashed to HK$2,550. Soon, companies holding portfolios of trading properties could not get rid of them fast enough. The stock-market was awash with property shares, making new equity issues impossible. Market turnover, meanwhile, was down to half of 1981 levels and falling.

Banks and deposit-taking companies (DTCs) which had generously extended credit to property traders and developers were feeling the pinch. The news of their exposure started some of the worst runs in the history of Hong Kong. At the end of the day, more than a dozen DTCs would go under and eight banks would change hands. 'It was like an outbreak of the measles,' recalls banking commissioner Robert Fell, 'only slightly more dangerous.'

By the autumn of 1982 the situation turned more grim. Margaret Thatcher visited Beijing in September to renegotiate Hong Kong's lease – due to expire in 1997 – from the Chinese government. The talks went badly. Thatcher's post-negotiations visit to Hong Kong failed to allay fears that China would regain control of the colony. The uncertainty over the future of Hong Kong created a devastating economic whiplash in the stock-market. Within a week, the Hang Seng index fell 170 points, losing one-fifth of its value. By December the stock-market's pre-Thatcher visit high of 986.36 would shrink to an all-time low of 676 points. At the same time, the Hong Kong dollar, the barometer of people's confidence, skidded to 9.20 against the US dollar, its late 1970s value severed in half. 'A lot of people felt Hong Kong had come to the end of its good days,' remembers Gerald Dobby of the Hong Kong Bank.

In light of the political uncertainty, investors were reluctant to sink money into fixed assets and the property market rather quickly dried up. Carrian had difficulty selling any properties, let alone the China Underwriters' Centre that it desperately needed to unload to service its debts. To compound its problem, Carrian's share price by mid-autumn fell to HK$1.50, down from almost HK$8 the year before. In October, Carrian announced 'temporary liquidity difficulties', causing the Hang Seng index to fall almost 10 per cent. It cancelled its interim dividend and turned to its bankers to formulate a rescheduling of its debt that it hoped would save it from liquidation. The restructuring, conducted by Wardley and Hambros, was full of revelations.

The new balance sheets for the group bore little or no relation to previously published figures. The value of CIL's assets was scarcely more than what would be required to pay its debts. Shares in CIL were therefore practically worthless. The result being that its parent, CHL, had virtually no assets to offset its own substantial borrowings.

The first reaction from banks was cool. The Hong Kong Bank, while keeping quiet about its own exposure to Carrian (estimated at the time to be between HK$1 billion to HK$2 billion), explained to the press that 'not very much' debt needed rescheduling. But Wardley's report, issued in January 1983, revealed a teetering empire on the brink of collapse. Together, CIL and CHL owed lenders HK$4.3 billion, but CIL's subsidiaries, such as Grand Marine, were also highly geared. The total group debt appeared to be a staggering US$1 billion.

In the wake of these revelations, some bankers who had refused loans to Carrian gloated. 'Would you lend money to a thing called "Outwit"?' asked one foreign banker, 'I'd turn them down just on the name alone.'[24] Chase Manhattan didn't see the humour. It was stuck with two million worthless CIL shares used to cover a HK$50 million Carrian loan.

One final deal emerged as a possible means of saving the conglomerate. It involved the purchase of China Underwriters' and Union Bank shares by a company called Fleuret. The only hitch was that Fleuret needed to borrow US$4 million in order to complete the deal. As with so many other transactions, Tan turned to Bumiputra Finance for the best terms in town. The man tasked with approving the loan was a gentle-faced new general manager, Jalil Ibrahim.

Jalil had just returned from home-leave the day his assistant, Henry Chin, placed the loan papers on his desk with the warning that there was a 4:30 p.m. signing deadline. If the loan went through, Carrian would receive US$4 million, an amount vital to creditors' desperate salvage operation on the shaking conglomerate. Without it, Carrian drew ever closer to liquidation proceedings.[25]

Around noontime, Jalil received a telephone call from a man identifying himself as Ibrahim Mohamed, a prominent Malaysian businessman. He was staying in Hong Kong and needed to cash some traveller's cheques, and asked Jalil, if he would, to meet him at his hotel. Jalil collected some HK$35,000 in traveller's cheques, tucked the notes inside a brief-case and made his way to the elegant Regent hotel in Kowloon.

Mak Foon Than, a small-time businessman from Kuala Lumpur, who sought credibility through links with Malaysian VIPs, was to admit later in court that he had placed the call to Jalil, using Tan Sri Ibrahim's name. Mak, a Malaysian citizen, and his wife had checked into the Hotel Regal Meridian, Hong Kong airport, on 7 July. While still registered there, Mak checked into the Regent hotel on 18 July. He did not carry any luggage.[26] In his statement to police, Mak allegedly said he took a room at the Regent on instructions from a Korean named 'Shin'. The Korean carried a Thai passport and said his boss was 'George'. The police asked Mak who 'George' was, and he replied George Tan.[27]

Mak told police he had had a telephone conversation with a man who identified himself as George Tan early in the afternoon of the 18th. In court it was alleged Mak remarked that, during his conversation, Tan complained that Jalil was a 'pain in the arse' and an 'obstacle' to his efforts to obtain a large loan from

Bumiputra Finance.[28] According to Mak's statement, Tan told him that Jalil wasn't co-operating in the loan negotiations.

Shortly after Mak checked into the Regent, Jalil arrived. The two men met in the hotel foyer and went up to Mak's room, ordered coffee and, after a while, some lunch from the room-service menu. During Jalil's visit, there was a 'Do Not Disturb' sign on the door.

While Jalil was meeting with Mak at the Regent, George Tan and his principal assistant, Bentley Ho, and Henry Chin, gathered in the boardroom of Bumiputra Finance, near Hong Kong's Central district. Over lunch, the two Carrian executives produced a letter from Fitarget that detailed how the loan was to be disbursed. During later testimony, Chin described how one of the signatures on the letter belonged to Mr Tan. The letter, he said, was addressed to Bumiputra Finance's general manager, Ibrahim Jaafar. But because Ibrahim was on holiday during July, Chin and Jalil would have to take care of the proposal. Chin explained to Tan and Ho that he had not been informed about the loan, but suggested to the Carrian pair that he would be in a better position to act on it if ordered to do so by Lorrain Osman, chairman of Bumiputra Finance.

After lunch, Tan and Ho went to the Hilton hotel to see Osman, who, conveniently, had arrived in Hong Kong over the weekend. Chin would later assert that Osman made the trip specifically to oversee the loan. At 2:30 p.m., Ho arrived at Bumiputra Finance's office and produced the letter for Chin. This time the letter bore the instruction from Osman, 'Henry, please proceed to implement immediately.'[29]

At about 3 p.m., Chin and Ho were going over the loan to Fitarget when Jalil called from Mak's hotel room. Jalil asked Chin to describe what was taking place at the office. Chin told Jalil that Bumiputra Finance's chairman, Lorrain Osman, had issued instructions that the proposed US$4 million loan to Fitarget be approved immediately.[30] Jalil wanted to know if the parent bank's five-man supervisory committee in Kuala Lumpur

264

had approved the loan. The committee had been formed in June 1983 to supervise the Hong Kong subsidiary. Prior to its formation, Osman had the power alone to approve Bumiputra Finance's loans. The new protocol meant that the Hong Kong unit had to contact one of three Bank Bumiputra officers before any loans could be granted. These included the chairman of the parent bank, Nawawi Mat Awin, the bank's executive director, Datuk Mohamed Hashim Shamsuddin, and the adviser to the bank, Wong Aun Phui.

Jalil, according to court records, questioned Chin about authorisation for the loan from Bank Bumiputra. He told Chin to review carefully the new loan procedures. Chin suggested that the bank's board may have authorised Osman to handle the Fitarget transaction. He urged Jalil to return to the office as soon as possible. Preparations for the loan continued in Jalil's absence.

Tan joined Ho at the Bumiputra Finance office shortly after 3:30 p.m. Chin remembers the Carrian chairman as 'irritated' because the loan hadn't been released and that the 4:30 p.m. deadline was fast approaching. Chin says he tried to stall the two to allow time for Jalil to return, but arranged with another bank officer to have the funds ready for release.[31]

At about 4:10 p.m. Chin left the boardroom and went to his office where he received a second call from Jalil, who was still in Mak's room at the Regent. Chin asked urgently when Jalil was coming back. Jalil replied, 'in a little while'. Chin told him that Tan was already in the boardroom and said completion of the loan arrangements couldn't be delayed much longer.[32] Once again, Chin urged him to come back to the office. Jalil said, 'Hold on a minute. . . .' And suddenly the line went dead. It was the last Chin would hear of Jalil. Chin stayed on the line for half a minute, he says, because he believed the line had been cut. Then, after thinking things through on his own for a few minutes, he decided to authorise the loan. The funds were transferred to an account with Bank of Communications.[33]

The next morning, Chin met Osman at the chairman's room at the Hilton hotel. Chin, in his testimony, told a court that Osman had instructed him to record the previous day's loan to Fitarget as a 'money market' transaction. He added that Osman explained 'this would be resolved' when Osman returned to Malaysia.[34] Jalil failed to come into the office Tuesday.

The following day, 20 July, Chin tried to contact him but to no avail. He informed the police of Jalil's disappearance and gave a detailed description of his colleague. Later that afternoon, homicide detectives requested Chin to come to the morgue to view a body discovered on Tuesday. A man had been brutally strangled and his body dumped in a remote banana grove near Tai Po Kao in the New Territories. The slain man, said Chin, was Jalil Ibrahim.

Michael Farnham, head of the Commercial Crime Bureau (CCB), assigned detective inspector Michael Rawlinson to assist the OSCB homicide investigation. Rawlinson, a unique blend of banker, cop and intelligence gatherer, was a natural choice. Paunchy, armed with a sense of humour and notable discretion, Rawlinson moves in Hong Kong's banking circles with a business card that, unlike most cops', is elegantly understated. The script is the same as an embassy drinks-party invitation and, instead of the crest of the Royal Hong Kong Police, it bears a subtle embossed 'PHQ', as in Police Headquarters.

Before joining the CCB in the early 1980s, Rawlinson worked for a while at the Hong Kong and Shanghai Bank in London, after which he spent three years in the foreign exchange department of Kleinwort Benson. In 1976, frustrated by the time constraints of his job, he left banking and the UK. Rawlinson travelled to Hong Kong and joined the Marine Police, and shortly thereafter, reported to Special Branch. It wasn't long before his combined banking and law-enforcement experience gained him a senior position in the CCB.

Rawlinson joined the homicide team in its pursuit for Jalil's assailant by first searching the office of Bumiputra Finance. Jalil had kept an extensive diary, jotting everything down that happened to him on the job with corresponding dates and times. At about 5 p.m. on the day of the search, Rawlinson located the diary and spotted the progression of a loan that looked highly suspicious. He sought guidance from a banking contact and then met with Farnham. Rawlinson had reason to believe that the investigation could evolve into a full fraud enquiry and he requested back up.

Farnham put Martin Barklem on to the case. Barklem, fair-haired, tall, tanned and athletic, had received an external law degree from London University and had experience in the Navy before joining the CCB. Together with Rawlinson, Barklem began piecing together Jalil's working pattern. 'It all focused on Jalil's notebook,' recalls Barklem. 'We tracked down all the people he'd been speaking to in the last few days. We pulled all of the loan files relating to any of those individuals or their companies.'

Barklem and Rawlinson studied credit valuations and with the assistance of willing bank employees and the absence of both Jaafar and Osman, the two inspectors were left alone to go through the paperwork. Round-the-clock uniformed guards watched to make sure no documents were smuggled out.

At Bumiputra Finance, located in Admiralty Towers, Barklem noticed that the chairman's office, adjacent to the boardroom, was filled with boxes of Carrian and Grand Marine share certificates that would normally be kept under lock and key. 'The administration,' says Barklem, 'was appalling.'

Despite the fact that trading in Carrian shares had been suspended, to Barklem it indicated that normal banking procedures were being ignored. In many instances, Barklem and Rawlinson learned, Bumiputra Finance did not have any recourse if the loans went bad, since they were basically unsecured.

'Jalil's job was to try and tighten up on all the security that had been promised for all the loans that had been granted,' says Barklem. 'Someone, somewhere up the line must have realised what was going on and said, "It's gone too far."'

In the early days of the investigation, Rawlinson and Barklem worked from Police Headquarters on Arsenal Street in Wanchai, a grey fortress complete with gun turrets. 'We were working under the guidance of the OSCB,' says Barklem. 'Whenever you get a homicide, it ranks above all other cases,' says Barklem, including fraud. 'Especially when there's a guy out on the loose.'

Rawlinson and Barklem sought assistance from Robert Tang, QC, and Michael Johnson, a senior partner at Arthur Andersen, the inspectors appointed by the Securities Commission, who had been investigating Carrian since April in the wake of suspect property deals. Primarily Tang and Johnson were looking into the credit worthiness of Carrian during rescue talks held between Robert Fell and creditor banks. Rawlinson and Barklem hoped Tang and Johnson would be versed in the relationship between the Carrian Group and Bumiputra Finance.

'Mike and I both realised that there was something very wrong with the whole way the bank was operating,' recalls Barklem. 'These Carrian loan files simply had ... in many cases, a single one-page report, giving details of the nominal capital of the company ... but no form of real evaluation.'

Barklem and Rawlinson zeroed in on the US$4 million loan that Jalil had been working on the day he was murdered. 'It was required by the escrow deed that it would be made on that day,' recalls Barklem, 'otherwise the whole thing fell apart and possibly the whole Carrian restructuring would have fallen apart. . . . Basically, the whole thing was on a knife-edge. . . . Obviously, we were vitally interested in what we felt was this very crucial sum of money.'

Barklem, Rawlinson, Tang and Johnson occupied the OSCB's

welfth-floor exhibits room, mounting a paper chase through undreds of documents, for the financial motive behind the nurder. Eventually, due to the volume of documents, the four noved up to the nineteenth floor, taking over a conference oom that belonged to the Deputy Director of Crime. In a natter of weeks, they had literally moved into the command ost of the entire Criminal Investigation Department.

'It was obviously getting big,' says Barklem. 'At that stage .. it became a distinct commercial crime investigation as vell as a homicide.' Rawlinson and Barklem 'straddled the ence', digging for leads for both the CCB and the OSCB. 'hings began to click. 'Once we'd discovered that there was n obvious flaw in the whole thing,' says Barklem, 'it looked s though Carrian money was being used to fund a supposed hird-party purchaser. In other words, Carrian was paying itself, vhich seemed incredible.'

Rawlinson and Barklem decided it was time to begin inter- iewing the principals in the case. On 31 July, ten days after he CCB had been put on the case, the two investigators took statement from Lorrain Osman. Three days later, the OSCB, oncluding its man-hunt for Jalil's murderer, arrested Mak Foon Than on 3 August. Than, hearing police knocking at the door, umped out his third-floor window, fracturing his pelvis. Held n a guarded hospital room, Mak recuperated in time for a trial ome eight months away. Before the case was heard, lawyers epresenting George Tan would petition to have the trial held n camera.

Less than a week after Mak's arrest, Rawlinson and Barklem nterviewed George Tan and his chief assistant, Bentley Ho. 'ollowing a review of the transcripts, the CCB executed search- varrants on Bumiputra Finance for the following weekend. After the search, two more detectives, Rod Starling and Roger toker, sorted through documents on the nineteenth floor at olice headquarters. Starling spotted a circular diagram jotted n a piece of paper. He passed it to Stoker. His reaction was instant: 'Bloody hell! I've seen this type of thing before.' Starling knew what Stoker was getting at.

'It was a sketch of a round robin of payments in the purchas of China Underwriters, that basically meant that technicall HK$230 million had been lent to Carrian,' says Starling. 'But a soon as China Underwriters had been purchased, the HK$23 million went back to Bumiputra Finance, so there was n substance to the transaction. When this money went back t Bumiputra, China Underwriters was left hollow.

'Indirectly, it looked as if Carrian had got a lot of money an was still quite intent on increasing its empire,' says Starling 'Secondly, China Underwriters, a public company in its ow right, looked as if it was cash rich. As such, it looked to al intents and purposes from the outside an interesting and legiti mate deal.'

China Underwriters Limited, an old-established insuranc firm (whose stock Carrian would seek to sell to Fleuret), wa bought over a period of time between June and Decembe 1981. The December transaction was when the $230 millio purportedly changed hands. Stoker had seen a similar patter in an earlier sensational case concerning Moscow Narodn Bank and businessman Amos Dawe. Both Stoker and Starlin described their discovery in a memo to Philip Layton. It state their belief that China Underwriters had been purchased b Carrian on a fraudulent basis. Starling's and Stoker's find woul become one of the focal points of the Carrian investigation.

When Layton, assistant superintendent of the CCB, read th memo, he realized that in order to obtain sufficient evidence o the transaction, there would have to be a search of the Carria offices. As more evidence from BMFL was gathered, the CC case became more airtight. The CCB began to focus its attentio on Carrian transactions. Rapidly it prepared for the biggest rai in its history.

In preparation for the execution of the 10 September search warrants on Carrian, the CCB turned to accountants Arthu

Andersen & Co. for professional advice. The firm soon became indispensable to the CCB, later appointed officially by the Director of Public Prosecutions to assist in the investigation.

Carrian had grown on the strengths and weaknesses of Hong Kong's most revered professional firms. The police were not only preparing to pull the curtain down on Carrian but also on key establishment figures. For all their planning, they could never have prepared for the storm on the horizon.

Typhoon Ellen's direct hit on Hong Kong in September 1983 was especially brutal. Gale-force winds with maximum speeds of 120 knots per hour pummelled the colony for three days. At the typhoon's peak, Robert Fell, Hong Kong's avuncular commissioner of banking, was scheduled to meet with the chairman and directors of the Carrian Group.

In January 1983, trading in Carrian stock had ceased in the wake of 'liquidity problems'. Now, nine months later, Fell was in the middle of orchestrating a final rescue package geared to provide assurance to panicked bankers who had loaned Carrian US$1.2 billion. In the midst of the typhoon, the meeting was postponed. 'Hong Kong,' says Fell, 'came to a complete standstill.'

In Kowloon's normally bustling Tsimshatsui district, neon signs that adorned hundreds of souvenir shops exploded like shrapnel. Shards of glass and overturned cars littered storm-swept streets. Winds ripped apart bamboo scaffolding, hurling fifteen-foot javelins through the air. Power outages plunged Hong Kong and its dazzling harbour into darkness. Anchor chains snapped, sending leviathans, such as the *Jin Hai*, a 21,000-ton Chinese cargo ship, aground. Other ships, unharnessed by vanishing docks, simply went out of control. Robert Johnson, a former CCB senior inspector, recalls seeing vessels 'doing cartwheels down the harbour'.

Johnson, a native of Shropshire, is a burly, moustached man in his early thirties. He spent the last night of typhoon Ellen gripping the French windows of his flat, in an attempt to keep them from blowing away. Bleary-eyed and exhausted, the next morning Johnson heard the number 10 typhoon signal had finally been lowered, a sign that the worst was over. Five minutes later, the phone rang. It was headquarters. The raid, he was told, was still on.

In the early morning hours before Johnson answered the call, detective inspector Martin Barklem put on a pair of flip-flops, shorts and a crash helmet. With the number 10 signal still hoisted, he had set out on foot, making his way from Braemer Hill to Victoria barracks. The CCB had for years been headquartered out of the old barracks, the base for the Commander Land Forces during the Second World War.

Being a bit of a romantic, Barklem had actually enjoyed previous Hong Kong typhoons. This time, it was different. Barklem was a key organiser of a full-scale commercial raid. The CCB's reputation would be pinned to its success or failure.

The autumn 1983 raid on Carrian and related companies was the result of several official investigations conducted by the CCB, the Securities Commission, the OSCB and the Independent Commission Against Corruption (ICAC). The duration and sheer force of typhoon Ellen meant that the raid, originally scheduled for 9 September, would have to be postponed. It was up to Barklem and a chosen few to reschedule and reorganise the entire event. Orchestrating the biggest commercial raid in Hong Kong history was difficult enough, comparable to an opening night at Covent Garden or a full-scale military invasion. But now there were hundreds of details that had to be re-examined. Ellen would be the first typhoon Barklem would grow to hate.

As he walked down littered boulevards and picked his way through narrow alleys, Barklem had a million things on his mind, namely what to do the next morning with 300 police officers, investigators and accountants. As he revamped the operational order in his head, the typhoon picked up strength

By the time it had passed, six people would be dead and the homes of more than 1,000 destroyed.

The wind still howled as the team of senior inspectors, Barklem, Johnson, Rod Starling, Mike Rawlinson and Roger Stoker, led by Philip Layton, reviewed search-warrants and finalised orders for raids on fourteen separate locations. These included banks, solicitors, finance houses, and an accountancy firm, all connected in some way to Carrian.

For these simultaneous raids, scheduled to begin Saturday morning, 10 September, police would execute the first of 365 search-warrants involving Carrian-related firms. For seventy-two hours, 170 CCB investigators, backed up by a team of chartered accountants and 120 members of Hong Kong's riot squad, would seize thousands of documents. There was no way that the group of senior officers could have anticipated what they were stepping into. For the moment, all that mattered was getting the creases out of the operational orders. Later that afternoon, the group broke up and headed for home and a good night's rest.

By nightfall, the typhoon had subsided. Bob Fell rescheduled his meeting with Carrian creditors. He was eager to share news of vital importance. The next morning Fell revealed that a major Carrian creditor withheld information about loans to the Carrian Group. The amount loaned exceeded HK$4 billion. He explained to the group that this particular creditor bank had been pursuing ways to improve its own security position outside the rescue scheme formulated by Wardleys and Hambros, the financial advisers of Carrian.[35] Until the raid, there had been an agreement, reluctantly reached by all known creditor banks, to scale down and stretch out Carrian's debt.

Fell's bombshell was a letter from George Tan to Bumiputra Finance. It was dated 15 January 1983:

> It is for the protection of your bank that we have not included your bank in a loan reduction program. We thought we have a great moral obligation to do so, since

our relationship is well established, long-term and world-wide. In other words, if anything happens in Carrian-Hong Kong, your exposure is still protected by overseas assets which by that time, we have taken out from the Hong Kong Companies of Carrian, which will be 'tightly controlled by committee' (as you quoted in your letter). . . . We do not want to put too much details or a time table for all these to happen. The above description is a very confidential strategy which should not be discussed or disclosed to other parties. So please keep this confidential only to your Board and if possible, destroy this letter afterwards.[36]

Fell wanted everyone present to provide urgent explanation for the matters raised in the letter, with particular attention to the understatement of the Carrian Group debt and the apparent preference shown to BMFL by at least George Tan.

While the letter raised eyebrows in the banking commissioner's office, at Victoria barracks, three platoons from the tactical unit, Hong Kong's standing riot squad, pulled up in wire-meshed, heavy goods vehicles, draped with faded green tarpaulins. The group of 120 'blue berets' were joined by the full strength of the CCB, over 170 officers and a dozen investigative accountants from Arthur Andersen. As the briefing began, operational orders were passed out to various section heads. To curtail any leaks, once the group assembled, all phone lines at the barracks were disconnected.

Layton delivered some background on Carrian and explained that the reason the CCB was raiding the company and related firms resulted from an on-going investigation into allegations of fraud. At this stage, in order to continue its investigation, Layton said, the CCB required further documentary evidence believed to be located in offices throughout the colony. 'It had to be totally co-ordinated,' remembers Johnson. 'This was the first major case we'd had. Everyone, from the Attorney General down to the lorry drivers, knew it was big.'

At end of the day, those in positions of power who had staked reputations on Tan's Carrian empire would become central characters in the most sensational, if not surreal trial in Hong Kong's history. Their standards of operation, in a place that cherishes secrecy, would be closely scrutinised. The raid conducted on the heels of a typhoon fuelled an investigation that uncovered the winners and losers of an alleged $1.2 billion fraud.

On a Saturday following the raid, Phil Layton was having lunch in Tsimshatsui with his wife and daughter. 'My pager went,' he recalls. 'It was Mike Farnham. He said, "There's a meeting in an hour's time in the Attorney General's office. Be there." I said, "Look, I'm not really dressed." "It doesn't matter," he said. "Be there."

'I rolled up there in my flip-flops, T-shirt and shorts. The AG (Attorney General) Michael Thomas was sitting next to his predecessor, John Griffiths. The Commissioner for the ICAC was there, the Commissioner of Police, the Director of Public Prosecutions, Mike Farnham and the Director of Operations. They were discussing whether there was sufficient evidence . . . what we should do. The sharp end of the stick is this: If the police had reasonable suspicion that a criminal offence had been committed, obviously, one has the power and the right to arrest. It's a question of timing.

'The Attorney General asked me: "Do you think you have reasonable suspicion to arrest George Tan and Bentley Ho as directors of Carrian? Do you think you can investigate this case . . . in a reasonable period of time?"

'What do you do?' asks Layton. 'They put you right on the spot with everyone there. I said, "Yes." Although in three to four months after that, I thought, You fool. You should have said "No"!'

Layton had every reason to regret his decision. 'People were running a mile from this,' recounts Richard Parry, Deputy Chief Inspector on the case. 'Shareholders were embarrassed to death for putting their life-savings in this crap. Nobody wanted to know. There was a lot of righteous indignation, but to say George Tan was brilliant and lose money, was just too much. . . .'

While the banking commission was trying to make Carrian come clean, or risk the abandonment of a final rescue package, Bentley Ho booked a seat on a plane to Kuala Lumpur. It was a Sunday afternoon, the day before the rescue deadline. He was carrying the value of HK$4,500 in US, Hong Kong, Singapore and Malaysian dollars when he was detained by Hong Kong immigration authorities at Kai Tek airport. Whether Ho was fleeing the colony or attempting to put together an eleventh-hour statement of Carrian's Bank Bumiputra accounts will probably never be known. When immigration contacted the CCB, the charges that the police had been working on since Jalil's murder were suddenly put into motion.

For the police it was an all-too-familiar scenario. An investigation heats up and a principal suspect exits to parts unextraditable. Ho was cautioned and handcuffed. His arrest would be meaningless, in the light of conspiracy charges, without similar action taken against Tan.

Earlier, Tan had mentioned that it would be quite simple for him to leave Hong Kong by sailing his yacht to one of his ships. Eventually, Rod Starling found Tan at the headquarters of the Independent Commission Against Corruption where Tan had been requested to report in connection with his arrest in April on bribery charges. Because the ICAC never disclose on-going investigations, when Starling later arrested him on CCB charges, the public learned for the first time of his previous scrape with the ICAC. Before he was handcuffed, Tan, dressed in a white T-shirt, pink jacket and a pair of baggy grey trousers, handed Starling a letter stating that he would not talk to police. It included details of his solicitors.

On Monday, 3 October 1983, Tan, 49, and Ho, 36, were

harged with violating Section 21 of Hong Kong's theft ordinance. Under the section, it is illegal for a director to 'deceive members or creditors' of his company about its affairs, or to publish 'misleading, false or deceptive' written statements or accounts. Ho was also charged with false accounting under Section 19 of the theft ordinance. Under this section it is illegal to destroy, deface, conceal or falsify' company accounts, or make misleading, false or deceptive entries in a company account or document. The two faced up to seven years' imprisonment.

The Hang Seng stock index reacted to the news by falling to its lowest level of the year, dropping more than forty points on Monday to close at 715.01. In court the following day, crown prosecutor Warrick Reid outlined the charges by stating that Carrian had sold shares in Union Bank of Hong Kong Ltd to Bylamson & Associates for HK$481 million on 31 December 1981 and that a HK$144-million deposit had been paid and the rest covered by a bank guarantee. The deposit, alleged the Crown, was a fiction and Ho falsified records to maintain the fiction. The 'deception' of the sale enabled Carrian to obtain additional loans.[37] Reid said further charges would be brought in connection with the 'sale' of China Underwriters' Centre to Bylamson. The prosecution alleged that 40 per cent of CIL's announced profit of HK$313 million for 1981 did not exist.

Reid told a magistrates' court there was 'evidence of a systematic scheme of deception and fraud' in relation to the rescue proposals. Reid said creditor banks had been 'induced' to join in the plans because Carrian had understated its debt. The prosecution announced that total debts of the Carrian Group came to HK$10 billion or US$1.2 billion, compared to the HK$6 billion previously indicated to creditor banks. Reid explained that in addition, HK$4.6 billion was owed to Bumiputra Finance by the Group (including Tan's private companies) and that of this total, HK$2 billion remained totally unaccounted for.[38]

Tan had been living illegally in Hong Kong since September

1972, said Reid. In addition, his Singapore passport had expired and his Paraguayan and Tongan passports would eventually provoke Singapore later to renounce his citizenship. The prosecution feared that Tan would abscond and, when he was ordered by the magistrate to be released on bail of HK$2 million, the prosecution, following an appeal to the Supreme Court, was able to have Tan's bail raised to HK$50 million, which was a record. Tan was required to pay a HK$2-million bond as part of his bail and, like Bentley Ho, who had to pay a HK$1-million bond and was on HK$1-million bail, was required to report to the police on a daily basis.

In court, Tan, who had spent the night in jail, looked drawn and haggard. His attorney, Michael Sherrard, called the prosecutor's court presentation 'absurd' and 'lurid' and accused Reid of trying to 'intimidate the court' into not granting bail for his client. Sherrard said it was 'just a little premature' to refer to the demise of the Carrian empire. 'It's totally wrong and unjust to make the assumption that the Carrian rescue operation is at an end.' The conglomerate, he said, 'hasn't collapsed and isn't in liquidation', and that 'no creditor has presented a petition to wind up' the group.[39]

Four days later, Saturday, 8 October, New York-based Bankers Trust Co., a Carrian creditor bank, filed a petition in Hong Kong's Supreme Court to wind up Carrian Investments Ltd. Accountants Arthur Young & Co. were immediately appointed provisional liquidators. The move was the final sign that the creditor banks had abandoned their rescue of Carrian. In a ten-minute liquidation hearing a month later, Carrian went down without a fight. By 7 November the empire was no more, having become the centre-piece in the biggest corporate failure in the history of Hong Kong.

Following the raid, the investigative team focused on conspiracy charges involving professionals linked to Carrian's suspect deals. During Carrian's hey-day, ten Price Waterhouse accountants moved over to Carrian,[40] Rodney Bell, a senior partner, became Carrian's finance director, and John Marshall, another senior partner at Price Waterhouse, became managing director and chairman designate.

Price Waterhouse accountants David Begg and Anthony Lo had been assigned to the 1981 audit of CIL's accounts. When they were interviewed by deputy chief inspector Stuart McDonald, both were viewed as potentially valuable witnesses for the prosecution. Before the meeting, Price Waterhouse's lawyers secured an agreement from the legal department that forbade police from making a recording of the interview. Instead, the lawyers would record the interviews and provide a transcript to the legal department. At the meeting, McDonald's assistant took notes, and, in accordance with the agreement, sent a draft to Price Waterhouse. In turn, Begg sent his version of the statement to McDonald, but important admissions in the earlier draft had been removed.

On 28 November 1983, McDonald and deputy inspector Richard Parry met with Begg and Tom Clydesdale, a senior partner at Price Waterhouse. For McDonald, who had listened to Begg's original statement, and realised its enormous value to the case, the version presented a whole new set of problems. The police investigation into the Price Waterhouse accountants heated up. In a short while Begg and Lo would no longer be witnesses but prime suspects.

For legal advice, Carrian had turned to Deacons Solicitors & Notaries Public, one of the largest and most prestigious firms in Hong Kong. In December, Rod Starling and deputy inspector Richard Parry served search-warrants on Peter Davies and John Wimbush of Deacons. Wimbush, a senior partner and past president of the Law Society of Hong Kong, strongly objected and requested that the police leave the warrants. Wimbush said documents would be supplied later. Starling refused and insisted that the documents requested be handed over immediately. Wimbush, visibly shaken, claimed that the documents were in storage and would take six weeks to retrieve. At that point, Russell Mason, superintendent of the CCB, joined Starling and Parry, and demanded the documents. Mason pointed out that 120 detectives were standing by to seal off and search Deacons. After redrafting their warrants, police eventually retrieved the documents, most of them the same night, the rest within a few days.

Police believed that Wimbush was directly involved in the creation of the complicated scheme that had enabled Carrian to announce the 'completion' of the sale of Gammon House to Bylamson for HK$1.68 billion, yielding a profit of HK$680 million. One of the intermediaries had been a company known as Wallop Investments, a company whose shareholders and directors were Deacons nominee companies: Anscode, Consade, Descona and Seconda, all anagrams of 'Deacons'.

By March, police had analysed evidence of the involvement of Deacons in the Gammon House transaction and drafted search-warrants for the homes of Wimbush and three other Deacons solicitors: Richard Wallis, Maurice Wong, who was on the board of China Underwriters, the publicly quoted Carrian subsidiary, and Simon Pun, whose name appeared on the Gammon House transaction.

At dawn on 4 April, police conducted raids on the solicitors' homes only to discover that Wimbush was in the UK on holiday and seeking legal advice, Wong was in the US receiving medical care for heart disease, and that Pun was nowhere to be found. Wallis was found and was placed on the immigration 'stop and detain' list. Wimbush was contacted in the UK by an associate and told that both he and Wallis were invited to assist police in their enquiries and, if they refused, they were to be arrested. Wallis assisted them by identifying some Carrian-related documents seized at Deacons. It was not until he was reached while on holiday that Wimbush fully realised the seriousness of the police probe.

Russ Mason made phone contact with Wimbush in the UK

and requested him to return to answer questions at the CCB regarding the Gammon House deal. The two men did not especially get along. Wimbush did not appreciate the effrontery of the police raiding his law firm. Mason did not fully trust Wimbush, but he respected him and assured Wimbush that he would not suffer the embarrassment of being detained at Kai Tak airport, since his name was not on the immigration 'stop list'. Unlike Wong and Pun who did not set foot back in Hong Kong, Wimbush came back of his own accord.

As immediate past president of the law society, Wimbush had considerable influence in Hong Kong. He was a local partner of Linklaters & Paines, the big London firm associated with Deacons. Wimbush, 46, was established, well respected, and known for his brilliance at conveyancing. He moved easily in Hong Kong's banking and business circles but his true dedication was to Deacons, where he had worked for the last twenty-two years.

His extraordinary loyalty to the firm coincided with his slight introversion, a product perhaps of a workaholic who found it hard to sleep at night. Wimbush took deep pride in his work and in the wake of the police investigation, he felt his reputation being threatened. When Rod Starling served the search-warrant on Wimbush back in December, Wimbush literally shook with rage. The police investigation into the firm was something Wimbush could not help but take personally. Deacons, said his colleagues, was his whole life.

On Wednesday, 11 April, Wimbush's wife, Julie, drove him to Gatwick. During the family holiday in the UK he had been depressed but he had told his wife it had to do with the uncertainty of Hong Kong's future. In Hong Kong, Wimbush's partner, John McClean, met him at Kai Tak airport. Wimbush seemed very depressed and looked unwell, as if he had not slept for days. He was tense and almost speechless. Wimbush took two sleeping tablets, and later when McClean spoke with him on the telephone at about 7:30 p.m. he seemed more relaxed.

In the afternoon, Wallis came by and spent an hour and a half with Wimbush, who he described as 'extremely tired and giving the impression of someone who had not slept for days'. He said Wimbush was unsteady on his feet, was depressed and their conversation, which focused on the Gammon House transaction, was full of Wimbush's 'long broody silences'.

During the afternoon, Wimbush's solicitor, Andrew Walker, contacted Mason to say that his client had returned, but was indisposed. A meeting was arranged for the following Monday. Wimbush never made it. In the early hours of Friday, 13 April, following an angry phone conversation with an unknown person, Wimbush allegedly committed suicide.

According to the coroner's verdict following an inquest into his death, Wimbush had tied a rope, attached to a 50 lb concrete manhole cover, around his neck. He then jumped into his swimming pool, and, unable to free himself, drowned. His body was found shortly after his death, at about 8:30 a.m.

Wimbush had left several apparent suicide notes. To his wife and family he wrote,

I have now had a further look at the situation and it's quite clear that I have acted honestly to the best of my ability. This transaction had gone so far wrong that nobody will ever believe me. I am afraid there is nothing that could be done. Your support over the last few days was wonderful and I drew a great strength from it . . . perhaps too much, as I should not have returned. The degree to which we are unprepared for this incident is I hope some comfort to you of my innocence. But I am afraid that long before that could be established, I should be in a quite hopeless position.

Wimbush's wife said the handwriting was neater than her husband's normal style and more horizontal.

To his partners, unnamed, he wrote,

I cannot find any words to express my sorrow and regret over our problems. A trial of this kind is not measured in days, weeks, or months but for years to come. What purpose is served if R.A.W. (business partner, Richard Allan Wallis) and I are acquitted in the end? Even if we are not ever charged, the problem is the same. So the end product is the same . . . we will be blamed for everything. I have no words to which I can express my grief. Hong Kong is my home and now I must stay here for ever.[41]

n a matter of weeks following Wimbush's death, Rod Starling liscovered the document that had undoubtedly caused the olicitor's extreme anxiety. Later known as the 'Wimbush Memorandum', it was a detailed formula outlining the highly uspect Gammon House transaction.

The news of Wimbush's violent death made public the CCB nvestigation into Carrian. It also acted as a reminder of the ther death associated with the Carrian saga. On 17 May, Mak Foon Than was convicted of murdering Jalil Ibrahim f Bumiputra Finance. Bank rescue plans for Tan's empire :ooled. In three days' time, a new drama in the Carrian saga vould unfold.

Following the advice of Harry Ognall, in agreement with the Director of Public Prosecutions, in consultation with Attorney General Michael Thomas, and on the recommendation of he CCB team, government prosecutors formally charged five nen with conspiracy to defraud shareholders and creditors f Carrian Investments Ltd. The accused were George Tan, Bentley Ho, Richard Wallis, junior partner at Deacons, David Begg and Anthony Lo, partner and auditor, respectively, at Price Waterhouse. The government also named as co-conspirators - but didn't charge - three other Deacons lawyers: Maurice Wong, Simon Pun and John Wimbush.

Leading off the indictments was the government accusation

that Tan and Ho and the Deacons lawyers committed a con
spiracy to defraud by failing to inform the public that the
Gammon House sale was not completed. The defendants were
also accused of 'creating and implementing a scheme designed
to conceal the true nature of the purported transaction'.

According to the second charge, CIL and the two Price
Waterhouse advisers made 'false and misleading statements'
on a number of 1981 transactions. Out of the HK$762 million
in profit that CIL reported, claimed the government, all bu
HK$95 million involved fraudulent accounting.

There were five separate deals involved in the third charge
The largest was the purported sale of Carrian's 17.2-million
shares of Union Bank of Hong Kong Ltd for a profit of HK$312
million. This transaction was the focus of fraud charges levied
against Tan and Ho in October when Warrick Reid alleged in
court that the sale never went through.

This time the government also accused CIL with faking a
profit of about HK$114 million from finance, management and
agency fees. It claimed Tan, Ho and the two Price Waterhouse
defendants were responsible for them. In addition, the four
faced charges in connection with the purchase in 1981 of
China Underwriters Life and General Insurance Co. Carrian
stated that it paid HK$230 million in cash for a 49 per cen
stake in China Underwriters. The government claimed tha
Tan, Ho, Begg and Lo failed to disclose that the sale actually
was made via an elaborate loan scheme. The government said
China Underwriters' own assets were used to secure the loan
for the purchase. All five faced maximum sentences of seven
years on each charge.

Preliminary arguments as to whether the defendants would
be required to stand trial were scheduled for the autumn. Bai
for each defendant was set at HK$100,000 cash. Wallis, Lo
and Begg had to post an additional HK$100,000 bond as
a means of ensuring their presence in court. Tan's record
HK$50 million bail and HK$2 million bond set in October

1983 would continue as well as Bentley Ho's HK$1-million bail and HK$1-million bond.

As the pressures mounted, the CCB and the prosecution worked at a fever pitch. Over one million documents would be submitted as evidence, but requests for copies from the defence, liquidators and the high court would multiply that number fivefold. Of those, the prosecution would also submit 6,000 exhibits to prove its case. 'No one could begin to conceive of the impact of Carrian,' recalls Parry.

When CIL first went into liquidation in October after the raid in 1983, Arthur Young sent out 500 telexes to banks and financial institutions, instructing them to freeze CIL's accounts. Arthur Young moved next to sell CIL's assets, most of which were property. In the middle of the liquidation proceedings, Arthur Andersen senior partner Ian Robinson, and his counterpart, Brian Stevenson, senior partner at Ernst and Whinney (who conducted the liquidation of Carrian Holdings Limited), made an amazing discovery. Tan had in his possession the Star of Asia, a 53.62-carat diamond pendant. The diamond was kept with Tan's mother in Singapore. The liquidators sold it to a Swiss dealer for US$2 million. 'It was a magnificent diamond,' says Robinson.

The gem was a highlight in an otherwise nightmarish liquidation. Robinson had 219 creditors with whom to negotiate settlements. In the beginning, Arthur Young geared up for the Carrian liquidation, one of the largest in history, by forming a team of sixty-five accountants. Extracting funds to pay off creditors was especially complicated as firms under group parent, Carrian Holdings Ltd, totalled 680. With still no end in sight by mid-1986, Arthur Young had spent 91,000 man-hours sorting through 5 million pages of documents, pertaining to the liquidation of CIL.

While Stevenson and Robinson both claim to have found the Star of Asia, Stevenson, in his efforts to seize assets on behalf of over 100 CHL creditors, decided to hold an auction, placing

Carrian and Tan's opulent furnishings under the hammer.

Stevenson raised cash by not only selling the paintings, marble statues, fountains and furniture but also by securing funds for oddities, such as an elevator that unexpectedly showed up in a Hong Kong parking lot, gold-plated sink taps with no sinks and nine million ceramic tiles. The search for Carrian assets opened Stevenson's eyes to a degree of opulence he compared to Adnan Khashoggi's yacht, *Nabila*. The proceeds of the furnishing auction that included a German grandfather clock, Italian-made French 'boudoir' furniture and Hong-Kong-made Ching dynasty pieces totalled HK$2.1 million, a drop in the bucket of CHL's estimated HK$3 billion debt.

To fortify their case against the accountants, the prosecution appointed Lord Henry Alexander Benson as an expert witness. Lord Benson, an adviser to Coopers & Lybrand, is regarded as a world leading authority on accountancy practices and has been appointed to several key commissions, including the UK Fraud Trials committee chaired by Lord Roskill.

Traditionally, in large fraud trials, conspiracy charges are favoured by prosecutors because of the amount of evidence that can be submitted in court. Also, says Johnson, 'Substantive charges, such as false accounting, property by deception and so on, are harder to prove. Each element of the offence has to be proved so it's harder. There is also little chance for concurrence. Conspiracy,' he says on the other hand, 'is easier to prove. All you have to do, basically, is show a story taking place and two people doing an unlawful act.'

The committal generated enormous interest. It had been postponed several times. Both sides were eager for justice to be served. Assuring the press of its opening date, Hong Kong's financial secretary, Sir John Brembridge, said, 'Let the bombs fall where they may.'

Representing the prosecution at the committal proceedings were Harry Ognall QC, senior assistant Crown prosecutor

John Sulan, senior Crown counsel Clive Grossman and Crown counsel Mark Rice.

It was the first time detailed evidence against the accused was presented and, in many ways, if the magistrate, Brian Suttill, ruled there was a case to answer, it would vindicate the prosecution's case. The committal was valuable: namely, it was a dress rehearsal for all of the evidence that the prosecution hoped would appear in the high-court trial. Suttill's opinion, following six months of testimony, would make or break the Crown's case. During the six-month-long proceedings, testimony would be heard from fifty-four witnesses. On the afternoon of 9 April 1985, Brian Suttill delivered his verdict.

He said the acquisition of China Underwriters' shares by CIL was, 'prima facie, an audacious fraud of breathtaking proportions'. He stated that testimony from Rodney Bell and John Marshall was 'objectively unbelievable'. But Bell and Marshall had been granted immunities.

For the defence counsel witnessing the proceedings, the two veteran Price Waterhouse accountants, in particular Bell, were of enormous interest. At the end of the day, Bell would become the perfect fall guy for the defence.

Turning to the Gammon House transactions, Suttill said, 'The evidence establishes that there was no sale of Gammon House to Bylamson. What there was instead was an elaborate charade, stage managed by the four named conspirators: Tan, Ho and the Lam brothers.'

Regarding David Begg and Anthony Lo, the Price Waterhouse accountants, Suttill said evidence established that the 1981 accounts they audited presented an untrue and unfair view. 'So unfair, untrue and misleading is the view that CIL, far from being the fast-growing, dynamic, going-concern shown by the accounts, was at 31 December 1981 teetering on the edge of bankruptcy.' He added that the false and misleading nature of the accounts was directly attributable to the six overt acts listed and established by evidence.

Acknowledging the presentation in court of various accounting guidelines, Suttill said, 'I make only one observation. When the view by the accounts is so divorced from the reality, it does not matter whose guidelines, standards or the like that have been used to achieve that view, those guidelines and standards are wrong.' He ruled that George Tan, Bentley Ho, Richard Wallis, David Begg and Anthony Lo all had a case to answer.

Preparations for the high-court trial began in earnest following the committal. For their outstanding work on the case, McDonald, Starling, Johnson and Stoker were awarded governor's commendations. Parry and two colleagues were awarded commissioner's commendations.

The euphoria did not last.

From the outset, the prosecution had trouble getting co-operating victims. 'The banks were extremely reluctant to come forward,' says John Sulan, who was the crown prosecutor during the committal. 'On the whole, we found that bankers ran for cover. They didn't really want to talk about it. Commercially, no bank really wants to have its dirty linen washed in public. Banks are interested in doing well in the future, not sitting moping about the past. Once they write off certain debts, they write them off and get on with making money in the future. A trial is time consuming and you've got important people involved. Bankers want to protect their own position as individuals because they have become far too close with an individual and perhaps accepted gifts which they shouldn't have accepted. I don't think they would like to get their money back at the expense of having to wash all their dirty linen on the line.'

Individuals who had invested in Carrian and lost big were also victims. But despite the number of shareholders who 'lost their shirts', says Neil Kaplan, the Hong Kong QC handling the trial for the prosecution, 'None of the shareholders was prepared to say they read the audited account and admit that based on the figures they bought shares in Carrian.'

The two QCs representing the Crown, Neil Kaplan and

Lionel Swift, were continually briefed by Grossman and Andrew Chung. The defence changed its line-up to Graeme Hamilton QC and Robert Kotewall for Tan, Warren Chan for Ho, Michael Beckman QC for Rogerio Lam, Barry Sceats for Stephen Lam, Anthony Scrivener QC and Adrian Huggins for Begg and Lo.

Presiding over the high-court trial was Justice Dennis Barker. Barker graduated from Oxford in 1949 with a first in jurisprudence from Queen's College. 'The guy was a genius,' recalls a high-ranking legal administrator in Hong Kong. 'He had to decide whether to be a concert pianist or a lawyer. He had a sterling record, but, suddenly, lots of personal and family tragedy entered his life. The crime cases he wound up handling were not enough for his intellectual mind.'

Barker arrived in Hong Kong in 1981 and fitted in well with the expatriate community. He soon became a member of the Hong Kong Club and Sheko Country Club, where he enjoyed playing golf. An immensely sociable man, Barker made friends and favoured the camaraderie of the Bowling Alley Bar at the Hong Kong Club where he often spent his lunch-hour.

With his merry eyes and chubby face, Barker looked like Dickens' Mr Pickwick. He took his country-club manners with him to court and often made a show of lightening the mood with familiarities and humour, referring on occasion to passages from Lewis Carroll's *Alice's Adventures in Wonderland* and to *Pickwick Papers*. Barker's behaviour both in and out of court would draw the concern of many connected to the trial. At the end of the day, he would cast the final verdict on the biggest fraud ever prosecuted in the free world.

The trial that began on 24 February 1986 was unusual for several reasons. To begin with, it would become the longest and most costly trial in Hong Kong history, lasting nineteen months. But even the physical aspects signalled that it was going to be different. Because of the welter of evidence: over one million documents copied for the defence, the jury and the judge and 5,000 exhibits, Barker abolished the dock, allowing defendants to sit, American-style, with their counsel. Bookcases were installed to contain the overflow of evidence, making the newly built courtroom 4 in the Supreme Court Buildings appear like an inexhaustible reference library.

In his opening remarks, Lionel Swift, dressed in black robes and a lambswool wig, described the different charges and said that the transactions conducted by Carrian to prop up its share price were 'designed to give the image of a dynamic, profitable company trading with conspicuous success'. Swift said, in fact, these were 'conjuring tricks with money – millions circulating through several bank accounts on the same day to give the illusion of genuine transactions'.[42] He described the Carrian empire as no more than a 'house of cards'.

With such an involved case, Swift attempted to make it simple: '31 December 1981 was an exceptionally busy day,' he said. 'HK$313 million of the HK$762-million profit for the year was made on that day.' The profit from the bank transaction, he added, was wholly 'fictitious'.[43] He clarified the point, stating that neither the Lam brothers nor their company, Bylamson, had the money to buy the 17.2 million shares. 'Not a penny piece passed. Not a cent passed. Not a share was transferred. Not a single condition was filled. Nothing.' He argued that the auditors became part of the conspiracy to defraud when they allowed the transaction to enter the company's accounts. 'The very fact that a transaction of this magnitude occurred on the last day of the year was something that would have alerted the auditors if they were honest and doing their job properly.'

Swift said that at the time of the transaction both CIL and CHL were 'going bankrupt'. At the end of 1981, according to Swift, Tan had pledged to lenders more than 380 million CIL shares with a market value of more than HK$2 billion at the prevailing December price of HK$5.50 a share – down from HK$9.55 in July.

'To keep the bankers at bay,' claimed Swift, 'the share price has got to be kept up. Because if the share price drops, Mr Tan has got to find some more shares (to pledge).' Swift underscored how desperate the situation was by explaining that a further HK$1 drop in CIL's share price would have produced pressure on Tan from his bankers to supply another HK$442 million of assets as loan collateral.[44]

George Tan's defence centred largely on his claim that, in his business deals, he had followed the professional advice given to him by leading lawyers, accountants and advisers. In addition, Tan's lawyers were eager to prove that he was not involved in a conspiracy intent on defrauding shareholders and creditors. At this critical moment in his life, Tan had turned to another professional, Graeme Hamilton QC.

For the prosecution, the chief problem with the conspiracy charge was that the volume of evidence presented gave the defence ample opportunity to trip up the Crown. For weeks, the barristers argued minor points covered by over one million pages of evidence. Normally the volume of evidence can work in favour of the prosecution, especially in a conspiracy case. But nothing about Carrian or its trial was normal.

'Barker,' says Kaplan, 'conducted the trial as if it were an arbitration, not a criminal trial. The atmosphere in court was not like any criminal trial any of us had ever been in before.' The first thing Barker did was to excuse defendants from appearing. 'When Tan came back after a long absence,' says Kaplan, 'the judge welcomed him as if he were a long lost friend.'

'One accepts that the judge was well minded to keep the atmosphere as friendly as possible,' says Kaplan, 'but it just got completely out of hand.' Even moments of high drama were tempered with courtroom antics. Anthony Scrivener's defence of the Price Waterhouse auditors was put to extreme test in the spring of 1987.

The prosecution's bottom line on the auditors was simple:

'The public relies on the imprint of the world's leading accounting firms, known as the "Big Eight",' said Kaplan. 'If you see a set of accounts of a company about which you know nothing, but you see one of the Big Eight accounting firms have been the auditors, and have given it a clean audit certificate, of course it means something to you. That's why banks make it a condition of loans, the seal of one of the Big Eight. Auditors cannot abdicate their responsibilities.

'One of the problems in Hong Kong has been that the Big Eight do the public company and a small Chinese firm handles the private company which actually owns the bulk of the public company,' says Kaplan. For instance, while Price Waterhouse accountants Begg and Lo conducted the audits on both CIL and CHL, they did not do a group of George Tan's private companies including Perak Pioneer and Plessey Investment (no relation to the British-based Plessey) which, according to the prosecution, shared loans of more than HK$2 billion from Bumiputra Finance. It was on this point, among others, that defence counsel for the auditors made their case.

If there was one person who could undermine Scrivener's case, it was Lord Benson, the prosecution's expert accountancy witness. At 76, Benson brought to the court a phenomenal amount of international business, government and accounting experience. He had been instrumental in the formation of the Council of British Industry (CBI), and was a director and president of the Institute of Chartered Accountants.

Referring to the Crown's allegations, that of CIL's 1981 pre-tax profits of HK$762 million, HK$620 million were fictitious, Benson said, 'In my experience of accountancy over sixty years, I have never come across another case where gifts of this magnitude and this character were approved for a listed company in order to enlarge the disclosed profits in a way which so distorted these accounts.'[45]

He added that the accountants were under a statutory obligation to disclose the items. He pointed out that Begg and

Lo should have stated, for instance, that the HK$309 million from the Union Bank deal should not have been included in the company report because essential conditions of the contract had not been fulfilled. Begg and Lo, said Benson, should also have reported that HK$473-million worth of assets had left the custody of the company as security for loans to a Tan-controlled company. He stated flatly that the accounts were not true and fair and did not comply with the Hong Kong Companies Ordinance.

Benson also said the auditors should have realised that Carrian Holdings Limited was on the point of bankruptcy by December 1981. At that time, testified Benson, the book value of the net assets was only $144 million. 'This is a dangerously small amount having regard to the size of the current liabilities of $2,961 billion. The conclusion to be drawn from these figures is that CHL was in financial crisis. Without massive restructuring its financial collapse was imminent.'

In Benson's opinion, 'Begg and Lo failed to comply with the audit responsibilities imposed on them by their own firm and in consequence, the accounts failed to show a true and fair view.'[46]

At one point, while Scrivener cross-examined Benson on the Union Bank deal, he asked Benson to assume that the auditors believed a 30-per-cent deposit was paid. Benson began to reply twice, saying the auditors knew they could not verify the deposit. Scrivener interrupted him twice. On the second occasion, Scrivener demanded the jury leave the courtroom, warning he would ask for a retrial of the case if Benson did not confine his answers to within the judge's rulings. Judge Barker intervened, telling Benson he had to go on the assumptions and not make statements.

'It may go against the grain for you,' said Barker, 'but Mr Scrivener is entitled to ask questions of the assumptions he makes and you must answer them on his assumptions and not assert any facts. I know you find it difficult and I understand your difficulties. I am sorry. You must abide by my rulings. If you don't, it's likely to cause untold trouble.'[47] Scrivener proceeded with the assumption that the accountants believed the deposit had been paid on the Union Bank deal and asked Benson if the accountants could take into account the payment when considering whether the outstanding amount was recoverable. Benson replied that if this was their 'honest and genuine belief', it would be proper to take it into account.

He queried another assumption he was asked to make – that the auditors had taken the view that the deal was completed. He said he had been asked no less than five times to make an assumption that was untrue. At that stage he was reminded again of the judge's ruling. At one point the ruling so constrained the ability of Benson to give evidence that he exclaimed 'What am I to do, my Lord? if the ruling conflicts with the oath I took to tell the truth. Do you wish me to abuse my oath?'[48]

During the trial, revelations about Carrian and George Tan emerged.

Business was clearly never boring at Carrian. There were so many deals taking place at any given time that it was hard to keep track. Carrian's financial controller, John Wong, first knew of a deal worth HK$481 million to Carrian when he read an announcement about it in the paper.

Many meetings of Tan-controlled private companies, in which minutes were taken, never took place. In effect, there were companies that continually held 'paper meetings'. Bentley Ho, George Tan's right-hand man, was the director of 300 such companies. Maureen Lai, Carrian's company secretary, said she bought shelf companies whenever Carrian was running low, selecting 'nice' names from a compiled list supplied by Deacons.[49] Tan's management style was restless and chaotic. He would dart from room to room, issuing plans and ideas to visitors, depositing a lighted Davidoff cigar in an ashtray as tangible assurance of his return.

The trial embarked on its second year and files began curling at the edges. In November 1986 the government reluctantly shelled out another HK$10.2 million for the trial that was already costing HK$34.6 million.

By May 1987, following fourteen months of testimony from 101 witnesses and many weeks of legal arguments, the trial was beginning to take its toll.

Barker sat day after day, his wig set square on his head, touching the collar of his red robes. His half-moon glasses perched on his Rugby-broken nose – evidence of his days as an Oxford Blue and Harlequin. It was hard to keep from wondering why he made the unprecedented move of stepping down from the Appeal Court to the High Court for the sake of the case.

The judge's attitude and behaviour were of creat concern to the lawyers participating in the Carrian trial.

On 6 February 1987, the 188th day of the proceedings, Judge Barker walked up a path leading to the Supreme Court building, following his lunch. He stumbled, falling badly on his face and knees. A policeman from the nearby Commercial Crime Bureau helped him up and led him back to his chamber. A clerk called Barker's wife but by the time she arrived Barker was unconscious. Barker spent only one night in hospital, against the advice of his doctor who wanted him to spend two full days under observation. In the fall, Barker lost two teeth, suffered bruises and facial lacerations, concussion and a fractured kneecap.

Unbelievably, Barker allowed himself: bruises, lacerations and chipped teeth, to be photographed for the *South China Morning Post*. What is most troubling about the photograph, apart from the fact that its subject at the time was presiding over one of the biggest fraud trials of all time, is that Barker beamed gleefully from the page, oblivious to the alarm his conduct raised in the hearts and minds of everyone connected to the trial.

Barker hobbled back into the courtroom a few days later and

told the assembled counsel that he was keen to get on with the case. 'If I find I am not able to concentrate properly then I shall tell you,' he said. 'If you think, or anybody thinks, I am not concentrating properly, I shall not be offended if you tell me.'[5] One month later, Barker's medical advisers made the decision for him. 'The powers that be have paid me the compliment of assuming I have a brain,' he joked, then announced he would be going into the hospital for a brain scan.

'The word around town was that he was drunk,' says Grossman. 'We got continual reports from other barristers and businessmen who frequented the same bars. He'd be seen at cocktail parties, drunk and talking about the case. Rumour had it he used to drink too much every lunchtime. He drinks wine mainly. When Barker fell down he looked terrible. Somebody found him and they called an ambulance and they carried him off. My own view, and I think the view of most of our team, is that his deterioration started from then.'

At one point Barker called the defence and prosecution team into his office to announce, according to Grossman, 'I'm under a great deal of strain. My registrar's face has come up in pimples . . . one of the shorthand writers has got a headache. . . .' 'What he wanted to do was sit shorter hours,' says Grossman. 'We said "No, that's not acceptable, we're not sitting long enough hours as it is. This case will just go on." And that's when he said he was going to have a brain scan.

'When you're in the most complex trial of all time and when you've just fallen flat on your face and you've banged your head, you don't say these things and then decline to give an answer [about the outcome] afterwards. . . .'

'What worried me was I thought his health was going to crack up completely because we had a team of eight,' says Scrivener. 'He was on his own without back up.' Scrivener was also concerned about the many rumours he heard during the case. 'I don't like the idea of a judge talking out of court. It always worries me,' he says. 'You get different versions

It's like watching a barometer. Totally unreliable. It shouldn't happen.'

'We were extremely concerned about the way the judge handled the case all the way through,' says Grossman. 'From a personal point of view, he was drinking too much and that worried us. . . . He's a big mouth. He used to go off to the Hong Kong Club and drink and hold court there. All of his mates would come back and you'd hear: "Barker didn't like this witness and Barker's fed up with him."'

Grossman said counsel heard months before the end of the trial what was going to happen. 'But you know,' he says, 'there's a major step between hearing rumours and actually going to the step of impeaching the judge. You just can't do it.'

'Hong Kong is a goldfish bowl,' says Richard Parry. 'He should have lived like a hermit.'

For the next five months, Judge Barker was tasked with deciding whether the defence had a case to answer. If it did, the trial would continue with a jury verdict delivered in the future. On 15 September 1987, the day Barker announced his decision, by 9:30 a.m., half an hour before he made his entrance, only standing-room remained in courtroom number 4. At 9:45 a.m., a fight broke out over a seat in the press section. As barristers in black robes milled in the 'trenches', some of their lambswool wigs had the look of nicotine-stained beards, their shabby condition underscoring how long the Carrian trial had lasted. Nearly four years had passed since Tan and the others were arrested.

Barker entered smiling. As he sat in the red-velvet high-backed chair, beneath an ornate British coat of arms, there was utter silence in the courtroom. He greeted his wife from the bench and began reading his judgement. It did not take long. The judgement ran to only twelve typescript pages, five of which were taken up with the details of the charges.

Barker described how the presence of deception practised by the participants on Begg and Lo was the antithesis of conspiracy. There was no evidence of any conspiracy against Begg and Lo and the case against them was stopped. He ruled that the other Defendants also had no case to answer, but on the basis that the indictment charged two different conspiracies and was therefore defective for duplicity. He called the jury into the courtroom and instructed them to acquit Rogerio and Stephen Lam, David Begg, Anthony Lo, Bentley Ho and George Tan. Tan stood up, blew his nose and wiped the sweat from his brow. Together, members of the Attorney General's chambers took a lift to the ground floor in silence. They walked in step as they headed into a firing-line of television cameras.

Later, George Tan took the same elevator with his solicitor, Monika Skowronska. The doors were slow to close and Skowronska began violently striking the button to shut them. Tan, wearing a light-grey suit, stood in the corner. He looked insignificant and embarrassed. Two native Hong Kong journalists began talking to him. Skowronska shouted, 'No speaking in Cantonese!' As the elevator descended, the tension rose. It was nothing compared to the mayhem outside the court. Tan escaped the barrage of reporters by quickly slipping into the back seat of a burgundy sedan. He did not look back.

Given the gravity and the importance of the case, Barker's judgement was seen to be inadequate both in length and substance. One judge remarked, 'It could easily have been written in one afternoon.'[51] The mountains of evidence and arguments of both prosecution and defence were brushed off in a few brief lines that found the accountants not only innocent but also without blame and let the Lams off on technicalities, stating that they may have been part of a conspiracy, but not the one charged. By extension, Barker said he was obliged to do the same with George Tan and Bentley Ho.

The shock of Barker's conclusion to the longest trial in Hong Kong history reverberated around the colony as people began tallying up expenditures. An estimated HK$100 million (US$12.8 million) was spent on legal fees and costs alone. The next week, the prosecution and defence were in court to decide who would carry that bill. Before the arguments were heard, Barker shocked the court by saying that, after ordering a jury to acquit the defendants half-way through the Carrian trial, he did not know the difference between discharging a defendant and acquitting him.

Barker said, rightly or wrongly, he had decided that the trial should come to an end and it had never occurred to him he should discharge the jury and the defendants. While he was explaining that he thought the accused were in the charge of the jury and that he could not direct a discharge because it had to come from them, Barker was interrupted by Lionel Swift who reminded him he was hearing argument on whether applications for the costs by two defendants should be postponed. On a discharge, the Crown could, if it wished, reframe the charges and prosecute once more; it cannot on an acquittal. Barker could have done much more than simply tossing the case out, some argued. He could have amended the indictment.

A month after the verdict, Hong Kong's Chief Justice, Sir Denys Roberts, ruled that Barker was wrong in law in acquitting the Lams, Tan and Ho. Begg and Lo who had been acquitted on the ground that there was no evidence against them were not included in the Attorney General's reference to the Court of Appeal. Roberts said the judge had confused two issues — quashing the indictment and finding no case to answer. He said that it was wrong to ask the jury to acquit the defendants and added that the proper course would have been to discharge the jury from giving a verdict, which means the defendants could be tried again on the same charge, if the Crown chose. That was not possible when the jury acquits, as it did in the Carrian case.

In its ruling, the Court of Appeal said:

If at the end of a trial of this magnitude, a judge says not a word about the evidence which has been adduced against D1 and D2 (Tan and Ho), acknowledged to have been the principal parties to the conspiracy charged, and bases 'acquittal' on the finding that the indictment was defective for duplicity, we cannot but take him at his word.

Political observers noted after the Carrian trial ruling that unless Hong Kong's judicial system can be viewed as performing better than it did during the Carrian trial, it will be hard to insist on the necessity of preserving the system post-1997, when the territory is handed back to the People's Republic of China.

'The judicial conduct of this case was a complete and utter disgrace and it puts our system back a number of years and does it no good at all,' says Kaplan. 'I'm sure the Chinese are laughing their heads off.'

On the heels of the Carrian trial, the Complex Commercial Crimes Bill was passed as a means of streamlining court cases so as not to run the risk of another judicial fiasco of Carrian proportions. The bill makes it possible to conduct an investigation and go straight to trial without a committal. In addition, the defence is not required to disclose its case before a trial.

Ultimately the cost of the Carrian affair has fallen hardest on the Bumiputras. The Malaysian government was forced to turn its back on the New Economic Policy and to sell Bank Bumiputra Malaysia Berhad (BBMB) to the Malaysian state oil company, the only entity with enough cash to rescue it. The assets it would chase were the remnants of the once great Carrian empire. Frozen within Hong Kong office towers, these tangibles had once been fruitlessly chased by the late Jalil Ibrahim.

Despite the acquittals, the Carrian saga is likely to continue for some years to come. George Tan faces twenty-three charges, nine of alleged conspiracy to defraud Bumiputra Finance, seven of offering advantages to Lorrain Osman and seven of offering advantages to former Bumiputra Finance director, Hashim Shamsudin. Carrie Woo, former managing director of many Carrian companies, is charged with one count of fraud and three of bribery. Bentley Ho faces seven fraud charges and one of bribery. Recently these criminal charges along with Woo's were temporarily dropped, permitting the crown to focus on the forthcoming corruption trial.

Several former Bumiputra Finance executives are named as co-conspirators in the eighty-five fraud and corruption charges that were made in December 1985 by the ICAC, when it was alleged BMF advanced over £600 million to Carrian companies between 1979 and 1983, in the world's biggest banking-fraud investigation.

Hashim Shamsudin was convicted in January 1987 and is currently serving a ten-year jail sentence after pleading guilty to four offences, including two charges of accepting corrupt advantages totalling HK$15 million from George Tan.

Rais Saniman, senior general manager of BBMB's international banking division, is the subject of extradition proceedings in France.

Lorrain Osman, founder director of BBMB and chairman of BMFL, continues to fight extradition from his jail cell in Pentonville prison, London, becoming, in the process, Britain's remand prisoner of longest duration.

Proceedings in at least nine other Carrian-related law suits have been initiated.

Ibrahim Jaafar, former BMFL general manager, is currently co-operating with the prosecution in its case against his former colleagues.

Judge Barker, following the appeal courts judgement, tendered his resignation. It was refused by the man who appointed him to the Carrian trial, Chief Justice Sir Denys Roberts. When

Roberts was replaced by T. L. Yang, Barker left his post an
moved to Cyprus where he died at the age of 63 from a motorin
accident on 13 November 1989.

Notes

1 What's the password?

Apart from noted references, information came directly from John Maxfield with additional commentary from Donn Parker. Physical description of Detroit and Maxfield's environs is based on a week-long visit to Detroit in May 1988. This chapter, through a key informant, looks at the earliest stages of computer fraud by reconstructing the hacking phenomena that swept America in the early 1980s. Background information on the 414 gang came from a variety of sources including *Newsweek* (5 September 1983). Reports issued by Coopers and Lybrand and Ernst and Whinney on the history of hacking were useful. An important first-hand account, 'Journey to the Center of the Mainframe' by Jeanne-Marie Laskas, appeared in *Pittsburgh* magazine in March 1988. The October 1983 issue of *Computer Crime Digest*, produced by the National Center for Computer Crime Data, provided important background as did a cover story on hacking in *USA Today* (6 December 1984), Joseph B. Treaster's series on the topic for the *New York Times* in autumn 1983 and the *Detroit News* and *Detroit Free Press* accounts of the Wizard of Arpanet's exploits (September–October 1983). The *Detroit News* of 30 March 1986 was especially informative. Interviews with Jay Bloombecker, director of the Los Angeles-based National Center for Computer Crime Data, and Chew Teck Soon, an expert in computer audit and security review at Coopers and Lybrand (at a Kuala Lumpur audit conference), provided vital background. Further sources include: *Computer-Related Fraud Casebook* by Dr K. K. Wong and W. F. N. Farquhar, 1986 edition, Business Intelligence Services, the First Annual Statistical Report of the

National Center for Computer Crime Data and reports from Boardscan.

Notes
1 *Detroit News*, 30 October 1986.
2 *Detroit Free Press*, 15 October 1983.
3 *Detroit News*, 30 March 1986.
4 'Computer World', as reprinted in *Computer Crime Digest*, October 1983.
5 *Detroit Free Press*, 19 May 1985.
6 *Computer-Related Fraud Casebook Update*, Dr K. K. Wong, Business Intelligence Services, 1988.
7 *The Times*, 19 September 1987.
8 Ernst and Whinney, 'Computer Fraud Report', presented to the National Commission on Fraudulent Financial Reporting.
9 The Investigation of Computer Crime by Jay J. Becker, Director US National Center for Computer Crime Data.
10 Ernst and Whinney, 'Computer Fraud Report', op. cit.

2 Chasing fakes

Research for this chapter was conducted world-wide. The stories from undercover agents at Carratu International and Commercial Trademark Services are eye-witness accounts that cover ground from Asia and South America to Europe. My undercover work, in co-operation with CTS, was conducted in Hong Kong, Taipei and Bangkok and took place during autumn 1987. To protect their identities, the real names of Steve Chan, Derek Lam, Catherine Sapphire and Eva Wong have been disguised in the text. Besides those references noted, for background I consulted Brian Freemantle's *The Steal*, the *International Chamber of Commerce Counterfeiting Intelligence Bureau Bulletin* and statistical briefs issued by the Hong Kong Trading Standards Investigation Bureau.

Notes
1 'Commercial Counterfeiting' by Vincent Carratu, *Trademark World*, issue 2, 1986.
2 *Counterfeiting Intelligence Report*, No. 2/86. International Chamber of Commerce Counterfeiting Intelligence Bureau.

3 The art of detection

This chapter relies primarily on interviews with Doreen Stoneham, authenticator at the Oxford Research Laboratory for Archaeology and the History of Art, and Pieter Meyers, head of conservation at the Los Angeles County Museum of Art. The dialogue at the beginning of the chapter is faithfully reconstructed from Stoneham's own account of the events. The Mahboubian caper was first told to me by Pieter Meyers and corroborated by Manhattan robbery squad detectives. A telephone interview with Mahboubian in London confirmed the latest development in the case. I consulted Stuart Fleming's book, *Authenticity in Art*, and Calvin Trillin's excellent story in *The New Yorker*, 'Frenchy and the Persians', published 29 June 1987. Academic papers on autoradiography and thermoluminescence supplied by the Oxford lab and the LA County Museum were also consulted. Background information came through interviews with Elizabeth Gams, leading investigator of art crimes at Interpol in Paris. Technical bulletins from the National Gallery (UK) and reports from the International Foundation for Art Research aided in both technical and criminal background in the field of art. The breaking case of forged Lloyd Rees paintings in Australia in autumn 1987, patiently described to me by curators of Sydney's Art Gallery of New South Wales, provided a brilliant introduction to the ruthlessness of art dealers. Colin Reeve, group chief security officer at Christie's, and Marcus Linell, financial director of Sotheby's, gave important auction-house perspectives.

Notes

1 'Genuine or Not?' by Michael C. Hughes in *Apollo*, September 1988.
2 *Independent*, 14 October 1988.
3 'Frenchy and the Persians' by Calvin Trillin, *The New Yorker*, 29 June 1987.
4 Ibid.
5 Ibid.
6 *Sunday Times*, 5 April 1987.
7 'Frenchy and the Persians' by Calvin Trillin, op. cit.
8 Ibid.
9 Ibid.
10 Ibid.
11 Ibid.

4 Adventures in the pirate trade

This chapter involved interviews in locations throughout Australasia and Hollywood. General source material was provided by the Motion Picture Association of America. Stories by Michael Cieply in the *Wall Street Journal* (19 April 1985) and David Bollier in *Channels* (March 1987) were particularly helpful. Material on Isaac Zafrani is based on the first-hand accounts of Charles Morgan, Michael Heuser and news reports. Steve Clug was interviewed in Singapore and Jakarta, Ray Stephenson in Sydney, Australia. Stephenson generously supplied numerous news releases from the Australasian Film and Video Security Office. Frank Fan, a prominent distributor in Taiwan, explained the devastating effects of piracy on distribution and introduced me to the latest twist in video piracy: MTV studios. Richard Bloeser provided useful perspectives on the Bel Air Circuit from his office at MPAA headquarters in Los Angeles. Vincent Garibaldi, attorney for the MPAA in Panama, provided the updates on Zafrani. Important statistical background was supplied by the MPAA and the MPEAA. Added information on the Zafrani raid was gleaned from: *Hollywood Reporter*, 28 September 1983; *Variety*, 28 September 1983; the *Wall Street Journal*, 28 September 1983. Additional helpful clips: *Newsweek*, 27 July 1987; *Variety*, 17 October 1985; *New York Times*, 23 June 1986 and 18 May 1987; *Straits Times*, 1 July 1986; *South China Morning Post*, 25 September 1987; *Hongkong Standard*, 24 March 1986; *Security Management*, November 1986; *Video Age*, August 1985.

Notes

1 *Hollywood Reporter*, 28 September 1983.
2 *Wall Street Journal*, 19 April 1985.
3 *Channels*, March 1979.

5 Sea crimes

Primary sources for this chapter were first-hand accounts by investigators at the International Maritime Bureau. Statistics were provided by Eric Ellen, director of the IMB, and bulletins and annual reports of the International Chamber of Commerce. Additional figures on world shipping were supplied by *Shipping*

Statistics and Economics, a monthly publication issued by Drewry Shipping Consultants Ltd. An interview with Arthur Klinghoffer provided background on the sinking of the *Salem*. Confidential information on the insurance market came through a well-placed and reliable source within the Lloyd's insurance market.

Notes
1 *International Maritime Fraud*, Ellen and Campbell, Sweet and Maxwell, 1981.

6 The enforcers

This chapter is based on interviews with over a dozen members of the SEC's division of enforcement in the spring of 1988. Apart from these fourteen interviews, I also spoke with former enforcement director and now federal judge, Stanley Sporkin, and Charles Carberry, the federal prosecutor who handled the criminal charges against Dennis Levine. Throughout my research on the SEC, Chiles Larson, the commission's press liaison, was unfailingly helpful. Information on recent insider trading legislation was gleaned from the *New York Law Journal* (5 December 1988). The story of Levine and Boesky has been written about in many publications but none as expertly as *Levine & Co.* by Douglas Frantz, to whom I am especially grateful. Another excellent source was Moira Johnston's pioneering work, *Takeover*. For information about Rudolph Guiliani, I read James B. Stewart's *The Prosecutors*. In order to draw comparisons between Gary Lynch and Eliot Ness, I referred to Martin Short's *Crime Inc.* I gleaned some statistics from Ivan Fallon and James Strodes's *Takeovers*. Many newspaper and magazine articles on the SEC, Boesky, Levine, Milken and insider-trading helped buttress my interviews: *LA Times*, 18 November 1986; *Denver Post*, 19 December 1987; *New York Times*, 14 June 1986; *Wall Street Journal*, 16 February 1989; *ABA Journal*, 1 March 1988; *Washington Post*, 25 May 1986; *Business*, Fall 1986; February 1987; *National Law Journal*, 9 June 1986; *Christian Science Monitor*, 11 February 1988; *Forbes*, 29 June 1987; *Regardies*, July 1986; *Guardian*, 4 April 1989; *Financial Times*, 6 September 1988; Connie Bruck's November 1980 profile of Stanley Sporkin; 'The Work of the SEC' by the Office of Public Affairs, SEC; the SEC's 52nd Annual Report.

Notes

1 *Christian Science Monitor*, 11 February 1988.
2 *Atlantic Monthly*, November 1980.
3 Ivan Fallon and James Strodes, *Takeovers*, Hamish Hamilto
  Ltd, 1987.
4 *Forbes*, 29 June 1987.
5 *Washington Post*, 26 May 1986.
6 *Takeover* by Moira Johnston, Arbor House, 1986, p. 126.
7 Ibid., p. 60.
8 *Washington Times*, 19 November 1986.
9 Oversight Committee, p. 69.

7 California scheming

This chapter relies primarily on interviews with key investigator
and my eye-witness account of the raid on Midwest Miner
Properties in the spring of 1988. Boiler-rooms have been th
subject of both fiction and non-fiction work (see Mamet's *Glengar
Glenross*). Generously provided to me were indictments, warrant
affidavits and police transcripts. These, in addition to 'pitch book
and lead cards obtained in raids, were supplied by Souther
California Investment Fraud Task Force investigators and th
Los Angeles US Attorney's Office. Peter Cary's story in *US New
& World Report*, 21 December 1987 and Marc Beauchamp's i
Forbes, 11 February 1987, became excellent background source
Interviews with victims delivered first-hand accounts and valuab
evidence for the chapter, i.e. threats of liquidation of accounts
more money was not handed over, etc. Statistical information cam
from the very comprehensive 1985–1986 Annual Report issue
by the US Attorney's Office/Southern California Investment Frau
Task Force.

8 Collapse of an empire

Between August and mid-October 1987, I lived in Hong Kor
and researched the Carrian case, gathering first-hand informatio
from participants. With them, I witnessed the final outcome
the trial. My main sources came from the criminal and corruptio
investigations. Bankers, accountants, investigators, journalist
barristers and their counsels generously gave of their time. At th

end of the day, I culled from thousands of documents, including many hours of transcribed interviews and valuable news cuttings. Among my best background sources were *The Carrian File* by Philip Bowring and Robert Cottrell and *Hot Money* by R. T. Naylor. Many people gave of their valuable time for this chapter. I am especially grateful to: Robert Fell, David Nendick, Gerald Dobby, Lindy Course, Rita Gourlay, Meocre Li, members of the Royal Hong Kong Police Commercial Crime Bureau, and of the Independent Commission Against Corruption, the crown and defence legal teams, as well as accountants and liquidators at Arthur Young, Arthur Andersen and Ernst and Whinney.

Notes

1 Noordin Report, p. 569.
2 *Fortune Magazine*.
3 *Far Eastern Economic Review*, 29 January 1987.
4 Report by Arthur Young (appointed liquidators); this amount included loans from Wardley, Way Foong Credit and HKSB Shipping.
5 *Far Eastern Economic Review*, 29 January 1987.
6 *The Carrian File* by Philip Bowring and Robert Cottrell, Far Eastern Economic Review Ltd, 1984.
7 *Asian Wall Street Journal*, 20 January 1983.
8 Ibid., 27 September 1982.
9 Ibid.
10 Ibid., 1 October 1983.
11 *New Straits Times*, 12 June 1986.
12 *Far Eastern Economic Review*, 20 March 1986, and Noordin Report.
13 *South China Morning Post*, 12 June 1986.
14 Noordin Report, Special Brief, p. 28.
15 *Asian Wall Street Journal*, 20 January 1983.
16 *Hot Money*, by R. T. Naylor, Unwin Hyman, 1987, p. 210, based on report in *Sunday Times*, 22 April 1984.
17 *Financial Times*, 11 March 1986.
18 *Asian Wall Street Journal*, 20 January 1983.
19 *South China Morning Post*, 25 March 1986.
20 Ibid., 2 March 1986 and 26 April 1986.
21 *The Carrian File*, op. cit.
22 *Far Eastern Economic Review*, 26 November 1982.

23 *South China Morning Post*, 5 August 1986.
24 *Asian Wall Street Journal*, 6 January 1984.
25 Ibid., 17 April 1984.
26 Ibid.
27 Ibid.
28 *Far Eastern Economic Review*, 26 April 1984.
29 *Asian Wall Street Journal*, 18 April 1984.
30 Ibid., 17 April 1984.
31 Ibid.
32 Ibid.
33 Ibid., 18 April 1984.
34 Ibid.
35 *South China Morning Post*, 15 September 1983.
36 Confidential Carrian report, p. 10, drafted by Robert Fell.
37 *Far Eastern Economic Review*, 13 October 1983.
38 Ibid., and *Asian Wall Street Journal*, 5 October 1983.
39 *Asian Wall Street Journal*, 5 October 1983.
40 *New Straits Times*, 14 May 1986.
41 *South China Morning Post*, 18 July 1984 and *Hong Kong Standard*, 19 July 1986.
42 *Asian Wall Street Journal*, 1 March 1986.
43 Ibid.
44 *Far Eastern Economic Review*, 13 March 1986.
45 *South China Morning Post*, 4 April 1987.
46 *South China Morning Post*, 5 May 1987.
47 Ibid., 11 May 1987.
48 *Far Eastern Economic Review*, 1 October 1987.
49 *South China Morning Post*, 12 April 1986.
50 Ibid., 10 February 1987.
51 *Far Eastern Economic Review*, 1 October 1987.